The Canadian System of Soil Classification

Canada Soil Survey Committee

Research Branch
Canada Department of Agriculture

Publication 1646
1978

© Minister of Supply and Services Canada 1977

Available by mail from

Printing and Publishing
Supply and Services Canada
Hull, Quebec K1A 0S9

or through your bookseller.

Catalogue No. A53-1646/1977   Canada: $ 9.00
ISBN 0-660-01620-6   Other countries: $10.80

Prices subject to change without notice.

RBT Printing Limited

OIA05-7-38904

This publication replaces Publication 1455, *The System of Soil Classification for Canada.*
Correct citation:
Canada Soil Survey Committee, Subcommittee on Soil Classification. 1978.
The Canadian system of soil classification. Can. Dep. Agric. Publ. 1646.
Supply and Services Canada, Ottawa, Ont. 164 pp.

CONTENTS

FIGURES

TABLES

PREFACE

This publication replaces *The System of Soil Classification for Canada* published by Canada Department of Agriculture as Publication 1455, Revised 1974. Some of the changes in the system were agreed upon at the 1973 and 1976 meetings of the Canada Soil Survey Committee (CSSC) and subsequent decisions have been made by the Subcommittee on Soil Classification.

The main changes are as follows:
1. The inclusion of a Cryosolic order for soils having permafrost close to the surface.
2. The elimination of subgroup modifiers and therefore a reduction in the number of subgroup combinations.
3. The deletion of soil type as a category in the system.
4. The increased uniformity of presentation of the soil orders.
5. The amplification of the introductory material to give more of the background and rationale of soil classification in Canada.

This publication presents the current state of soil taxonomy in Canada. The Canadian system was influenced by history, regional biases, new information on soils in Canada and elsewhere, and international concepts of soil. It represents the views of most Canadian pedologists, but not all the details are satisfactory to any one pedologist. This is a stage in the evolution of an improved system that will result from further knowledge of soils and an improved arrangement of the information.

The history and rationale of soil classification in Canada are outlined briefly to point out the changes in concepts and the current point of view on soil taxonomy. This is followed by chapters that define soil, soil horizons, and other basic terms, and explain how to key out the classification of a soil. A chapter is devoted to each of the nine soil orders and the great groups and subgroups within each order. The orders are arranged alphabetically, but great groups and subgroups are arranged as they were in previous versions of the system. Chapters on the family and series categories and on soil phases follow. The recently developed landform classification system for soil surveys that was approved by CSSC in 1976 is included as a separate chapter. For additional information see: Canada Department of Agriculture (1976), Clayton et al. (1977), Working Group on Soil Survey Data (1975), and soil survey reports available from provincial soil survey units.

This revision was prepared by the Subcommittee on Soil Classification of the Canada Soil Survey Committee: T. M. Lord, British Columbia; W. W. Pettapiece, Alberta; R. J. St. Arnaud, Saskatchewan; R. E. Smith, Manitoba; C. J. Acton, Ontario; R. Baril, Quebec; G. J. Beke and C. Wang, Atlantic Provinces; and J. H. Day, J. A. McKeague, J. L. Nowland, and J. A. Shields, all of Ottawa.

The Subcommittee wishes to thank all those who shared in the preparation of this publication. Many pedologists critically reviewed drafts of sections and made useful suggestions. Janet Lyons typed several drafts of the manuscript. B. Baker, Graphics Section, Research Program Service, prepared the drawings.

Readers are invited to send their questions and suggestions to the chairman of the Canada Soil Survey Committee, Soil Research Institute, Agriculture Canada, Ottawa.

J. A. McKeague
Chairman
Subcommittee on Soil Classification

Chapter 1   INTRODUCTION

HISTORY OF SOIL CLASSIFICATION IN CANADA

The early years, 1914–1940

The classification of soils in Canada began with the first soil survey in Ontario in 1914. When A. J. Galbraith set out to map the soils of southern Ontario, concepts of soil and methods of soil classification were rudimentary in North America. G. N. Coffey, formerly of the U.S. Bureau of Soils, advised Galbraith during the early stages of the survey and the system of classification used was that of the U.S. Bureau of Soils based largely upon geological material and texture (Ruhnke 1926). Nine "soil series" were mapped in all of Ontario south of Kingston by 1920. The broad scope of "series," which were somewhat analogous to geological formations at that time, has narrowed progressively to the present.

Changes in the system of classifying the soils of Canada have resulted from the combined effects of international developments in concepts of soils and increasing knowledge of Canadian soils. Canadian pedologists were influenced from the time of the first surveys by the concept of soil as a natural body integrating the accumulative effects of climate and vegetation acting on surficial materials. This concept was introduced by Dokuchaev about 1870, developed by other Russian soil scientists, and proclaimed to western Europe by Glinka in 1914 in a book published in German. Marbut's translation of this book made the Russian concept of soil as a natural body easily available to the English-speaking world (Glinka 1927). The concept is of paramount importance in soil science because it makes possible the classification of soils on the basis of properties of the soils themselves rather than on the basis of geology, climate, or other factors. Classification systems based on the inherent properties of the objects classified are called natural or taxonomic systems.

Recognition of the relationships between soil features and factors of climate and vegetation was not limited to Russian scientists. In the United States, Hilgard had noted this association in a book published in 1860 (Jenny 1961), and Coffey had recognized soils as natural bodies by 1912 (Kellogg 1941). However, the development of the concept of soils as natural bodies with horizons that reflect the influences of soil-forming factors, particularly climate and vegetation, may be credited to the Russians.

In the earliest soil surveys undertaken in the Prairie Provinces during the 1920s classification was

on the basis of texture, but an increased awareness of soil zones and of the soil profile is evident in soil survey reports published during that decade. Preliminary soil zone maps of Alberta and Saskatchewan were presented by Wyatt and Joel at the first International Congress of Soil Science in 1927. They showed the broad belts of brown, black, and gray soils. The Congress and the associated field tours brought Canadian pedologists into close contact with world concepts of soil and systems of soil classification.

Developments in soil classification occurred independently in each province because surveys were carried out by university departments of soils or chemistry. For example, a numbering system indicating the soil zone, nature of parent material, mode of deposition, profile features, and texture was developed in Alberta. J. H. Ellis in Manitoba recognized the impossibility of developing a scientific soil taxonomy based on the limited knowledge of Canadian soils in the 1920s. Influenced by concepts of C. C. Nikiforoff in Minnesota, Ellis developed a field system of soil classification that was useful in soil mapping and endures in various revised forms to this day. The system identified "associations" of soils formed on similar parent materials and "associates" that differed according to topographic position within the association (Ellis 1932, 1971).

During the 1930s soil surveys proceeded in Ontario and the Prairie Provinces and were started in British Columbia in 1931, Quebec and Nova Scotia in 1934, and New Brunswick in 1938. Soil surveys began in Prince Edward Island in 1943, the Northwest Territories in 1944, and Newfoundland in 1949. A few soil surveyors were employed on a permanent basis by federal and provincial departments of agriculture in the 1930s and they worked cooperatively with personnel of university soils departments. By 1936 about 15 000 000 ha (1.7% of the land area of Canada) had been surveyed, mainly in Alberta, Saskatchewan, and Ontario. Soil classification was limited by the fragmentary knowledge of the soils of Canada.

Canadian pedologists were influenced in the 1930s by Marbut's developing ideas on soil classification, Ellis's system of field classification (Ellis 1932), and the classification system of the U.S. Department of Agriculture (USDA) described by Baldwin, Kellogg, and Thorp (1938). The latter system divided soils at the highest category among three orders:

1. Zonal soils, which are those with well-developed characteristics that reflect the influence of the active factors of soil genesis such as climate

and organisms, particularly vegetation, e.g. Podzol.

2. Intrazonal soils, which are soils having more or less well-defined characteristics that reflect the dominant influence of some local factor of relief or parent material over the normal effects of climate and vegetation, e.g. Humic Gley.

3. Azonal soils, which are soils without well-developed characteristics due either to their youth or to some condition of relief or parent material, e.g. Alluvial soils.

Zonal soils were divided at the suborder level on the basis of climatic factors, and suborders were subdivided into great groups more or less similar to the great groups of today.

Canadian experience showed that the concept of zonal soils was useful in the western plains, but was less applicable in Eastern Canada where parent material and relief factors had a dominant influence on soil properties and development in many areas. However, the 1938 USDA system was used in Canada and it influenced the subsequent development of the Canadian system.

From 1940 to 1976

The formation of the National Soil Survey Committee of Canada (NSSC) was a milestone in the development of soil classification and of pedology generally in Canada. The initial organization meeting was held in Winnipeg in 1940 by the Soils Section of the Canadian Society of Technical Agriculturists (Ellis 1971). Subcommittees were established to prepare reports on six major topics including soil classification. At the suggestion of E. S. Archibald, Director of the Experimental Farms Service, the NSSC became a committee of the National Advisory Committee on Agricultural Services. The first executive committee of the NSSC consisted of: A. Leahey, chairman; P. C. Stobbe, secretary; F. A. Wyatt, western representative; and G. N. Ruhnke, eastern representative. Terms of reference for the NSSC were developed by A. Leahey, G. N. Ruhnke, and C. L. Wrenshall. They were modified and restated in 1970 by the Canada Soil Survey Committee (CSSC) as follows:

To act as a coordinating body among the soil survey organizations in Canada supported by the Canada Department of Agriculture, provincial departments of agriculture, research councils, and departments of soil science at universities. Its functions include:

1. Improvement of the taxonomic classification system for Canadian soils and revision of this system because of new information.

2. Improvement of the identification of physical features and soil characteristics used in the description and mapping of soils.

3. Review of methods, techniques, and nomenclature used in soil surveys and recommending changes necessary for a greater measure of uniformity or for their improvement.

4. Recommending investigations of problems affecting soil classification, soil formation, and the interpretation of soil survey information.

5. Recommending and supporting investigations on interpretations of soil survey information for soil ratings, crop yield assessments, soil mechanics, and other purposes.

6. Cooperating with specialists in soil fertility, agronomy, agrometeorology, and other disciplines in assessing interrelated problems.

Much of the credit for the present degree of realization of these objectives is due to A. Leahey, chairman from 1940 until 1966, and P. C. Stobbe, secretary from 1940 until 1969. W. A. Ehrlich was chairman from 1966 to 1971 and was succeeded by J. S. Clark. In 1969 the name of the committee was changed to the Canada Soil Survey Committee (CSSC).

Developments in soil classification in Canada since 1940 are documented in the reports of the meetings of the NSSC held in 1945, 1948, 1955, 1960, 1963, 1965, 1968, and of the CSSC in 1970, 1973, and 1976. Soil classification was one of the main items on the agenda of the first meeting and a report by P. C. Stobbe provoked a prolonged and lively discussion. He and his committee recommended a system of field classification similar to that developed in Manitoba by Ellis (1932). The proposed system was a hierarchical one with seven categories as follows:

Soil Regions—tundra, woodland, and grassland soils.

Soil Zones—broad belts in which a dominant kind of soil occurs, such as podzol or black soil.

Soil Subzones—major subdivisions of soil zones, such as black and degraded black.

Soil Associations or Catenas—the group of soils that are associated together on the same parent material to form a land pattern.

Soil Series, Members, or Associates—the individual kinds of soils that are included in an association.

Soil Type or Soil Class—subdivisions of associations or of series based upon texture.

Soil Phase—subdivisions of mapping units based upon external soil characteristics such as stoniness and topography.

This was a field system of classification or a system of classifying the units of soils mapped at various scales. The classes at all levels, phase to region, were segments of the landscape that included all of the soil variability within the area designated. Thus a soil zone was a land area in which a "zonal great soil group occurred as a dominant soil." The system was not intended to be a scientific or taxonomic one in which the classes at all levels had clearly defined limits based on a reasonably thorough knowledge of the properties of the entire population of soils in Canada. Unfortunately, a degree of confusion about the distinction between the nature of a soil taxonomic system and a system of classifying and naming soil mapping units persists to this day. Several of the issues debated at that first NSSC meeting in 1945 remain as controversial issues today. The system proposed was accepted for trial by the committee, which represented all provinces. Thus, an important step was taken in the development of a national system of classifying the units of soil mapped in soil surveys.

The first Canadian taxonomic system of soil classification was presented by P. C. Stobbe at the NSSC meeting in 1955. This system was a marked departure from the mapping or field classification system proposed in 1945 and it probably resulted from the following circumstances:

The greater knowledge of Canadian soils.

The desire to classify soils, even at the highest categorical level, on the basis of properties of the soils themselves.

The need for a taxonomic system better than the old USDA system (Baldwin, Kellogg, and Thorp 1938) that focused unduly on "normal" soils. The Soil Conservation Service had begun the development of a new system in 1951, but the 4th approximation of that system was judged to be too complicated and too tentative for Canadian needs (NSSC Report 1955).

Unfortunately, formal discussion of field systems of classifying soils or soil mapping systems was dropped for several years at NSSC meetings, but the need for such systems was recognized by leaders in pedology. This need can be illustrated by an example of mapping soils at a particular scale and classifying the kinds of soil that occur.

If the map is at a scale of 1:100 000 and the smallest area delineated is a square measuring 1 cm on each side, that area represents 100 ha. Such an area commonly includes upland and lowland positions in the landscape and the associated kinds of soils. The kinds of soils within that area are identified by digging pits at different topographic positions in the landscape. At each of these points the profile exposed usually has a rather narrow range of properties that reflects the influence of soil-forming factors at that point. Thus the soils at each point of observation can be classified as a single class in a taxonomic system, but the area delineated on the map cannot be classified as a single class in such a system because it includes several kinds of soils. However, the area mapped can be classified as a kind of soil mapping unit such as a soil association in the system of Ellis (1932). Thus the need was evident for both a taxonomic system to permit the naming and the ordering of information about specific kinds of soils, and a mapping system to permit the ordering of information about the areas delineated on soil maps and the naming of them.

The taxonomic system outlined in 1955, which is the basis of the system used today, had six unnamed categorical levels corresponding to the order, great group, subgroup, family, series, and type. The seven taxa separated at the order level were: Chernozemic, Halomorphic, Podzolic, Forested Brown, Regosolic, Gleisolic, and Organic. Taxa were defined only in general terms down to the subgroup level. Although this was inevitable because of the lack of sufficient information, it led to differences of interpretation of the taxa in various provinces and some lack of uniformity in the use of the system. The need for correlation was clearly recognized by senior Canadian pedologists.

Progress in the development of the Canadian system of soil classification since 1955 has been toward more precise definitions of the taxa at all categorical levels and an increasing emphasis on soil properties as taxonomic criteria. This is evident from the reports of NSSC meetings held in 1960, 1963, 1965, and 1968, at which the main topic of discussion was soil classification. Some changes in taxa at the order, great group, and subgroup levels were made at these meetings. For example, in 1963 the Meadow and Dark Gray Gleisolic great groups were combined as Humic Gleysol; in 1965 a system of classifying soils of the Organic order was presented and accepted; in 1968 the former Podzolic order was divided into Luvisolic (clay translocation) and Podzolic (accumulation of Al and Fe organic complexes) orders, and the concept and classification of Brunisolic soils were revised. Criteria of classification involving morphological, chemical, and physical properties became increasingly specific through this period. The bases of classifying soils at the family level were outlined and the series and type categories were defined more specifically.

Following the publication of *The System of Soil Classification for Canada* in 1970, topics other than soil taxonomy were emphasized at CSSC meetings. However, in 1973 a Crysolic order was proposed to classify the soils with permafrost close to the surface, and some refinements were made in several orders.

Between 1945 and 1970 very little consideration was given at NSSC meetings to systems of naming and classifying soil mapping units. In 1970 a report was presented on the Biophysical Land Classification System, which is a hierarchical system with four levels for classifying the units of land mapped. The 1973 CSSC meeting included reports on mapping units in surveys of forest land and permafrost areas, and miscellaneous land types. The main topic at a CSSC meeting in 1976 was soil mapping units. With the achievement of a reasonably satisfactory taxonomic system, the emphasis in the CSSC has swung to the equally basic matter of a system of defining the nature and distribution of soils within mapping units and of naming these units.

RATIONALE OF SOIL TAXONOMY IN CANADA

During some 60 years of pedological work in Canada, concepts of soil and systems of classification have progressed as a result of new knowledge and new concepts developed in Canada and elsewhere. An attempt is made here to enunciate the current rationale of soil taxonomy based on the historical material outlined in the previous section and on recent publications on pedology in Canada.

The nature of soil

The concept of soil in Canada and elsewhere (Cline 1961; Knox 1965; Simonson 1968) has changed greatly since 1914 when the first soil survey was started in Ontario. No specific definition is available from that early work, but clearly soil was thought of as the uppermost geological material. Texture was apparently considered to be its most important attribute. Currently, soil is defined in general terms by pedologists as the naturally occurring, unconsolidated, mineral or organic material at the earth's surface that is capable of supporting plant growth. Its properties usually vary with depth and are determined by climatic factors and organisms, as conditioned by relief and hence water regime, acting on geological materials and producing genetic horizons that differ from the parent material. In the landscape soil merges into nonsoil entities such as exposed, consolidated rock or permanent bodies of water at arbitrarily defined boundaries.

Specific definitions of soil and nonsoil are given in Chapter 2.

Because soil occurs at the surface of the earth as a continuum with variable properties, it is necessary to decide on a basic unit of soil to be described, sampled, analyzed, and classified. Such a unit was defined by United States' pedologists (Soil Survey Staff 1960) and is accepted in Canada. It is called a pedon and is the smallest, three-dimensional body at the surface of the earth that is considered as a soil. Its lateral dimensions are 1–3.5 m and its depth is 1–2 m. Pedon is defined more specifically in Chapter 2.

Nature and purpose of soil classification

Soil classification systems are not truths that can be discovered but methods of organizing information and ideas in ways that seem logical and useful (Soil Survey Staff 1960). Thus no classification system is either true or false; some systems are more logical and useful for certain objectives than others. A classification system reflects the existing knowledge and concepts concerning the population of soils being classified (Cline 1949). It must be modified as knowledge grows and new concepts develop.

Both the theoretical and practical purposes of soil classification have been discussed in the literature (Cline 1949, 1963; De Bakker 1970). The general purpose of soil classification in Canada may be stated as follows:

To organize the knowledge of soils so that it can be recalled systematically and communicated and that relationships may be seen among kinds of soils, among soil properties and environmental factors, and among soil properties and suitabilities of soils for various uses.

The related purposes of soil classification are: to provide a framework for the formulation of hypotheses about soil genesis and the response of soil to management, to aid in extending knowledge of soils gained in one area to other areas having similar soils, and to provide a basis for indicating the kinds of soils within mapping units. Soil classification is essential to soil surveys, to the teaching of soils as a part of natural science, and to meeting the practical needs related to land use and management.

The overall philosophy of the Canadian system is pragmatic; the aim is to organize the knowledge of soils in a reasonable and usable way. The system is a natural or taxonomic one in which the classes (taxa) are based upon properties of the soils themselves and not upon interpretations of the soils for various uses. Interpretations involve a second step that is essential if the information is to be used effectively. If the taxa are defined on properties and the boundaries of these classes or of combinations of them are shown on a map, any interpretation based upon properties implied in the class definitions can be made.

Misconceptions about soil taxonomy

Misconceptions about the functions of a system of soil taxonomy are evident periodically. Some of these are listed to warn users of the Canadian system against unrealistic expectations.

1. It is a misconception that a good system results in the assignment of soils occurring close together to the same taxon at least at the higher categorical levels. This is neither possible nor desirable in some areas. Pedons a few metres apart may differ as greatly as pedons hundreds of kilometres apart within a climatic region.
2. Another common misconception is that a good national system provides the most suitable groupings of soils in all areas. This is not possible because criteria based upon properties of the whole population of soils in the country are bound to be different from those developed on the basis of properties of soils in any one region. Criteria developed for a national system will inevitably result in areas where most of the soils have properties that straddle the boundary line between two taxa.
3. The idea that if the system was soundly based there would be no need for changes every few years is erroneous. As new areas are surveyed, as more research is done, and as concepts of soil develop, changes in the system become inevitable to maintain a workable taxonomy.
4. Another unfortunate hope is that a good system will ensure that taxa at the order level at least can be assigned unambiguously and easily in the field. Actually in a hierarchical system the divisions between orders must be defined just as precisely as those between series. With pedons having properties close to class boundaries at any taxonomic level, classification is difficult and laboratory data may be necessary.
5. The assumption is made by some that a good system permits the classification of soils occurring within mapped areas as members of not more than three series. Clearly this is not reasonable because the number of taxonomic classes occurring within a mapping unit depends upon the complexity of the pattern of soils in the landscape, on the scale of the map, and on the narrowness of class limits.
6. The idea that a good system is simple enough to be clear to any layman is erroneous. Unfortunately, soil is complex and although the general ideas of the taxonomy should be explainable in simple terms the definitions of taxa must be complex in some instances.
7. Another misconception is that a good system makes soil mapping easy. Ease of mapping depends more upon the complexity of the landscape, the access, and the predictability of the pattern of soils within segments of the landscape than upon taxonomy.

Attributes of the Canadian system

The development of soil taxonomy in Canada has been toward a system with the following attributes:

1. It provides taxa for all known soils in Canada.
2. It involves a hierarchical organization of several categories to permit the consideration of soils at various levels of generality. Classes at high categorical levels reflect, to the extent possible, broad differences in soil environments that are related to differences in soil genesis.
3. The taxa are defined specifically so as to convey the same meaning to all users.
4. The taxa are concepts based upon generalizations of properties of real bodies of soils rather than idealized concepts of the kinds of soils that would result from the action of presumed genetic processes. The criteria chosen define taxa in accordance with the desired groupings of soils. The groupings are not decided upon initially on the basis of arbitrary criteria.
5. Differentiae among the taxa are based upon soil properties that can be observed and measured objectively in the field or, if necessary, in the laboratory.
6. It is possible to modify the system on the basis of new information and concepts without destroying the overall framework. Periodically, however, the entire framework of the system will be reevaluated.

Although taxa in the Canadian system are defined on the basis of soil properties, the system has a genetic bias in that properties or combinations of properties that reflect genesis are favored as differentiae in the higher categories. For example, the chernozemic A and the podzolic B imply genesis. The reason for the genetic bias is that it seems reasonable to combine at high categorical levels soils that developed their particular horizonation as a result of similar dominant processes resulting from broadly similar climatic conditions. Classification is not based directly on presumed genesis because soil genesis is incompletely understood, is subject to a wide variety of opinion, and cannot be measured simply.

Bases of criteria for defining taxa at various categorical levels

The bases of differentiation of taxa at the various categorical levels are not clear cut. In a hierarchical system of soil classification, logical groupings of soils that reflect environmental factors cannot be obtained by following any rigid systematic framework in which all taxa at the same categorical level are differentiated on the basis of a uniform specific criterion such as acidity or texture. The fact that criteria must be based on soil properties rather than directly on environmental factors or use evaluation was recognized by some pedologists half a century ago (Joel 1926). The general bases of the different categorical levels can be inferred from a study of the system and these are presented below. They apply better to some taxa than to others; for example, the statement for order applies more clearly to Chernozemic and Podzolic soils than to Regosolic and Brunisolic soils.

Order. Taxa at the order level are based on properties of the pedon that reflect the nature of the soil environment and the effects of the dominant, soil-forming processes.

Great group. Great groups are soil taxa formed by the subdivision of each order. Thus each great group carries with it the differentiating criteria of the order to which it belongs. In addition, taxa at the great group level are based on properties that reflect differences in the strengths of dominant processes or a major contribution of a process in addition to the dominant one. For example, in Luvic Gleysols the dominant process is considered to be gleying, but clay translocation is also a major process.

Subgroup. Subgroups are formed by subdivisions of each great group. Therefore they carry the differentiating criteria of the order and the great group to which they belong. Also, subgroups are differentiated on the basis of the kind and arrangement of horizons that indicate: conformity to the central concept of the great group, Orthic; intergrading toward soils of another order, e.g. Gleyed, Brunisolic; or additional special features within the control section, e.g. Ortstein.

Family. Taxa at the family level are formed by subdividing subgroups. Thus they carry the differentiating criteria of the order, great group, and subgroup to which they belong. Families within a subgroup are differentiated on the basis of parent material characteristics such as texture and mineralogy, and soil climatic factors and soil reaction.

Series. Series are formed by subdivisions of families. Therefore they carry all the differentiating criteria of the order, great group, subgroup, and family to which they belong. Series within a family are differentiated on the basis of detailed features of the pedon. Pedons belonging to a series have similar kinds and arrangements of horizons whose color, texture, structure, consistence, thickness, reaction, and composition fall within a narrow range. A series is a category in the taxonomic system; thus it is a conceptual class in the same sense as an order.

A pedon is a real unit of soil in the landscape; a series is a conceptual class with defined limits based on the generalization of properties of many pedons. A particular pedon may be classified as a series if its attributes fall within the limits of those of an established series. However, it is not, strictly speaking, a series because the attributes of any one pedon do not encompass the complete range of attributes allowable within a series. Thus, it is not correct to study part of a pedon and to declare, "this is X series." Rather it should be stated, "this pedon has properties that fall within the limits of the X series," or "this pedon is classified in the X series."

Type. Type is no longer a category in the Canadian system. Surface texture may be indicated as a phase.

Relationship of taxonomic classes to environments

A general relationship exists between kinds of environments and taxa at various levels in the system. This follows from the basis of selection of diagnostic criteria for the taxa; the primary basis at the higher levels is properties that reflect the environment and properties resulting from processes of soil genesis. Although the system may look like a key with classes defined precisely but arbitrarily on the basis of specific properties, it is one in which the taxa reflect, to as great an extent as possible, genetic or environmental factors.

The Podzolic order, for example, is defined on the basis of morphological and chemical properties of the B horizon. However, these properties are associated with humid conditions, sandy to loamy parent materials, and forest or heath vegetation. Although the great groups within the order are defined on the basis of the amounts of organic C and extractable Fe and Al in the B horizons, they have broad environmental significance. Humic Podzols are associated with very wet environments, high water tables, periodic or continuous reducing conditions, hydrophytic vegetation, and often a peaty surface. Ferro-Humic Podzols occur in areas of high effective precipitation, but they are not under reducing conditions for prolonged periods. Humo-Ferric Podzols occur generally in less humid environments than the other great groups in the order. There is an interrelation of climatic and vegetative factors and parent material and relief in determining the occurrence of these classes of Podzolic soils. Similarly, there are general relationships between other orders, great groups, and soil environmental factors. However, these relationships are much less clear for some Regosolic and Brunisolic soils than they are for most soils of other orders. At lower categorical levels in general, relationships between soil taxa and factors of the soil environment become increasingly close.

Relationship of the Canadian system to other systems of soil taxonomy

The numerous national systems of soil taxonomy might be looked upon as indications of the youthfulness of soil science. Knowledge of the properties of the soils of the world is far from complete, therefore it is not possible to develop an international system of classification for the whole population of known and unknown soils. Probably even after such a system has been developed, national systems will remain in use because they are familiar and are thought to be more useful for the restricted population of soils within the country. The soil units defined for the FAO-Unesco world soil map project are useful in international soil correlation, but they do not constitute a complete system of soil taxonomy (FAO 1974). The closest approach to a comprehensive system of soil taxonomy is that produced by the USDA Soil Survey Staff (1975), which has been under development since 1951. Like previous U.S. systems, it has had a major influence on soil taxonomy in Canada and elsewhere.

The Canadian system of soil taxonomy is more closely related to the U.S. system than to any other. Both are hierarchical and the taxa are defined on the basis of measurable soil properties. However, they differ in several respects. The Canadian system is designed to classify only soils that occur in Canada and is not a comprehensive system. The U.S. system has a suborder, which is a category that the Canadian system does not have. In the Canadian system Solonetzic, Gleysolic, and Cryosolic soils are differentiated at the highest categorical level as in the Russian and some other European systems. These soils are differentiated at the suborder or great group level in the U.S. system. Perhaps the main difference between the two systems is that all horizons to the surface may be diagnostic in the Canadian system, whereas horizons below the depth of plowing are emphasized in the U.S. system. This may be a consequence of the fact that 90% of the area of Canada is not likely to be cultivated.

SUMMARY

The Canadian system is a hierarchical one in which the classes are conceptual based upon the generalization of properties of real bodies of soil. Taxa are defined on the basis of observable and measurable soil properties that reflect processes of soil genesis and environmental factors. The development of the system has progressed with the increasing knowledge of the soils of Canada obtained through pedological surveys carried out over a 60-yr period. The system has been influenced strongly by concepts developed in other countries, but some aspects are uniquely Canadian. The system is imperfect because it is based on a limited knowledge of the vast population of soils in the country. However, the system does make possible the assignment of the soils throughout Canada to taxa at various levels of generalization and the organization of the knowledge about soils in such a way that relationships between factors of the environment and soil development can be seen. It is possible to define the kinds of soils that occur within units on soil maps, and to provide a basis for evaluating mapped areas of soil for a variety of potential uses.

Soil taxonomy in Canada is based on properties of the soil. Therefore, there is a need for definitions of soil as opposed to nonsoil and of the unit of soil being classified. These and the equally basic definitions of soil horizons are given in this chapter.

SOIL AND NONSOIL

Bodies of soil and nonsoil occur as a continuum at the surface of the earth. They merge into one another often at imperceptible though arbitrarily defined boundaries. Soil is defined herein as the naturally occurring, unconsolidated mineral or organic material at least 10 cm thick that occurs at the earth's surface and is capable of supporting plant growth. In this definition "naturally occurring" includes disturbance of the surface by activities of man such as cultivation and logging but not displaced materials such as gravel dumps and mine spoils. Unconsolidated material includes material compacted or cemented by soil-forming processes. Soil extends from the earth's surface through the genetic horizons, if present, into the underlying material to the depth of the control section. Soil may have water covering its surface to a depth of 60 cm or less either at low tide in coastal areas or during the driest part of the year in areas inland. A soil covered by a surface mantle of new material at least 50 cm thick is considered to be a buried soil. Soil development involves climatic factors and organisms, as conditioned by relief and hence water regime, acting through time on geological materials and thus modifying the properties of the parent material.

Nonsoil is the aggregate of surficial materials that do not meet the preceding definition of soil. It includes soil materials displaced by unnatural processes such as dumps of earth fill along a highway under construction, unconsolidated mineral or organic material thinner than 10 cm overlying bedrock, exposed bedrock, and unconsolidated material covered by more than 60 cm of water throughout the year. Nonsoil also includes organic material thinner than 40 cm overlying water.

The definitions reflect the fact that bodies of soil and nonsoil have a continuum of properties. For example, the thickness of soil material overlying bedrock might range from 1 m at the base of a slope to 20 cm at midslope and gradually thin out to exposed bedrock at the top. The exposed bedrock is nonsoil, but the thickness of unconsolidated material over bedrock that should qualify as soil is not obvious. To avoid ambiguity and permit uniformity of classification, an arbitrary depth limit of 10 cm

is used. Similarly, bodies of periodically submerged soil merge into bodies of water in the natural landscape.

PEDON, THE BASIC UNIT OF SOIL

The pedon as defined by pedologists of the United States (Soil Survey Staff 1975) serves as the basic unit of soil in the Canadian classification system. It is the smallest, three-dimensional unit at the surface of the earth that is considered as a soil. Its lateral dimensions are 1 m if ordered variation in genetic horizons can be sampled within that distance or if these horizons are few and faintly expressed. If horizons are cyclical or intermittent and are repeated in a lateral distance of 2–7 m, the lateral dimensions of the pedon are half the cycle (1–3.5 m). The vertical dimension of the pedon is to the depth of the control section. A contiguous group of similar pedons is called a polypedon, which is indicated in *Soil Taxonomy* (Soil Survey Staff 1975) as a unit of classification.

The pedon concept applies to the classification of all soils, but its relevance to soils having cyclic variation, such as Turbic Cryosols, is most apparent. Examples of pedons are illustrated in Figs. 1, 2, and 3. In Fig. 1 the profiles beneath the stone circles and the intercircle material differ markedly. However, the variation is cyclic and occurs repeatedly over a lateral distance of about a metre. Thus the pedon includes a full cycle from the midpoint of one circle through the intercircle material to the midpoint of another circle. All of the variability within the pedon is included in the concept of the taxonomic class used from order to series. In this case classification would be based upon the properties of the intercircle material as it is dominant in extent. If the circles were further apart such that a full cycle was 2–7 m in diameter, the pedon would include half a cycle. Thus it would extend from the midpoint of a circle to the midpoint of the intercircle material. If the lateral dimension of the cycle was greater than 7 m, two soils would be identified, one associated with the circles and the other with the intercircle material.

Cyclic variation involving tonguing of Ah horizon material into the IICk horizon is shown in Fig. 2. The full cycle has lateral dimensions of about 1 m or less so that the pedon includes a full cycle. All of the variability in thickness of the Ah is included in the concept of the soil series.

The pedon is half of the cycle in the example of hummocky terrain resulting from tree throw shown in Fig. 3. In such cases the hummocks are

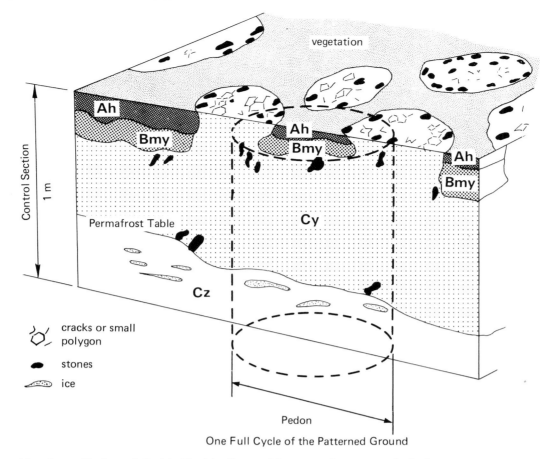

vegetation

Ah
Bmy
Ah
Bmy
Ah
Bmy

Control Section

1 m

Permafrost Table

Cy

Cz

cracks or small polygon

stones

ice

Pedon

One Full Cycle of the Patterned Ground

Fig. 1.   Pedon of Orthic Turbic Cryosol in area of nonsorted circles.

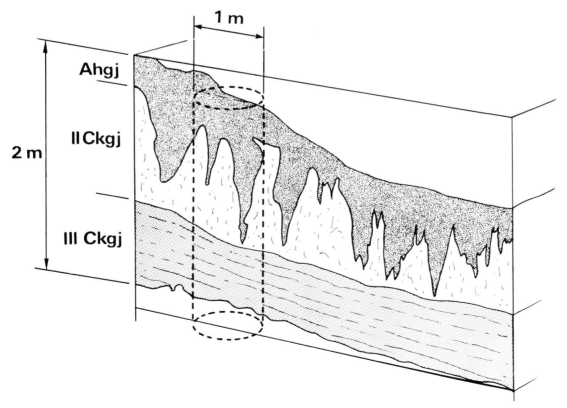

1 m

Ahgj

II Ckgj

III Ckgj

2 m

Fig. 2.   Pedon of Gleyed Rego Black, grumic phase, with tongueing Ah horizon.

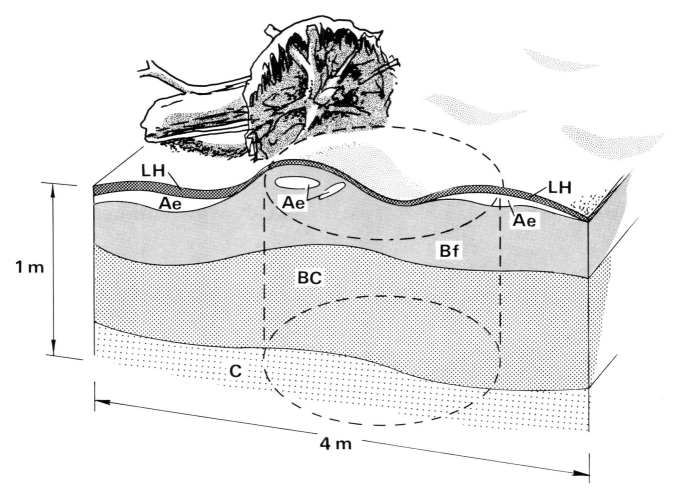

Fig. 3.   Pedon of Orthic Humo-Ferric Podzol, turbic phase, in hummocky terrain due to blowdown of trees.

usually not regularly distributed and the dimensions of the pedon may vary appreciably over short distances.

CONTROL SECTION

The control section is the vertical section of soil upon which classification is based.

Mineral soils

For mineral soils in general, the control section extends either from the mineral surface to 25 cm below the upper boundary of the C or IIC, or to a depth of 2 m, whichever is less. Exceptions are:

1. If the upper boundary of the C or IIC is less than 75 cm from the mineral surface, the control section extends to a depth of 1 m.
2. If bedrock occurs at a depth of less than 1 m, the control section is from the surface to the lithic contact.

Organic soils

For Organic soils the control section extends from the surface either to a depth of 160 cm or to a lithic contact. The control section is divided into tiers, which are used in classification. The tiers are layers based upon arbitrary depth criteria.

Surface tier. The surface tier is 40 cm thick exclusive of loose litter, crowns of sedges and reeds, or living mosses. Mineral soil on the surface of the profile is part of the surface tier, which is used to name the soil family. Shallow lithic Organic soils may have only a surface tier.

Middle tier. The middle tier is 80 cm thick. It establishes the great group classification if no terric, lithic, or hydric substratum is present. Otherwise the dominant kind of organic material in this and the surface tier establishes the great group classification. The nature of the subdominant organic material in the middle or bottom tier assists in establishing the subgroup classification.

Bottom tier. The bottom tier is 40 cm thick. The material in this tier establishes in whole or in part the subgroup classification.

A control section is necessary to provide a uniform basis for soil classification. In general, pedons should be sampled at least to the depth of the control section. The properties of the material beneath the control section are important for many interpretive purposes. Therefore, the underlying material should be examined and its properties recorded whenever possible.

SOIL HORIZONS AND OTHER LAYERS

The definitions of classes in the Canadian system are based mainly on the kinds, degrees of development, and the sequence of soil horizons and other layers in pedons. Therefore, the clear definition and designation of soil horizons and other layers are basic to soil classification. A soil horizon is a layer of mineral or organic soil or soil material approximately parallel to the land surface that has characteristics altered by processes of soil formation. It differs from adjacent horizons in properties such as color, structure, texture, and consistence, and in chemical, biological, and mineralogical composition. The other layers are either nonsoil layers such as rock and water or layers of unconsolidated material considered to be unaffected by soil-forming processes. For the sake of brevity these other layers are referred to simply as layers, but it is recognized that soil horizons are also layers. In previous editions of this publication and in the *Glossary of Terms in Soil Science* organic materials are designated as layers and not horizons.

The major mineral horizons are A, B, and C. The major organic horizons are L, F, and H, which are mainly forest litter at various stages of decomposition, and O, which is derived mainly from bogs, marsh, or swamp vegetation. Subdivisions of horizons are labeled by adding lower case suffixes to some of the major horizon symbols as with Ah or Ae. Well-developed horizons are readily identified in the field. However, in cases of weak expression or of borderline properties, as between Ah and H, laboratory determinations are necessary before horizons can be designated positively. Many of the laboratory methods required are outlined in a manual prepared by a subcommittee of CSSC (McKeague 1976). Some other methods pertaining to organic horizons are outlined near the end of this chapter.

The layers defined are R, rock; W, water; and IIC or other nonconforming, unconsolidated mineral layers, IIIC, etc. below the control section that are unaffected by soil-forming processes. Theoretically a IIC affected by soil-forming processes is a horizon; for example a IICca is a horizon. In practice, it is usually difficult to determine the lower boundary of soil material affected by soil-forming processes. Thus the following are considered as horizons: C(IC), any unconforming layer within the control section, and any unconforming layer below the control section that has been affected by pedogenic processes (e.g. IIBc, IIIBtj). Unconforming layers below the control section that do not appear to have been affected by pedogenic processes are considered as layers. The tiers of Organic soils are also considered as layers.

Mineral horizons and layers

Mineral horizons contain 17% or less organic C (about 30% organic matter) by weight.

A — This is a mineral horizon formed at or near the surface in the zone of leaching or eluviation of materials in solution or suspension, or of maximum in situ accumulation of organic matter or both. The accumulation of organic matter is usually expressed morphologically by a darkening of the surface soil (Ah), and conversely the removal of organic matter is usually expressed by a lightening of the soil color usually in the upper part of the solum (Ae). The removal of clay from the upper part of the solum (Ae) is expressed by a coarser soil texture relative to the underlying subsoil layers. The removal of iron is indicated usually by a paler or less red soil color in the upper part of the solum (Ae) relative to the lower part of the subsoil.

B — This is a mineral horizon characterized by enrichment in organic matter, sesquioxides, or clay; or by the development of soil structure; or by a change of color denoting hydrolysis, reduction, or oxidation. The accumulation in B horizons of organic matter (Bh) is evidenced usually by dark colors relative to the C horizon. Clay accumulation is indicated by finer soil textures and by clay cutans coating peds and lining pores (Bt). Soil structure developed in B horizons includes prismatic or columnar units with coatings or stainings and significant amounts of exchangeable sodium (Bn) and other changes of structure (Bm) from that of the parent material. Color changes include relatively uniform browning due to oxidation of iron (Bm), and mottling and gleying of structurally altered material associated with periodic reduction (Bg).

C — This is a mineral horizon comparatively unaffected by the pedogenic processes operative in A and B, (C), except the process of gleying (Cg), and the accumulation of calcium and magnesium carbonates (Cca) and more soluble salts (Cs, Csa). Marl, diatomaceous earth, and rock no harder than 3 on Mohs' scale are considered to be C horizons.

R — This is a consolidated bedrock layer that is too hard to break with the hands (>3 on Mohs' scale) or to dig with a spade when moist and does not meet the requirements of a C horizon. The boundary between the R layer and any overlying unconsolidated material is called a lithic contact.

W — This is a layer of water in Gleysolic, Organic, or Cryosolic soils. Hydric layers in Organic soils are a kind of W layer.

Lowercase suffixes

b — A buried soil horizon.

c — A cemented (irreversible) pedogenic horizon. Ortstein, placic, and duric horizons of Podzolic soils, and a layer cemented by $CaCO_3$ are examples.

ca — A horizon of secondary carbonate enrichment in which the concentration of lime exceeds that in the unenriched parent material. It is more than 10 cm thick, and its $CaCO_3$ equivalent exceeds that of the parent material by at least 5% if the $CaCO_3$ equivalent is less than 15% (13% vs 8%), or by at least 1/3 if the $CaCO_3$ equivalent of the horizon is 15% or more (28% vs 21%). If no IC is present, this horizon is more than 10 cm thick and contains more than 5% by volume of secondary carbonates in concretions or in soft, powdery forms.

cc — Cemented (irreversible) pedogenic concretions.

e — A horizon characterized by the eluviation of clay, Fe, Al, or organic matter alone or in combination. When dry, it is usually higher in color value by one or more units than an underlying B horizon. It is used with A (Ae).

f — A horizon enriched with amorphous material, principally Al and Fe combined with organic matter. It usually has a hue of 7.5YR or redder or its hue is 10YR near the upper boundary and becomes yellower with depth. When moist the chroma is higher than 3 or the value is 3 or less. It contains at least 0.6% pyrophosphate-extractable Al + Fe in textures finer than sand and 0.4% in sands (coarse sand, sand, fine sand, and very fine sand). The ratio of pyrophosphate-extractable Al + Fe to clay

(<0.002 mm) is more than 0.05 and organic C exceeds 0.5%. Pyrophosphate-extractable Fe is at least 0.3%, or the ratio of organic C to pyrophosphate-extractable Fe is less than 20, or both are true. It is used with B alone (Bf), with B and h (Bhf), with B and g (Bfg), and with other suffixes. These criteria do not apply to Bgf horizons. The following f horizons are differentiated on the basis of the organic C content:

Bf — 0.5–5% organic C

Bhf — more than 5% organic C

No minimum thickness is specified for a Bf or a Bhf horizon. Thin Bf and Bhf horizons do not qualify as podzolic B horizons as defined later in this chapter.

Some Ah and Ap horizons contain sufficient pyrophosphate-extractable Al + Fe to satisfy this criterion of f but are designated Ah or Ap.

g — A horizon characterized by gray colors, or prominent mottling, or both, indicative of permanent or periodic intense reduction. Chromas of the matrix are generally 1 or less. It is used with A and e (Aeg); B alone (Bg); B and f (Bfg, Bgf); B, h, and f (Bhfg); B and t (Btg); C alone (Cg); C and k (Ckg); and several others. In some reddish parent materials matrix colors of reddish hues and high chromas may persist despite long periods of reduction. In these soils, horizons are designated as g if there is gray mottling or marked bleaching on ped faces or along cracks.

Aeg — This horizon must meet the definitions of A, e, and g.

Bg — This horizon is analogous to a Bm horizon but has colors indicative of poor drainage and periodic reduction. It includes horizons occurring between A and C horizons in which the main features are: (i) Colors of low chroma, that is: chromas of 1 or less, without mottles on ped surfaces or in the matrix if peds are lacking; or chromas of 2 or less in hues of 10YR or redder, on ped surfaces or in the matrix if peds are lacking, accompanied by more prominent mottles than those in the C horizon; or hues bluer than 10Y, with or without mottles on ped surfaces or in the matrix if peds are lacking. (ii) Colors indicated in (i) and a change in structure from that of the C horizon. (iii) Colors indicated in (i) and illuviation of clay too slight to meet the requirements of Bt, or an accumulation of iron oxide too slight to meet the limits of Bgf. (iv) Colors indicated in (i) and the removal of carbonates. Bg horizons occur in some Orthic Humic Gleysols and some Orthic Gleysols.

Bfg, Bhfg, Btg, and others — When used in any of these combinations the limits set for f, hf, t, and others must be met.

Bgf — The dithionite-extractable Fe of this horizon exceeds that of the IC by 1% or more. Pyrophosphate-extractable Al + Fe is less than the minimum limit specified for f horizons. This horizon occurs in Fera Gleysols and Fera Humic Gleysols and possibly below the Bfg of gleyed Podzols. It is distinguished from the Bfg of gleyed Podzols on the basis of the extractability of the Fe and Al. The Fe in the Bgf horizon is thought to have accumulated as a result of the oxidation of ferrous iron. The iron oxide formed is not associated intimately with organic matter or with Al and is sometimes crystalline. The Bgf horizons are usually prominently mottled; more than half of the soil material occurs as mottles of high chroma.

Cg, Ckg, Ccag, Csg, Csag — When g is used with C alone, or with C and one of the lowercase suffixes k, ca, s, or sa the horizon must meet the definition for C and for the particular suffix as well as for g.

h — A horizon enriched with organic matter. It is used with A alone (Ah), or with A and e (Ahe), or with B alone (Bh), or with B and f (Bhf).

Ah — A horizon enriched with organic matter, it has a color value at least one unit lower than the underlying horizon or 0.5% more organic C than the IC or both. It contains less than 17% organic C by weight.

Ahe — An Ah horizon that has undergone eluviation as evidenced, under natural conditions, by streaks and splotches of different shades of gray and often by platy structure. It may be overlain by a dark-colored Ah and underlain by a light-colored Ae.

Bh — This horizon contains more than 1% organic C, less than 0.3% pyrophosphate-extractable Fe, and has a ratio of organic C to pyrophosphate-extractable Fe of 20 or more. Generally the color value and chroma are less than 3 when moist.

Bhf — Defined under f.

j — This is used as a modifier of suffixes e, f, g, n, and t to denote an expression of, but failure to meet, the specified limits of the suffix it modifies. It must be placed to the right and adjacent to the suffix it modifies. For example, Bfgj means a Bf horizon with a weak expression of gleying; Bfjgj means a B horizon with weak expression of both f and g features.

Aej — It denotes an eluvial horizon that is thin, discontinuous, or slightly discernible.

Btj — It is a horizon with some illuviation of clay but not enough to meet the limits of Bt.

Btgj, Bmgj — These are horizons that are mottled but do not meet the criteria of Bg.

Bfj — It is a horizon with some accumulation of pyrophosphate-extractable Al + Fe but not enough to meet the limits of Bf.

Btnj or Bnj — These are horizons in which the development of solonetzic B properties is evident but insufficient to meet the limits for Bn or Bnt.

k — Denotes the presence of carbonate as indicated by visible effervescence when dilute HC1 is added. It is used mostly with B and m (Bmk) or C (Ck) and occasionally with Ah or Ap (Ahk, Apk), or organic horizons (Ofk, Omk).

m — A horizon slightly altered by hydrolysis, oxidation, or solution, or all three to give a change in color or structure, or both. It has:
  1. Evidence of alteration in one of the following forms:
    a. Higher chromas and redder hues than the underlying horizons.
    b. Removal of carbonates either partially (Bmk) or completely (Bm).
    c. A change in structure from that of the original material.
  2. Illuviation, if evident, too slight to meet the requirements of a Bt or a podzolic B.
  3. Some weatherable minerals.
  4. No cementation or induration and lacks a brittle consistence when moist.
This suffix can be used as Bm, Bmgj, Bmk, and Bms.

n — A horizon in which the ratio of exchangeable Ca to exchangeable Na is 10 or less. It must also have the following distinctive morphological characteristics: prismatic or columnar structure, dark coatings on ped surfaces, and hard to very hard consistence when dry. It is used with B as Bn or Bnt.

p — A horizon disturbed by man's activities such as cultivation, logging, and habitation. It is used with A and O.

s — A horizon with salts, including gypsum, which may be detected as crystals or veins, as surface crusts of salt crystals, by depressed crop growth, or by the presence of salt-tolerant plants. It is commonly used with C and k (Csk), but can be used with any horizon or combination of horizon and lowercase suffix.

sa — A horizon with secondary enrichment of salts more soluble than Ca and Mg carbonates; the concentration of salts exceeds that in the unenriched parent material. The horizon is at least 10 cm thick. The conductivity of the saturation extract must be at least 4 mS/cm and exceed that of the C horizon by at least one-third. (The unit mho has been replaced by siemens [S].)

t — An illuvial horizon enriched with silicate clay. It is used with B alone (Bt), with B and g (Btg), with B and n (Bnt), etc.

Bt — A Bt horizon is one that contains illuvial layer-lattice clays. It forms below an eluvial horizon but may occur at the surface of a soil that has been partially truncated. It usually has a higher ratio of fine clay to total clay than the IC. It has the following properties:
  1. If any part of an eluvial horizon remains and there is no lithologic discontinuity between it and the Bt horizon, the Bt horizon contains more total clay than the eluvial horizon as follows:
    a. If any part of the eluvial horizon has less than 15% total clay in the fine earth fraction (<2 mm), the Bt horizon must contain at least 3% more clay, e.g. Ae 10% clay; Bt minimum 13% clay.
    b. If the eluvial horizon has more than 15% and less than 40% total clay in the fine earth fraction, the ratio of the clay in the Bt horizon to that in the eluvial horizon must be 1.2 or more, e.g. Ae 25% clay; Bt at least 30% clay.

     c. If the eluvial horizon has more than 40% total clay in the fine earth fraction, the Bt horizon must contain at least 8% more clay, e.g. Ae 50% clay; Bt at least 58% clay.

2. A Bt horizon must be at least 5 cm thick. In some sandy soils where clay accumulation occurs in the lamellae, the total thickness of the lamellae should be more than 10 cm in the upper 150 cm of the profile.
3. In massive soils the Bt horizon should have oriented clay in some pores and also as bridges between the sand grains.
4. If peds are present, a Bt horizon has clay skins on some of the vertical and horizontal ped surfaces and in the fine pores or has illuvial oriented clays in 1% or more of the cross section as viewed in thin section.
5. If a soil shows a lithologic discontinuity between the eluvial horizon and the Bt horizon, or if only a plow layer overlies the Bt horizon, the Bt horizon need show only clay skins in some part, either in some fine pores or on some vertical and horizontal ped surfaces. Thin sections should show that the horizon has about 1% or more of oriented clay bodies.
    Btj and Btg are defined under j and g.

u — A horizon that is markedly disrupted by physical or faunal processes other than cryoturbation. Evidence of marked disruption such as the inclusion of material from other horizons or the absence of the horizon must be evident in at least half of the cross section of the pedon. Such turbation can result from a blowdown of trees, mass movement of soil on slopes, and burrowing animals. The u can be used with any horizon or subhorizon with the exception of A or B alone; e.g. Aeu, Bfu, BCu.

x — A horizon of fragipan character. A fragipan is a loamy subsurface horizon of high bulk density and very low organic matter content. When dry, it has a hard consistence and seems to be cemented. When moist, it has moderate to weak brittleness. It frequently has bleached fracture planes and is overlain by a friable B horizon. Air-dry clods of fragic horizons slake in water.

y — A horizon affected by cryoturbation as manifested by disrupted and broken horizons, incorporation of materials from other horizons, and mechanical sorting in at least half of the cross section of the pedon. It is used with A, B, and C alone or in combination with other subscripts, e.g. Ahy, Ahgy, Bmy, Cy, Cgy, Cygj.

z — A frozen layer. It may be used with any horizon or layer, e.g. Ohz, Bmz, Cz, Wz.

Named diagnostic horizons and layers of mineral soils

Chernozemic A — This is an A horizon having all of the following characteristics:
1. It is at least 10 cm thick.
2. Its color value is darker than 5.5 dry and 3.5 moist, and its chroma is lower than 3.5 moist.
3. Its color value is at least one Munsell unit darker than that of the IC horizon.
4. In soils disturbed by cultivation or other means the Ap horizon is thick and dark enough to provide 15 cm of surface material that meets the color criteria stated in 2 and 3 above.
5. Its organic C content is 1–17% and its C:N ratio is less than 17.
6. Characteristically it has sufficiently good structure so that it is neither massive and hard nor single grained when dry.
7. Its base saturation (neutral salt) is more than 80% and Ca is the dominant exchangeable cation.
8. A chernozemic A horizon is restricted to soils having a mean annual soil temperature of 0°C or higher and a soil moisture regime subclass drier than humid.
    To meet the requirements of a chernozemic A, a dark-colored surface horizon must occur in a soil that meets the soil climatic specifications given in the preceding sentence and have the seven characteristics specified previously. Usually chernozemic A horizons are associated with well to imperfectly drained soils having cold semiarid to subhumid soil climates.

Duric horizon — This is a strongly cemented horizon that does not satisfy the criteria of a podzolic B horizon. Usually it has an abrupt upper boundary to an overlying podzolic B or to a Bm horizon and a diffuse lower boundary more than 0.5 m below. Cementation is usually strongest near the upper boundary, which occurs commonly at a depth of 40–80 cm from the mineral surface. The color of the duric horizon usually differs little from that of the moderately coarse textured to coarse textured parent material, and the structure is usually massive or very coarse platy. Air-dry clods of duric horizons do not slake when immersed in water, and moist clods at least 3 cm thick usually cannot be broken in the hands.

Fragipan — See definition of "x".

Ortstein — This is a strongly cemented Bh, Bhf, or Bf horizon at least 3 cm thick that occurs in more than one-third of the exposed face of the pedon. Ortstein horizons are generally reddish brown to very dark reddish brown.

Placic horizon — This is a thin layer (commonly 5 mm or less thick) or a series of thin layers that are irregular or involuted, hard, impervious, often vitreous, and dark reddish brown to black. Placic horizons may be cemented by Fe, Al-organic complexes (Bhfc or Bfc), hydrated Fe oxides (Bgfc), or a mixture of Fe and Mn oxides.

Podzolic B horizon — This diagnostic horizon is defined by the following morphological and chemical properties:
Morphological
1. It is at least 10 cm thick.
2. The moist crushed color is either black, or the hue is 7.5YR or redder or 10YR near the upper boundary and becomes yellower with depth. The chroma is higher than 3 or the value is 3 or less.
3. The accumulation of amorphous material is indicated by brown to black coatings on some mineral grains or brown to black microaggregates. Also there is a silty feel when the material is rubbed wet, unless it is cemented.
4. The texture is coarser than clay.
Chemical
Two kinds of podzolic B horizons are differentiated chemically.
1. Very low Fe. Such a podzolic B horizon (Bh) must be at least 10 cm thick and have more than 1% organic C, less than 0.3% pyrophosphate-extractable Fe, and a ratio of organic C to pyrophosphate-extractable Fe of 20 or more.
2. Contains appreciable Fe as well as Al. Such a podzolic B horizon (Bf or Bhf) must be at least 10 cm thick and have an organic C content of more than 0.5%. It contains 0.6% or more pyrophosphate-extractable Al + Fe in textures finer than sand and 0.4% or more in sands (coarse sand to very fine sand). The ratio of pyrophosphate-extractable Al + Fe to clay ($<2~\mu$m) is more than 0.05. Pyrophosphate-extractable Fe is at least 0.3%, or the ratio of organic C to pyrophosphate-extractable Fe is less than 20, or both are true.

Not all Bh, Bhf, and Bf horizons are podzolic B horizons because a podzolic B has a depth requirement and Bh, Bhf, and Bf horizons do not.

Solonetzic B horizon — The term includes both Bn and Bnt horizons. These horizons have prismatic or columnar primary structure that breaks to blocky secondary structure; both structural units have hard to extremely hard consistence when dry. The ratio of exchangeable Ca to Na is 10 or less.

Lithic layer — This is a consolidated bedrock layer (R) within the control section below a depth of 10 cm. The upper surface of a lithic layer is a lithic contact.

Mull — This is a zoogenous, forest humus form consisting of an intimate mixture of well-humified organic matter and mineral soil with crumb or granular structure that makes a gradual transition to the horizon underneath. Because of the activity of burrowing microfauna, (mostly earthworms), partly decomposed organic debris does not accumulate as a distinct layer (F layer) as in mor and moder. The organic matter content is usually 5–20% and the C:N ratio 10–15. It is a kind of Ah horizon.

Organic horizons

Organic horizons are found in Organic soils and commonly at the surface of mineral soils. They may occur at any depth beneath the surface in buried soils or overlying geologic deposits. They contain more than 17% organic C (approximately 30% organic matter) by weight. Two groups of these horizons are recognized, the O horizons and the L, F, and H horizons.

O — This is an organic horizon developed mainly from mosses, rushes, and woody materials. It is divided into the following subhorizons.
Of — This is an O horizon consisting largely of fibric materials that are readily identifiable as to botanical origin. A fibric horizon (Of) has 40% or more of rubbed fiber by volume and a pyrophosphate index of 5 or more. If the rubbed fiber volume is 75% or more, the pyrophosphate criterion does not apply. Fiber is defined as the organic material retained on a 100-mesh sieve (0.15 mm), except for wood fragments that cannot be crushed in the hand and are larger than 2 cm in the smallest dimension.

Rubbed fiber is the fiber that remains after rubbing a sample of the layer about 10 times between the thumb and forefinger. Fibric material usually is classified in the von Post scale of decomposition as class 1 to class 4. Three kinds of fibric horizons are named. Fenno horizons are derived from rushes, reeds, and sedges. Silvo horizons are derived from wood, moss with less than 75% of the volume being *Sphagnum* spp., and other herbaceous plants. Sphagno horizons are derived from sphagnum mosses.

Om — This is an O horizon consisting of mesic material, which is at a stage of decomposition intermediate between fibric and humic materials. The material is partly altered both physically and biochemically. It does not meet the requirements of either a fibric or a humic horizon. Mesic material usually is classified in the von Post scale of decomposition as class 5 or 6.

Oh — This is an O horizon consisting of humic material, which is at an advanced stage of decomposition. The horizon has the lowest amount of fiber, the highest bulk density, and the lowest saturated water-holding capacity of the O horizons. It is very stable and changes very little physically or chemically with time unless it is drained. The rubbed fiber content is less than 10% by volume and the pyrophosphate index is 3 or less. Humic material usually is classified in the von Post scale of decomposition as class 7 or higher and rarely as class 6.

The methods of determining the properties of fibric, mesic, and humic materials are outlined later in this chapter.

Oco — This is coprogenous earth, which is a limnic material that occurs in some Organic soils. It is deposited in water by aquatic organisms such as algae or derived from underwater and floating aquatic plants subsequently modified by aquatic animals.

L, F, and H — These are organic horizons that developed primarily from the accumulation of leaves, twigs, and woody materials with or without a minor component of mosses. Usually they are not saturated with water for prolonged periods.

L — This is an organic horizon that is characterized by an accumulation of organic matter derived mainly from leaves, twigs, and woody materials in which the original structures are easily discernible.

F — This is an organic horizon that is characterized by an accumulation of partly decomposed organic matter derived mainly from leaves, twigs, and woody materials. Some of the original structures are difficult to recognize. The material may be partly comminuted by soil fauna as in moder, or it may be a partly decomposed mat permeated by fungal hyphae as in mor.

H — This is an organic horizon that is characterized by an accumulation of decomposed organic matter in which the original structures are indiscernible. This horizon differs from the F by having greater humification due chiefly to the action of organisms. It is frequently intermixed with mineral grains, especially near the junction with a mineral horizon.

Named layers and materials of Organic soils

Fibric, mesic, and humic materials were defined under Of, Om, and Oh. Some typical physical properties of fibric and humic materials are listed below. Mesic material has intermediate physical properties.

	Fibric material	Humic material
bulk density (g/cm³)	<0.075	>0.195
total porosity (% vol)	>90	<85
0.1 bar H_2O content (% vol)	<48	>70
hydraulic conductivity (cm/hr)	>6	<0.1

Limno layer — This is a layer or layers 5 cm or more thick of coprogenous earth (sedimentary peat), diatomaceous earth, or marl. Except for some of the coprogenous earths containing more than 30% organic matter, most of these limno materials are inorganic.

Coprogenous earth is composed of aquatic plant debris modified by aquatic animals. It makes slightly viscous water suspensions and is slightly plastic but not sticky. The material shrinks upon drying to form clods that are difficult to rewet and often tend to crack along horizontal planes. It has very few or no plant fragments recognizable to the naked eye, a pyrophosphate index of 5 or more, and a dry color value of less than 5. The cation exchange capacity (CEC) is less than 240 meq/100 g organic matter. It is designated Oco in horizon descriptions.

Diatomaceous earth is composed mainly of the siliceous shells of diatoms. It has a matrix color value of 4 ± 1, if not previously dried, that changes on drying to the permanent, light gray or whitish color of diatoms. The diatom shells can be identified by microscopic (440 X) examination. Diatomaceous earth has a pyrophosphate index of 5 or more. It is frequently more nearly mineral than organic in composition. It is designated C in horizon descriptions.

Marl is composed of the shells of aquatic animals and $CaCO_3$ precipitated in water. It has a moist color value of 6 ± 1 and effervesces with dilute HCl. The color of the matrix usually does not change on drying. Marl contains too little organic matter to coat the carbonate particles. It is designated Ck in horizon descriptions.

Cumulo layer — This consists of a layer or layers of mineral material in Organic soils. Either the combined thickness of the mineral layers is more than 5 cm or a single mineral layer 5–30 cm thick occurs. One continuous mineral layer more than 30 cm thick in the middle or bottom tier is a terric layer.

Terric layer — This is an unconsolidated mineral substratum not underlain by organic matter, or one continuous unconsolidated mineral layer (with less than 17% organic C) more than 30 cm thick in the middle or bottom tiers underlain by organic matter, within a depth of 160 cm from the surface.

Lithic layer — This is a consolidated mineral layer (bedrock) occurring within 10–160 cm of the surface of Organic soils.

Hydric layer — This is a layer of water that extends from a depth of not less than 40 cm from the organic surface to a depth of more than 160 cm.

Tests for distinguishing organic layers

Unrubbed and rubbed fiber. *See* methods 2.71 and 2.72 in *Manual on Soil Sampling and Methods of Analysis* (McKeague 1976).

Pyrophosphate index. Place 1 g of sodium pyrophosphate in a small plastic, screw-topped container, add 4 ml of water and stir. With a syringe measure a 5 cm³ sample of moist organic material as in method 2.71 and place it in the plastic container, stir, and let stand overnight. Mix the sample thoroughly the next day. Using tweezers insert one end of a strip of chromatographic paper about 5 cm long vertically into the suspension. With the screw top in place to avoid evaporation, let the paper strip stand in the suspension until it is wetted to the top. Remove the paper strip with tweezers, cut off and discard the soiled end, and blot the remainder of the strip on absorbent paper. Read the value and chroma of the strip using good illumination and viewing the strip through the holes in the Munsell chart. The pyrophosphate index is the difference between the Munsell value and chroma of the strip.

von Post scale of decomposition. In this field test squeeze a sample of the organic material within the closed hand. Observe the color of the solution that is expressed between the fingers, the nature of the fibers, and the proportion of the original sample that remains in the hand. Ten classes are defined as follows:

1—Undecomposed; plant structure unaltered; yields only clear water colored light yellow brown.
2—Almost undecomposed; plant structure distinct; yields only clear water colored light yellow brown.
3—Very weakly decomposed; plant structure distinct; yields distinctly turbid brown water, no peat substance passes between the fingers, residue not mushy.
4—Weakly decomposed; plant structure distinct; yields strongly turbid water, no peat substance escapes between the fingers, residue rather mushy.
5—Moderately decomposed; plant structure clear but becoming indistinct; yields much turbid brown water, some peat escapes between the fingers, residue very mushy.
6—Strongly decomposed; plant structure somewhat indistinct but clearer in the squeezed residue than in the undisturbed peat; about a third of the peat escapes between the fingers, residue strongly mushy.
7—Strongly decomposed; plant structure indistinct but recognizable; about half the peat escapes between the fingers.
8—Very strongly decomposed; plant structure very indistinct; about two-thirds of the peat escapes between the fingers, residue almost entirely resistant remnants such as root fibers and wood.
9—Almost completely decomposed; plant structure almost unrecognizable; nearly all the peat escapes between the fingers.
10—Completely decomposed; plant structure unrecognizable; all the peat escapes between the fingers.

Rules concerning horizon and layer designations

1.   Do not use the uppercase letters A, B, and O singly for horizons in pedon descriptions, but accompany them by a lowercase suffix (e.g. Ah, Bf, or Om) indicating the estimated nature of the modification of the horizon from the parent material. The horizon and layer designations L, F, H, R, and W may be used alone, and the horizon designation C may be used alone except when the material is affected by reducing conditions (Cg), cementation (Cc), salinity (Cs or Csa), or $CaCO_3$ (Ck or Cca).

2.   Unless otherwise specified, additional lowercase suffixes indicate a feature or features in addition to those characteristic of the defined main horizon. For example, the symbol Btg indicates that in addition to illuvial clay in the B horizon there is evidence of strong gleying. Some combinations such as Bmj are not used. In some cases, such as Bgf and Bhf, the combination of suffixes has a specific meaning that differs from the sum of the two suffixes used singly.

3.   All horizons except A and B, and B and A may be vertically subdivided by consecutive numeral suffixes. The uppermost subdivision is indicated by the numeral 1; each successive subdivision with depth is indicated by the next numeral. This convention is followed regardless of whether or not the horizon subdivisions are interrupted by a horizon of a different character. For example, an acceptable subdivision of horizons would be: Ae1, Bf, Ae2, Bt1, Bt2, C1, C2. In some instances it may be useful for sampling purposes to subdivide a single horizon, for example, Bm1-1, Bm1-2, Bm1-3.

4.   Roman numerals are prefixed to horizon and layer designations to indicate parent material discontinuities in the profile. The Roman numeral I is understood for the uppermost material and is not written. Subsequently, contrasting materials are numbered consecutively in the order in which they are encountered downward, that is II, III, and so on.

5.   For transitional horizons only uppercase letters are used as follows:

   If the transition is gradual, use AB, BC, etc.

   If the horizons are interfingered in the transitional zone, use A and B, B and C, etc.

   The dominance of horizons in the transitional zone may be shown by order, AB or BA, etc.

6.   The designations for diagnostic horizons must be given in the sequence shown in the horizon definitions, e.g. Ahe not Aeh.

7.   Where j is used, the suffix or suffixes that it modifies are written after other horizon suffixes, e.g. Btnj, Bntj, Bfjtj, Bfcjgj.

Although definitions are given for all horizon symbols, all possible combinations of horizon designations have not been covered and all horizons having the same designation do not have identical properties. Therefore horizon descriptions are necessary.

Need for precise definitions of horizons and layers

In many cases the definitions of soil horizons may seem almost pedantically specific. For example, the suffix "t" indicates a horizon enriched with silicate clay. However, a Bt horizon must have a clay content exceeding that of the overlying eluvial horizon by specified amounts depending upon texture. For example, if the clay content of the Ae is 10%, that of the Bt must be 13% or more; if the clay content of the Ae is 40%, that of the Bt must be 48% or more. Also a Bt horizon must have a thickness that meets specified limits and clay skins on ped surfaces or oriented clay in pores.

Some B horizons that are slightly enriched with silicate clay are not Bt horizons. For example, two pedons X and Y have clay contents as follows: X: Ae—20%, B—22%; C—21%; Y: Ae—20%, B—25%, C—21%. If there is no parent material discontinuity in either pedon and both have B horizons more than 5 cm thick with clay skins on ped surfaces, the B horizon of pedon Y is a Bt, but that of pedon X is not. The two pedons would probably be closely similar if they were derived from similar materials in the same area, but they would be classified in different orders (Luvisolic and Brunisolic) because one has a Bt horizon and the other does not. Yet the difference in the clay contents of the B horizons is only 3% and it could result from an analytical error. If the descriptions of the pedons indicated no difference in the development of B horizons, the particle size data would be checked. In most cases, clay skins would be thicker and more continuous in the B horizon of pedon Y than in that of pedon X.

From the point of view of the soil surveyor in the area, pedons X and Y are closely similar soils that belong in the same class even at the series level and certainly at the order level. However, for the soil taxonomist concerned with ordering the information on the whole population of soils in the country the classification of pedons X and Y in different orders is inevitable for two reasons. Soils have a continuum of properties, and specific limits are essential if soil taxonomy is to be applied in a uniform manner by users of the system. The classification of pedons X and Y in different orders does not imply that the use interpretations must be different nor that the pedons must be separated and delineated in mapping. This depends on the pattern of distribution of the pedons X and Y and the scale of mapping. The indication that pedon X does not have a Bt horizon and that pedon Y does simply informs pedologists that the two B horizons have properties such that they are on opposite sides of the man-made line through the continuum of properties indicating the development of a horizon enriched in silicate clay. The alternatives of vague specifications of limits of diagnostic horizons or of relying on individual judgments lead to chaos in the ordering of soil information throughout the country.

The specific horizon definitions are based on the generalization of properties of horizons of real soils that are thought to be representative of the main soil classes and reflect the kinds and degrees of soil development. Whenever possible, the specifications are based on observable or easily measurable properties and they are modified as the knowledge of soils increases and as concepts change. Because of the lack of sufficient knowledge, some soil horizons are not defined adequately.

Chapter 3

OUTLINE OF THE SYSTEM AND KEY TO THE CLASSIFICATION OF A PEDON

OUTLINE OF THE SYSTEM

The Canadian system of soil classification at the order, great group, and subgroup levels is tabulated alphabetically according to the names of the orders. For each subgroup the abbreviation of the name is appended.

Order	Great Group	Subgroup
Brunisolic	Melanic Brunisol	Orthic Melanic Brunisol O.MB
		Eluviated Melanic Brunisol E.MB
		Gleyed Melanic Brunisol GL.MB
		Gleyed Eluviated Melanic Brunisol GLE.MB
	Eutric Brunisol	Orthic Eutric Brunisol O.EB
		Eluviated Eutric Brunisol E.EB
		Gleyed Eutric Brunisol GL.EB
		Gleyed Eluviated Eutric Brunisol GLE.EB
	Sombric Brunisol	Orthic Sombric Brunisol O.SB
		Eluviated Sombric Brunisol E.SB
		Duric Sombric Brunisol DU.SB
		Gleyed Sombric Brunisol GL.SB
		Gleyed Eluviated Sombric Brunisol GLE.SB
	Dystric Brunisol	Orthic Dystric Brunisol O.DYB
		Eluviated Dystric Brunisol E.DYB
		Duric Dystric Brunisol DU.DYB
		Gleyed Dystric Brunisol GL.DYB
		Gleyed Eluviated Dystric Brunisol GLE.DYB
Chernozemic	Brown	Orthic Brown O.B
		Rego Brown R.B
		Calcareous Brown CA.B
		Eluviated Brown E.B
		Solonetzic Brown SZ.B
		Gleyed Brown GL.B
		Gleyed Rego Brown GLR.B
		Gleyed Calcareous Brown GLCA.B
		Gleyed Eluviated Brown GLE.B
		Gleyed Solonetzic Brown GLSZ.B
	Dark Brown	Orthic Dark Brown O.DB
		Rego Dark Brown R.DB
		Calcareous Dark Brown CA.DB
		Eluviated Dark Brown E.DB
		Solonetzic Dark Brown SZ.DB
		Gleyed Dark Brown GL.DB
		Gleyed Rego Dark Brown GLR.DB
		Gleyed Calcareous Dark Brown GLCA.DB
		Gleyed Eluviated Dark Brown GLE.DB
		Gleyed Solonetzic Dark Brown GLSZ.DB
	Black	Orthic Black O.BL
		Rego Black R.BL
		Calcareous Black CA.BL
		Eluviated Black E.BL

Order	Great Group	Subgroup
		Solonetzic Black SZ.BL
		Gleyed Black GL.BL
		Gleyed Rego Black GLR.BL
		Gleyed Calcareous Black GLCA.BL
		Gleyed Eluviated Black GLE.BL
		Gleyed Solonetzic Black GLSZ.BL
	Dark Gray	Orthic Dark Gray O.DG
		Rego Dark Gray R.DG
		Calcareous Dark Gray CA.DG
		Solonetzic Dark Gray SZ.DG
		Gleyed Dark Gray GL.DG
		Gleyed Rego Dark Gray GLR.DG
		Gleyed Calcareous Dark Gray GLCA.DG
		Gleyed Solonetzic Dark Gray GLSZ.DG
Cryosolic	Turbic Cryosol	Orthic Turbic Cryosol O.TC
		Brunisolic Turbic Cryosol BR.TC
		Regosolic Turbic Cryosol R.TC
		Gleysolic Turbic Cryosol GL.TC
	Static Cryosol	Orthic Static Cryosol O.SC
		Brunisolic Static Cryosol BR.SC
		Regosolic Static Cryosol R.SC
		Gleysolic Static Cryosol GL.SC
	Organic Cryosol	Fibric Organic Cryosol FI.OC
		Mesic Organic Cryosol ME.OC
		Humic Organic Cryosol HU.OC
		Terric Fibric Organic Cryosol TFI.OC
		Terric Mesic Organic Cryosol TME.OC
		Terric Humic Organic Cryosol THU.OC
		Glacic Organic Cryosol GC.OC
Gleysolic	Humic Gleysol	Orthic Humic Gleysol O.HG
		Rego Humic Gleysol R.HG
		Fera Humic Gleysol FE.HG
	Gleysol	Orthic Gleysol O.G
		Rego Gleysol R.G
		Fera Gleysol FE.G
	Luvic Gleysol	Orthic Luvic Gleysol O.LG
		Humic Luvic Gleysol HU.LG
		Fera Luvic Gleysol FE.LG
		Fragic Luvic Gleysol FR.LG
Luvisolic	Gray Brown Luvisol	Orthic Gray Brown Luvisol O.GBL
		Brunisolic Gray Brown Luvisol BR.GBL
		Podzolic Gray Brown Luvisol PZ.GBL
		Gleyed Gray Brown Luvisol GL.GBL
		Gleyed Brunisolic Gray Brown Luvisol GLBR.GBL
		Gleyed Podzolic Gray Brown Luvisol GLPZ. GBL
	Gray Luvisol	Orthic Gray Luvisol O.GL
		Dark Gray Luvisol D.GL
		Brunisolic Gray Luvisol BR.GL
		Podzolic Gray Luvisol PZ.GL

Order	Great Group	Subgroup
		Solonetzic Gray Luvisol SZ.GL
		Fragic Gray Luvisol FR.GL
		Gleyed Gray Luvisol GL.GL
		Gleyed Dark Gray Luvisol GLD.GL
		Gleyed Brunisolic Gray Luvisol GLBR.GL
		Gleyed Podzolic Gray Luvisol GLPZ.GL
		Gleyed Solonetzic Gray Luvisol GLSZ.GL
		Gleyed Fragic Gray Luvisol GLFR.GL
Organic	Fibrisol	Typic Fibrisol TY.F
		Mesic Fibrisol ME.F
		Humic Fibrisol HU.F
		Limno Fibrisol LM.F
		Cumulo Fibrisol CU.F
		Terric Fibrisol T.F
		Terric Mesic Fibrisol TME.F
		Terric Humic Fibrisol THU.F
		Hydric Fibrisol HY.F
	Mesisol	Typic Mesisol TY.M
		Fibric Mesisol FI.M
		Humic Mesisol HU.M
		Limno Mesisol LM.M
		Cumulo Mesisol CU.M
		Terric Mesisol T.M
		Terric Fibric Mesisol TFI.M
		Terric Humic Mesisol THU.M
		Hydric Mesisol HY.M
	Humisol	Typic Humisol TY.H
		Fibric Humisol FI.H
		Mesic Humisol ME.H
		Limno Humisol LM.H
		Cumulo Humisol CU.H
		Terric Humisol T.H
		Terric Fibric Humisol TFI.H
		Terric Mesic Humisol TME.H
		Hydric Humisol HY.H
	Folisol	Typic Folisol TY.FO
Podzolic	Humic Podzol	Orthic Humic Podzol O.HP
		Ortstein Humic Podzol OT.HP
		Placic Humic Podzol P.HP
		Duric Humic Podzol DU.HP
		Fragic Humic Podzol FR.HP
	Ferro-Humic Podzol	Orthic Ferro-Humic Podzol O.FHP
		Ortstein Ferro-Humic Podzol OT.FHP
		Placic Ferro-Humic Podzol P.FHP
		Duric Ferro-Humic Podzol DU.FHP
		Fragic Ferro-Humic Podzol FR.FHP
		Luvisolic Ferro-Humic Podzol LU.FHP
		Sombric Ferro-Humic Podzol SM.FHP
		Gleyed Ferro-Humic Podzol GL.FHP
		Gleyed Ortstein Ferro-Humic Podzol GLOT.FHP
		Gleyed Sombric Ferro-Humic Podzol GLSM.FHP

Order	Great Group	Subgroup
	Humo-Ferric Podzol	Orthic Humo-Ferric Podzol O.HFP
		Ortstein Humo-Ferric Podzol OT.HFP
		Placic Humo-Ferric Podzol P.HFP
		Duric Humo-Ferric Podzol DU.HFP
		Fragic Humo-Ferric Podzol FR.HFP
		Luvisolic Humo-Ferric Podzol LU.HFP
		Sombric Humo-Ferric Podzol SM.HFP
		Gleyed Humo-Ferric Podzol GL.HFP
		Gleyed Ortstein Humo-Ferric Podzol GLOT.HFP
		Gleyed Sombric Humo-Ferric Podzol GLSM.HFP
Regosolic	Regosol	Orthic Regosol O.R
		Cumulic Regosol CU.R
		Gleyed Regosol GL.R
		Gleyed Cumulic Regosol GLCU.R
	Humic Regosol	Orthic Humic Regosol O.HR
		Cumulic Humic Regosol CU.HR
		Gleyed Humic Regosol GL.HR
		Gleyed Cumulic Humic Regosol GLCU.HR
Solonetzic	Solonetz	Brown Solonetz B.SZ
		Dark Brown Solonetz DB.SZ
		Black Solonetz BL.SZ
		Alkaline Solonetz A.SZ
		Gleyed Brown Solonetz GLB.SZ
		Gleyed Dark Brown Solonetz GLDB.SZ
		Gleyed Black Solonetz GLBL.SZ
	Solodized Solonetz	Brown Solodized Solonetz B.SS
		Dark Brown Solodized Solonetz DB.SS
		Black Solodized Solonetz BL.SS
		Dark Gray Solodized Solonetz DG.SS
		Gray Solodized Solonetz G.SS
		Gleyed Brown Solodized Solonetz GLB.SS
		Gleyed Dark Brown Solodized Solonetz GLDB.SS
		Gleyed Black Solodized Solonetz GLBL.SS
		Gleyed Dark Gray Solodized Solonetz GLDG.SS
		Gleyed Gray Solodized Solonetz GLG.SS
	Solod	Brown Solod B.SO
		Dark Brown Solod DB.SO
		Black Solod BL.SO
		Dark Gray Solod DG.SO
		Gray Solod G.SO
		Gleyed Brown Solod GLB.SO
		Gleyed Dark Brown Solod GLDB.SO
		Gleyed Black Solod GLBL.SO
		Gleyed Dark Gray Solod GLDG.SO
		Gleyed Gray Solod GLG.SO

Photographs of some subgroup profiles are shown in Figs. 4–25.

Fig. 4.   Orthic Melanic Brunisol, Ontario.

Fig. 5.   Eluviated Eutric Brunisol, British Columbia.

Fig. 6.   Eluviated Dystric Brunisol, Saskatchewan.

Fig. 7.   Orthic Brown Chernozemic, Alberta.

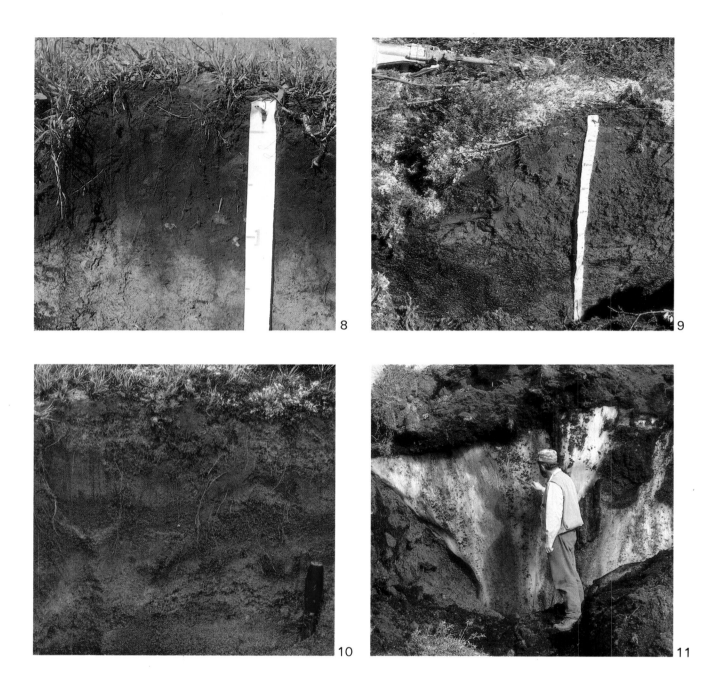

Fig. 8.   Orthic Black Chernozemic, Alberta.

Fig. 9.   Orthic Turbic Cryosol, Northwest Territories.

Fig. 10.   Brunisolic Static Cryosol, Northwest Territories.

Fig. 11.   Glacic Organic Cryosol, Northwest Territories.

Fig. 12.   Orthic Humic Gleysol, Ontario.

Fig. 13.   Rego Gleysol, peaty phase, Ontario.

Fig. 14.   Fera Gleysol, Ontario.

Fig. 15.   Orthic Gray Brown Luvisol, Ontario.

Fig. 16. **Orthic Gray Luvisol**, Alberta.

Fig. 17. Mesic Fibrisol, Alberta.

Fig. 18. Humic Mesisol, British Columbia.

Fig. 19. Orthic Humic Podzol, Newfoundland.

Fig. 20.   Orthic Ferro-Humic Podzol, Quebec.

Fig. 21.   Orthic Humo-Ferric Podzol, Nova Scotia.

Fig. 22.   Orthic Regosol, Northwest Territories.

Fig. 23.   Cumulic Regosol, Northwest Territories.

Fig. 24.   Brown Solodized Solonetz, Saskatchewan.

Fig. 25.   Brown Solod, Saskatchewan.

CLASSIFYING A PEDON

The taxonomic class of a pedon can be determined by using the definitions and key in this and other chapters. A knowledge of soil horizon definitions and soil terminology as presented in this publication is required to use the key. Definitions of these terms related to soil climate may be found in Chapter 13. A key to soil orders is presented in this chapter. In the chapter on an order, the definition of each great group is followed by a definition of the Orthic subgroup, if any, of that great group. Other subgroups are defined in terms of differences in properties from those required of the Orthic subgroup. The families and series within subgroups are not included in this publication. However, family differentiae are specified in the chapter on the soil family and an up-to-date listing of approved series (*CanSIS Canadian Soil Names File*) is maintained by the Canada Soil Survey Committee.

To key out the classification of a pedon use the following procedure.
1.   Expose a vertical section through the pedon, describe it, and take appropriate samples if the designation of some horizons must be checked by laboratory analysis. In some cases the final classification must await the laboratory data.
2.   Study the key to soil orders in this chapter and select the first order in the key that apparently includes the pedon involved.
3.   Turn to the page indicated and read the definition of the order to ensure that it includes the pedon concerned. Then study the key to the great groups following the order definition and select the appropriate great group.
4.   Study the definitions of the subgroups within the selected great group and choose the appropriate subgroup.
5.   To classify the pedon at the family level, turn to the chapter on the soil family and select the family designation that applies; e.g. loamy, mixed, shallow, acid, cold, humid.
6.   For the classification of the pedon at the series level, refer to a recent soil survey report for the area or confer with the soil correlator of the province or territory.

For those familiar with Canadian soil taxonomy and the soils of the area under study, the detailed step-by-step procedure usually is not necessary. However, even experienced pedologists must await laboratory data before classifying some pedons. Periodically users of the system will encounter pedons that do not appear to fit any of the soil classes defined. If the pedon represents an area of more than 200 ha, then describe it thoroughly, collect samples for analysis, indicate the properties that make it impossible to classify, and inform the soil correlator of the province or territory involved.

Key to soil orders

A. Soils that have permafrost within 1 m of the surface or 2 m if strongly cryoturbated.

Cryosolic order

B. Other soils that:
1. Have organic horizons (more than 17% organic C by weight) that extend from the surface to one of the following:
    a. A depth of 60 cm or more if the surface layer is fibric material (Of) having a bulk density of less than 0.1 g/cm³.
    b. A depth of 40 cm or more if the surface layer consists of mesic or humic material (Om or Oh) having a bulk density greater than 0.1 g/cm³.
    c. A depth of at least 10 cm if a lithic contact occurs at a depth less than 60 cm. Mineral material less than 10 cm thick may overlie the lithic contact, but the organic material (O or LFH) must be more than twice as thick as the mineral layer.

2. Have at least one mineral horizon or layer within 40 cm of the surface in addition to the organic horizons (O) as follows:
    a. If a mineral horizon thinner than 40 cm occurs at the surface, the organic horizon or horizons must have a total thickness of at least 40 cm.
    b. If one or more mineral horizons or layers occur within 40 cm of the surface, the organic material must occupy more than 40 cm of the upper 80 cm of the control section.

Organic order

C. Other soils that have a podzolic B horizon and do not have a Bt horizon within 50 cm of the mineral surface.

Podzolic order

D. Other soils that are saturated with water and under reducing conditions either continuously or during some period of the year as indicated either by direct measurements of the water table and the oxidation-reduction status or by any of the following morphological features within 50 cm of the mineral surface:
1. Chromas of 1 or less, without mottles, on ped surfaces or in the matrix if peds are lacking in materials that develop higher chromas under oxidizing conditions.
2. Chromas of 2 or less, in hues of 10YR or redder, on ped surfaces or in the matrix if peds are lacking, accompanied by prominent mottles.
3. Chromas of 3 or less, in hues yellower than 10YR, on ped surfaces or in the matrix if peds are lacking, accompanied by prominent mottles.
4. Hues bluer than 10Y, with or without mottles, on ped surfaces or in the matrix if peds are lacking.

Gleysolic order

E. Other soils that have a solonetzic B horizon.

Solonetzic order

F. Other soils that have a chernozemic A horizon and any one of the following:
1. No Ae horizon.
2. A weakly expressed Ae horizon (Aej) with a dry color value lower than 5.
3. An Ae horizon thinner than an overlying Ah or Ap horizon that does not appear to be eluviated.
4. An Ae horizon not more than 5 cm thick if the chernozemic A is eluviated (Ahe) as indicated by gray streaks and splotches when the soil is dry.

Chernozemic order

G. Other soils that have a Bt horizon.

Luvisolic order

H. Other soils that have either Bm, Btj, or Bfj horizons at least 5 cm thick.

Brunisolic order

I. Other soils.

Regosolic order

Great Group	*Subgroup*
Melanic Brunisol	Orthic Melanic Brunisol O.MB Eluviated Melanic Brunisol E.MB Gleyed Melanic Brunisol GL.MB Gleyed Eluviated Melanic Brunisol GLE.MB
Eutric Brunisol	Orthic Eutric Brunisol O.EB Eluviated Eutric Brunisol E.EB Gleyed Eutric Brunisol GL.EB Gleyed Eluviated Eutric Brunisol GLE.EB
Sombric Brunisol	Orthic Sombric Brunisol O.SB Eluviated Sombric Brunisol E.SB Duric Sombric Brunisol DU.SB Gleyed Sombric Brunisol GL.SB Gleyed Eluviated Sombric Brunisol GLE.SB
Dystric Brunisol	Orthic Dystric Brunisol O.DYB Eluviated Dystric Brunisol E.DYB Duric Dystric Brunisol DU.DYB Gleyed Dystric Brunisol GL.DYB Gleyed Eluviated Dystric Brunisol GLE.DYB

A diagrammatic representation of profiles of some subgroups of the Brunisolic order is given in Fig. 26. A common horizon sequence is given for each subgroup; diagnostic horizons are underlined and some other commonly occurring horizons are listed. The subgroup includes soils having horizon sequences different from those shown.

Soils of the Brunisolic order have sufficient development to exclude them from the Regosolic order, but they lack the degree or kind of horizon development specified for soils of other orders. The central concept of the order is that of soils under forest having brownish-colored Bm horizons, but the order also includes soils of various colors with both Ae horizons and weakly expressed B horizons of accumulation of either clay (Btj), or amorphous Al and Fe compounds (Bfj), or both. Soils having a Bf horizon less than 10 cm thick are a part of this order.

A Bm horizon may have any or all of the following: stronger chroma and redder hue than the underlying material, partial or complete removal of carbonates, slight illuviation based mainly on the occurrence of an overlying Ae horizon, a change in structure from that of the original material. They may develop in materials of any color, such as gray, brown, black or red, which vary in texture from gravel to clay.

Brunisolic soils include some that are calcareous to the surface and very slightly weathered, and others that are strongly acid and apparently weathered to about the same extent as the associated Podzolic soils. Most Brunisolic soils are well to imperfectly drained, but some that have been affected by seepage water are poorly drained although not strongly gleyed. They occur in a wide range of climatic and vegetative environments including Boreal Forest; mixed forest, shrubs, and grass; and heath and tundra.

Brunisolic soils have a Bm, Bfj, thin Bf, or Btj horizon at least 5 cm thick, and they lack the diagnostic properties specified for soils of other orders. Thus they do not have any of the following: a solonetzic or podzolic B horizon, a Bt horizon, evidence of gleying as specified for soils of the Gleysolic order, organic horizons thicker than 40 cm if mesic or humic or 60 cm if fibric, permafrost within 1 m of the surface, or 2 m if cryoturbated. Some Brunisolic soils have an Ah horizon, but it does not meet the specifications for a chernozemic A either because of its inherent properties or the associated soil climate.

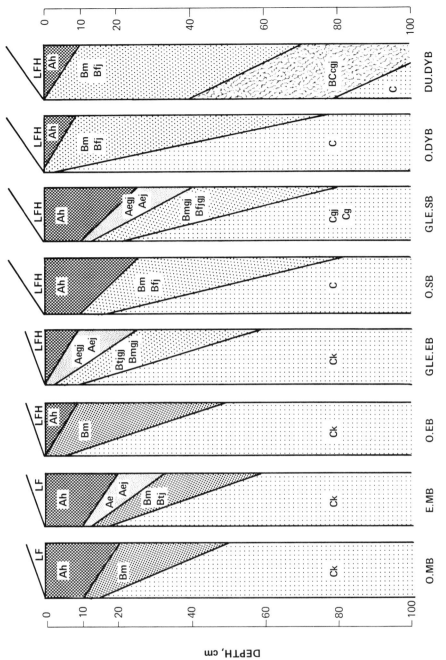

Fig. 26. Diagrammatic horizon pattern of some subgroups of the Brunisolic order.

DISTINGUISHING BRUNISOLIC SOILS FROM SOILS OF OTHER ORDERS

Guidelines for distinguishing Brunisolic soils from soils of other orders with which they might be confused follow. To a degree the Brunisolic order can be considered as an intergrade order between the Regosolic soils and soils of several other orders. The distinctions are based more upon the degree than the kind of development.

Chernozemic. Some Brunisolic soils and many Chernozemic soils have an Ah or dark Ap horizon and either a Bm or a Btj horizon. These soils are classified as Chernozemic only if they have a chernozemic A horizon as defined in Chapter 2. For example, Melanic Brunisols of the St. Lawrence Lowlands lack a chernozemic A and so are excluded from the Chernozemic order because their soil moisture subclass is humid.

Soils of subalpine, alpine, and very cold northern areas having Ah and Bm horizons are classified as Chernozemic if they have a chernozemic A horizon. Many similar soils in these areas do not have a chernozemic A either because of soil climate that is humid or colder than 0°C or because of some inherent property of the Ah horizon such as low base saturation. These soils are classified as Brunisolic. Further studies of these soils may lead to improved criteria of differentiation of Brunisolic and Chernozemic soils. Current information indicates that many Ah horizons of soils at high altitudes and latitudes have the following characteristics that differ from the Ah horizons of Chernozemic soils:

Low degree of incorporation of organic matter with mineral material, moder. This includes the turfy A horizons of some alpine soils. Bulk density less than 1.0.

In addition, some of these soils at high elevations have the following properties that differ from those of Chernozemic soils:

Appreciable content of pyrophosphate-extractable Al + Fe in the Ah horizon, especially in soils containing volcanic ash.

More than 1% organic carbon in the B horizon.

Luvisolic. Luvisolic soils must have a Bt horizon, but Brunisolic soils do not. However, it is difficult to distinguish a Bt from a Btj horizon and micromorphological examination may be required.

Podzolic. Podzolic soils must have a podzolic B horizon and Brunisolic soils do not. However, the colors of some Bm and Bfj horizons are within the range of that of podzolic B horizons, and some of these horizons contain concentrations of amorphous complexes of Al and Fe with organic matter close to the minimum concentration diagnostic for Bf horizons. Therefore, chemical analysis is required to differentiate some Brunisolic soils from Podzolic soils. Soils having a Bf horizon thinner than 10 cm are classified as Brunisolic.

Regosolic. Brunisolic soils must have a Bm, Bfj, thin Bf, or a Btj horizon at least 5 cm thick; Regosolic soils do not.

Cryosolic. Cryosolic soils have permafrost within 1 m of the mineral surface or 2 m if strongly cryoturbated, but Brunisolic soils do not.

The Brunisolic order is divided into four great groups: Melanic Brunisol, Eutric Brunisol, Sombric Brunisol, and Dystric Brunisol based on acidity and the presence or absence of an Ah horizon, as indicated below.

Brunisolic Order

Melanic Brunisol	Eutric Brunisol	Sombric Brunisol	Dystric Brunisol
Thick Ah (>10 cm) pH >5.5	No Ah or thin Ah (<10 cm) pH >5.5	Thick Ah (>10 cm) pH <5.5	No Ah or thin Ah (<10 cm) pH <5.5

Subgroups are separated on the basis of the kind and sequence of the horizons. Some former subgroup features (lithic, andic, turbic, and cryic) are now recognized taxonomically at either the family or series level, but different names are used for some of them. Alternatively, these features may be indicated as phases of subgroups, great groups, or orders.

MELANIC BRUNISOL

These are Brunisolic soils having a dark-colored Ah horizon and a relatively high degree of base saturation as indicated by their pH. They occur typically under deciduous or mixed forest vegetation on materials of high base status in areas of boreal to mesic temperature class and humid moisture subclass, but they are not restricted to such environments. Many uncultivated Melanic Brunisols have a forest mull Ah horizon associated with the activity of soil fauna, especially earthworms.

Melanic Brunisols have an Ah horizon more than 10 cm thick or an Ap horizon with a moist color value of less than 4 and either a Bm, Bfj, or Btj horizon at least 5 cm thick. The pH (0.01 M $CaCl_2$) is 5.5 or more in some part or all of the uppermost 25 cm of the B horizon, or in some part or all of the B horizon and the underlying material either to a total depth of 25 cm or to a lithic contact above that depth. Melanic Brunisols may have L, F, and H horizons and Ae or Aej horizons, but they do not have solonetzic or podzolic B horizons, or Bt horizons. The Ah horizons of some Melanic Brunisols have all of the properties diagnostic of a chernozemic A except the associated soil climate. If cultivated, these soils are classified as Melanic Brunisols if part of the Bm, Btj, or Bfj horizon remains below the Ap and as Humic Regosols if the Ap includes all of the former B horizon.

Orthic Melanic Brunisol

Common horizon sequence: Ah, Bm, C, or Ck

These soils have the general properties specified for the Brunisolic order and the Melanic Brunisol great group. Characteristically, they have a forest mull Ah horizon with fine to medium granular structure and a brownish-colored Bm horizon with a chroma of 3 or more. The color of the B horizon normally fades with depth. Commonly, the C horizon is calcareous.

Orthic Melanic Brunisols are identified by the following properties:

1. They have either an Ah horizon 10 cm thick or more or an Ap horizon at least 10 cm thick with a moist color value less than 4. The A horizon does not meet the requirements of a chernozemic A.
2. They have a pH (0.01 M $CaCl_2$) of 5.5 or more as specified for the great group.
3. They have a Bm horizon at least 5 cm thick.
4. They lack an eluvial horizon, Ae or Aej, at least 2 cm thick.
5. They lack mottles indicative of gleying as specified for Gleyed Melanic Brunisols.

Orthic Melanic Brunisols and all other subgroups of Brunisolic soils may have a lithic contact within 50 cm of the surface or turbic or andic features. These features are separated taxonomically at the family (lithic, some andic) or series (turbic) levels, or as phases of any taxonomic level above the family.

Eluviated Melanic Brunisol

Common horizon sequence: L, Ah, Ae or Aej, Bm or Btj, C or Ck.

These soils have the general properties specified for soils of the Brunisolic order and the Melanic Brunisol great group. They differ from the Orthic Melanic Brunisols by having an eluvial horizon, Ae or Aej, at least 2 cm thick. The underlying horizon may be a Btj with thin clay skins on some surfaces or, less commonly, a Bfj. Otherwise, they have the diagnostic properties of Orthic Melanic Brunisols.

Gleyed Melanic Brunisol

Common horizon sequence: L, Ah, Bmgj, Cgj, or Cg

These soils have the general properties specified for soils of the Brunisolic order and the Melanic Brunisol great group. They differ from the Orthic Melanic Brunisols by having faint to distinct mottles within 50 cm of the mineral surface, or distinct or prominent mottles at depths of 50–100 cm. Otherwise, they have the diagnostic properties of Orthic Melanic Brunisols.

Gleyed Eluviated Melanic Brunisol

Common horizon sequence: L, Ah, Ae or Aej, Bmgj or Btgj, Cgj or Cg

These soils have the general properties specified for soils of the Brunisolic order and the Melanic Brunisol great group. They differ from Eluviated Melanic Brunisols by having mottles indicative of gleying. Gleyed Eluviated Melanic Brunisols have either an Ae or an Aej horizon at least 2 cm thick, and mottles as specified for Gleyed Melanic Brunisols.

EUTRIC BRUNISOL

These are Brunisolic soils that have a relatively high degree of base saturation as indicated by their pH and lack a well-developed mineral-organic surface horizon. They occur mainly on parent material of high base status under forest or shrub vegetation in a wide range of climates.

Eutric Brunisols have either a Bm, Bfj, or Btj horizon at least 5 cm thick, and a pH (0.01 M $CaCl_2$) of 5.5 or more in some part or all of the uppermost 25 cm of the B horizon, or some part or all of the B horizon and the underlying material either to a total depth of 25 cm or to a lithic contact above that depth. Eutric Brunisols may have L, F, and H horizons, Ae or Aej horizons, and an Ah horizon less than 10 cm thick, but they do not have either Bt or podzolic B horizons. If cultivated, these soils are classified as Melanic Brunisols if the Ap horizon is at least 10 cm thick and has a moist color value less than 4 and part of the Bm, Bfj, or Btj remains below the Ap. They are classed as Eutric Brunisols if the Ap horizon does not meet the above specifications and part of the Bm horizon remains below the Ap. If the Ap includes all of the former B horizon, they are classified as Humic Regosols or Regosols, depending on the Ap.

Orthic Eutric Brunisol

Common horizon sequence: LFH, Bm, C or Ck

These soils have the general properties specified for the Brunisolic order and the Eutric Brunisol great group. Usually they have an organic surface horizon overlying a brownish-colored, base-saturated B horizon. The C horizon is commonly calcareous.

Orthic Eutric Brunisols are identified by the following properties:

1. They have a pH (0.01 M $CaCl_2$) of 5.5 or more as specified for the great group.
2. They have a Bm horizon at least 5 cm thick.
3. They lack an eluvial horizon, Ae or Aej, at least 2 cm thick.
4. They lack mottles indicative of gleying as specified for Gleyed Melanic Brunisols.
5. They lack an Ah horizon at least 10 cm thick and an Ap horizon with a moist color value of 4 or less.

Eluviated Eutric Brunisol

Common horizon sequence: LFH, Ae or Aej, Bm or Btj, C or Ck

These soils have the general properties specified for soils of the Brunisolic order and the Eutric Brunisol great group. They differ from the Orthic Eutric Brunisols by having an eluvial horizon, Ae or Aej, at least 2 cm thick. The underlying horizon may be a Btj with thin clay skins on some surfaces or, less commonly, a Bfj. Otherwise, they have the diagnostic properties of Orthic Eutric Brunisols.

Gleyed Eutric Brunisol

Common horizon sequence: LFH, Bmgj, Cgj or Cg

These soils have the general properties specified for soils of the Brunisolic order and the Eutric Brunisol great group. They differ from the Orthic Eutric Brunisols by having faint to distinct mottles within 50 cm of the mineral surface, or distinct or prominent mottles at depths of 50–100 cm. Otherwise, they have the diagnostic properties of Orthic Eutric Brunisols.

Gleyed Eluviated Eutric Brunisol

Common horizon sequence: LFH, Ae or Aej, Bmgj or Btjgj, Cgj or Cg

These soils have the general properties specified for soils of the Brunisolic order and the Eutric Brunisol great group. They differ from Eluviated Eutric Brunisols by having mottles indicative of gleying. Gleyed Eluviated Eutric Brunisols have either an Ae or an Aej horizon at least 2 cm thick and mottles as specified for Gleyed Eutric Brunisols.

SOMBRIC BRUNISOL

These are acid Brunisolic soils having a dark-colored Ah horizon and a relatively low base saturation as indicated by their pH. Minor areas of this great group occur widely in association with Podzolic soils.

Sombric Brunisols have an Ah horizon more than 10 cm thick or an Ap horizon with a moist color value of less than 4, and a Bm, Bfj, thin Bf, or Btj horizon at least 5 cm thick. The pH (0.01 M $CaCl_2$) is less than 5.5 throughout the uppermost

25 cm of the B horizon, or throughout the B horizon and the underlying material to a total depth of at least 25 cm or to a lithic contact above that depth. Sombric Brunisols may have L, F, and H horizons and Ae or Aej horizons, but they do not have solonetzic or podzolic B horizons, or Bt horizons.

Orthic Sombric Brunisol

Common horizon sequence: LFH, Ah, Bm, C

These soils have the general properties specified for the Brunisolic order and the Sombric Brunisol great group. Usually they have an organic layer at the surface, a dark grayish brown to black Ah horizon, a brown acid B horizon, and an acid C horizon.

Orthic Sombric Brunisols are identified by the following properties:

1. They have an Ah horizon at least 10 cm thick or an Ap horizon with a moist color value less than 4.
2. They have a pH (0.01 M CaCl$_2$) of less than 5.5 as specified for the great group.
3. They have a Bm horizon at least 5 cm thick.
4. They lack an eluvial horizon, Ae or Aej, at least 2 cm thick.
5. They lack mottles indicative of gleying as specified for Gleyed Sombric Brunisols.
6. They lack a duric horizon.

Eluviated Sombric Brunisol

Common horizon sequence: LFH, Ah, Ae or Aej, Bm or Bfj, C

These soils have the general properties specified for soils of the Brunisolic order and the Sombric Brunisol great group. They differ from the Orthic Sombric Brunisols by having an eluvial horizon, Ae or Aej, at least 2 cm thick. The underlying horizon may be a Btj with thin clay skins on some surfaces or, more commonly, a Bfj. Otherwise, these soils have the diagnostic properties of Orthic Sombric Brunisols.

Duric Sombric Brunisol

Common horizon sequence: LFH, Ah, Bm or Bfj, Bc or BCc, C

These soils have the general properties specified for the Brunisolic order and the Sombric Brunisol

great group. They differ from the Orthic Sombric Brunisols by having a duric horizon within the control section. They may also have Ae and Btj or Bfj horizons and mottles indicative of gleying. A duric horizon is a strongly cemented acidic horizon that does not meet the requirements of a podzolic B and usually has a color similar to that of the parent material. This horizon has either an abrupt or a clear upper boundary and a diffuse lower boundary usually at least 50 cm below. Air-dry clods do not slake when immersed in water.

Gleyed Sombric Brunisol

Common horizon sequence: LFH, Ah, Bmgj or Bfjgj, Cgj or Cg

These soils have the general properties specified for soils of the Brunisolic order and the Sombric Brunisol great group. They differ from the Orthic Sombric Brunisols by having faint to distinct mottles within 50 cm of the mineral surface or distinct or prominent mottles at depths of 50–100 cm. Otherwise, these soils have the diagnostic properties of Orthic Sombric Brunisols.

Gleyed Eluviated Sombric Brunisol

Common horizon sequence: LFH, Ah, Aegj, Bmgj or Bfjgj, Cgj or Cg

These soils have the general properties specified for soils of the Brunisolic order and the Sombric Brunisol great group. They differ from Eluviated Sombric Brunisols by having mottles indicative of gleying. Gleyed Eluviated Sombric Brunisols have either an Ae or an Aej horizon at least 2 cm thick and mottles as specified for Gleyed Sombric Brunisols.

DYSTRIC BRUNISOL

These are acid Brunisolic soils that lack a well-developed mineral-organic surface horizon. They occur widely usually on parent materials of low base status and typically under forest vegetation.

Dystric Brunisols have a Bm, Bfj, thin Bf, or Btj horizon at least 5 cm thick, and a pH (0.01 M CaCl$_2$) of less than 5.5 throughout the upper 25 cm of the B horizon, or throughout the B horizon and the underlying material to a total depth of at least 25 cm or to a lithic contact above this depth. Dystric Brunisols may have L, F, and H horizons; an Ae or Aej horizon, and an Ah horizon less than 10 cm thick, but they do not have either a Bt or a podzolic B horizon. If cultivated, these soils are classified as Sombric Brunisols when the Ap horizon is at least 10 cm thick and has a moist color value less than 4 and part of the B horizon remains below the Ap. If the Ap horizon does not meet the above specifications but part of the B horizon remains below the Ap, then the soils are Dystric Brunisols. The classification is Humic Regosol or Regosol, depending on the Ap, if the Ap includes all of the former B horizon.

Orthic Dystric Brunisol

Common horizon sequence: LFH, Bm, C

These soils have the general properties specified for the Brunisolic order and the Dystric Brunisol great group. Usually they have organic surface horizons and brownish-colored, acid B horizons overlying acid C horizons.

Orthic Dystric Brunisols are identified by the following properties:

1. They have a pH (0.01 M CaCl$_2$) of less than 5.5 as specified for the great group.
2. They have a Bm horizon at least 5 cm thick.
3. They lack an eluvial horizon, Ae or Aej, at least 2 cm thick.
4. They lack mottles indicative of gleying as specified for Gleyed Dystric Brunisols.
5. They lack a duric horizon.
6. They lack an Ah horizon at least 10 cm thick and an Ap horizon with a moist color value of 4 or less.

Eluviated Dystric Brunisol

Common horizon sequence: LFH, Ae or Aej, Bm or Bfj, C

These soils have the general properties specified for soils of the Brunisolic order and the Dystric Brunisol great group. They differ from the Orthic Dystric Brunisols by having an eluvial horizon, Ae or Aej, at least 2 cm thick. The underlying horizon is commonly a Bfj, but it may be a Btj or a Bm. Otherwise, they have the diagnostic properties of Orthic Dystric Brunisols.

Duric Dystric Brunisol

Common horizon sequence: LFH, Bm or Bfj, Bc or BCc, C

These soils have the general properties specified for soils of the Brunisolic order and the Dystric Brunisol great group. They differ from the Orthic Dystric Brunisols by having a duric horizon within the control section. Also they may have Ae and Btj or Bfj horizons and mottles indicative of gleying.

Gleyed Dystric Brunisol

Common horizon sequence: LFH, Bmgj or Bfjgj, Cgj or Cg

These soils have the general properties specified for soils of the Brunisolic order and the Dystric Brunisol great group. They differ from the Orthic Dystric Brunisols by having faint to distinct mottles within 50 cm of the mineral surface, or distinct or prominent mottles at depths of 50–100 cm. Otherwise, they have the diagnostic properties of Orthic Dystric Brunisols.

Gleyed Eluviated Dystric Brunisol

Common horizon sequence: LFH, Ae or Aej, Bmgj or Bfjgj, Cgj or Cg

These soils have the general properties specified for soils of the Brunisolic order and the Dystric Brunisol great group. They differ from Eluviated Dystric Brunisols by having mottles indicative of gleying. Gleyed Eluviated Dystric Brunisols have either an Ae or an Aej horizon at least 2 cm thick and mottles as specified for Gleyed Dystric Brunisols.

Chapter 5   CHERNOZEMIC ORDER

Great Group	Subgroup
Brown	Orthic Brown O.B
	Rego Brown R.B
	Calcareous Brown CA.B
	Eluviated Brown E.B
	Solonetzic Brown SZ.B
	Gleyed Brown GL.B
	Gleyed Rego Brown GLR.B
	Gleyed Calcareous Brown GLCA.B
	Gleyed Eluviated Brown GLE.B
	Gleyed Solonetzic Brown GLSZ.B
Dark Brown	Subgroups the same as for Brown except for the great group name.
Black	Subgroups the same as for Brown except for the great group name.
Dark Gray	Orthic Dark Gray O.DG
	Rego Dark Gray R.DG
	Calcareous Dark Gray CA.DG
	Solonetzic Dark Gray SZ.DG
	Gleyed Dark Gray GL.DG
	Gleyed Rego Dark Gray GLR.DG
	Gleyed Calcareous Dark Gray GLCA.DG
	Gleyed Solonetzic Dark Gray GLSZ.DG

A diagrammatic representation of profiles of some subgroups of the Chernozemic order is given in Fig. 27. A common horizon sequence is given for each subgroup; diagnostic horizons are underlined and some other commonly occurring horizons are listed. The subgroups include soils having horizon sequences different from those shown.

The general concept of the Chernozemic order is that of well to imperfectly drained soils having surface horizons darkened by the accumulation of organic matter from the decomposition of xerophytic or mesophytic grasses and forbs representative of grassland communities or of grassland-forest communities with associated shrubs and forbs. The major area of Chernozemic soils is the cool, subarid to subhumid Interior Plains of Western Canada. Minor areas of Chernozemic soils occur in some valleys and mountain slopes in the Cordilleran Region extending in some cases beyond the tree line. Most Chernozemic soils are frozen during some period each winter and their sola are dry at some period each summer. Their mean annual temperature is higher than 0°C and usually less than 5.5°C, but some Chernozemic soils in dry valleys of British Columbia have higher temperatures.

The specific definition is as follows: soils of the Chernozemic order have an A horizon in which organic matter has accumulated (Ah, Ahe, Ap) and that meets the requirements of a chernozemic A horizon. A chernozemic A has the following properties:

1. It is at least 10 cm thick.
2. Its color value is darker than 5.5 dry and 3.5 moist, and its chroma is less than 3.5 moist.
3. Its color value is at least one Munsell unit darker than that of the IC horizon.
4. In soils disturbed by cultivation or other means the Ap horizon must be thick and dark enough to provide 15 cm of surface material that meets the color criteria given above.
5. It contains 1–17% organic C and its C:N ratio is less than 17.
6. Usually it has sufficiently good structure so that it is neither massive and hard nor single grained when dry.
7. Its base saturation (neutral salt) is more than 80% and Ca is the dominant exchangeable cation.
8. It is restricted to soils having a mean annual temperature of 0°C or higher and a soil moisture subclass drier than humid. Chernozemic soils may have an Ae horizon and a Bm or a Bt horizon.

They do not have any of the following: solonetzic B, podzolic B, evidence of gleying strongly enough expressed to meet the criteria of Gleysolic soils, or permafrost within 2 m of the surface.

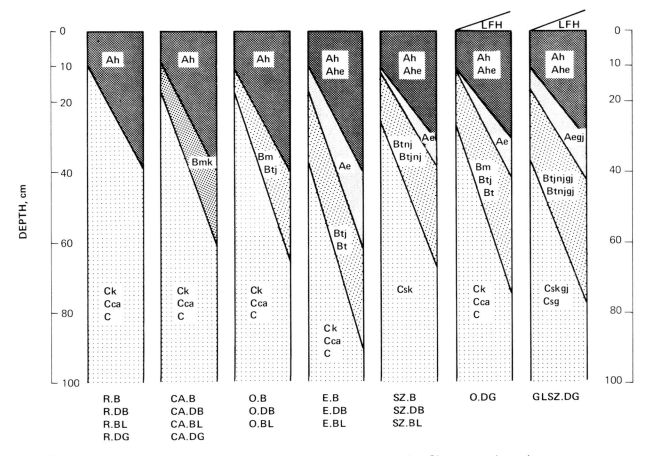

Fig. 27. Diagrammatic horizon pattern of some subgroups of the Chernozemic order.

DISTINGUISHING CHERNOZEMIC SOILS FROM SOILS OF OTHER ORDERS

Throughout the major area of Chernozemic soils in Canada there is little difficulty in distinguishing them from soils of other orders. However, soils of several other orders may have dark-colored Ah horizons. The bases for distinguishing Chernozemic soils from such soils are outlined below.

Solonetzic. These soils have a solonetzic B horizon, but Chernozemic soils do not.

Luvisolic. Some Dark Gray Luvisols and some Chernozemic soils have all of the following: a chernozemic A horizon, an Ae horizon, a Bt horizon, and a subhumid soil moisture regime. The classification of these soils at the order level is done according to these guidelines:

1. If the chernozemic A horizon is eluviated as evidenced by gray streaks and splotches when the soil is dry, and if the Ae extends to a depth of at least 5 cm below the overlying Ah, Ahe, or Ap, the soil is Luvisolic (Dark Gray Luvisol).
2. If the chernozemic A is not eluviated as described above, the soil is classified as Chernozemic unless the Ae horizon has a dry color value higher than 5 and a thickness greater than that of the Ah. In the latter case, the soil is classified as Luvisolic (Dark Gray Luvisol).

Podzolic. These soils have a podzolic B horizon, but Chernozemic soils do not.

Brunisolic. Brunisolic soils having dark-colored, mineral-organic surface horizons are distinguished from Chernozemic soils. They do not have a chernozemic A horizon because their mean annual temperature is below 0°C, or because their moisture subclass is humid or wetter, or the A horizon is acid or has a high C:N ratio. A degree of ambiguity remains on the basis of separation of some Melanic Brunisols from Chernozemic soils, especially in subalpine and alpine areas. Further work on these soils may disclose definitive differences between their A horizons and those of Chernozemic soils (*see* Chapter 4, Brunisolic order).

Regosolic. These soils do not have a chernozemic A horizon.

Gleysolic. Some of these soils have a chernozemic A horizon. They are excluded from the Chernozemic order because of evidence of reduction and poor drainage as specified in the Gleysolic order definition.

Chernozemic soils are divided into four great groups: Brown, Dark Brown, Black, and Dark Gray mainly on the basis of the color of the chernozemic A horizon, which reflects differences in the nature and amount of organic matter incorporated with the mineral material because of differences in climate and vegetation. The bases of the great group separations are tabulated below.

Chernozemic Order

	Brown	Dark Brown	Black	Dark Gray
Color value (dry)	4.5–5.5	3.5–4.5	<3.5	<4.5
Chroma	>1.5	>1.5	1.5 or less	<1.5
Climate	subarid to semiarid	semiarid	subhumid	subhumid

Subgroups are separated on the basis of the kind and sequence of the horizons indicating conformity with the central concept of the great group or intergrades to soils of other orders, or additional features. Some of the former subgroup features (grumic, carbonated, saline, and lithic) are now recognized taxonomically at either the family or series level. They may be indicated also as phases of subgroups, great groups, or orders. The former Solonetzic and Solodic subgroups are now combined into a single subgroup Solonetzic, which includes all the intergrades to the Solonetzic order.

BROWN

These are soils that occur in the most arid segment of the climatic range of Chernozemic soils and have brownish-colored A horizons. They are associated with xerophytic and mesophytic grass and forb vegetation. In virgin Brown soils the upper part of the Ah horizon is commonly as light as or lighter in color value than the lower part of the Ah or the upper B horizon.

Brown soils have chernozemic Ah or Ap horizons with color values darker than 3.5 moist and 4.5–5.5 dry. The chroma of the A horizon is usually higher than 1.5. The soil climate of this great group is typically cold, rarely mild, and subarid to semiarid (*see* the chapter on soil family).

Orthic Brown

Common horizon sequence: <u>Ah</u>, <u>Bm</u>, Cca or Ck

The Orthic Brown subgroup may be thought of as the central concept of Brown soils. It encompasses the properties specified for the Chernozemic order and the Brown great group. Orthic Brown soils are well drained and their B horizons are usually brown with prismatic macrostructure. The prismatic peds are usually coarse in coarse-textured soils. With increasing clay content, the peds become smaller and have an increasing tendency to crush to fine blocky and granular aggregates. Thin clay coatings occur occasionally to commonly on ped surfaces in the B horizon. A light-colored horizon of carbonate accumulation usually occurs below the brownish B horizon.

Orthic Brown soils are identified by the following properties:

1. They have a chernozemic A horizon with a color value darker than 3.5 moist and 4.5–5.5 dry.

2. They have a B horizon (Bm, Btj, or Bt) at least 5 cm thick that contains no alkaline earth carbonates.
3. They lack an Ae horizon at least 2 cm thick.
4. They lack a Bnjtj horizon or a similar horizon characteristic of intergrades to the Solonetzic order.
5. They lack evidence of gleying as indicated by faint to distinct mottling within 50 cm of the surface.

Orthic Brown soils and all other subgroups of Chernozemic soils may have any of the following features that are separated either at the family or series level taxonomically or as phases of any taxonomic level above the family: lithic, saline, grumic, and carbonated.

Rego Brown

Common horizon sequence: <u>Ah</u>, C or Cca, or Ck

These soils have the general properties specified for the Chernozemic order and the Brown great group. They differ from the Orthic Brown soils by lacking a B horizon or having a B horizon (Bm) less than 5 cm thick. Usually Rego Brown soils have an AC profile. They may have grumic or saline features.

Calcareous Brown

Common horizon sequence: <u>Ah</u>, <u>Bmk</u>, Cca or Ck

These soils have the general properties of the Chernozemic order and the Brown great group. They differ from the Orthic Brown soils by having a B horizon from which primary alkaline earth carbonates have not been removed completely (Bmk). Otherwise, they have the general properties of Orthic Brown soils.

Eluviated Brown

Common horizon sequence: <u>Ah</u>, <u>Ae</u>, <u>Btj</u> or <u>Bt</u>, Cca or Ck

These soils have the general properties of the Chernozemic order and the Brown great group. They differ from the Orthic Brown soils by having an eluvial horizon or horizons at least 2 cm thick (Ahe, Ae, Aej) usually underlain by a weakly to moderately developed illuvial Btj or Bt horizon. Commonly, the eluvial horizon is slightly to moderately acid. Two variations of this subgroup may be recognized.

One variation has pedons in which eluviation is indicated by light-colored, relic, macroprismatic structure below the Ah or Ap. The prismatic units break into coarse to medium platy peds that commonly have vesicular or tubular voids. This suggests the development of an eluvial horizon from a former prismatic B. The Bt or Btj horizon underlying the eluvial horizon usually has well-developed macroprismatic structure that breaks to blocky peds of lower color value and slightly higher chroma than the eluvial horizon.

The other variation has cumulic pedons in which the periodic deposition of transported soil materials modifies the normal horizon differentiation caused by leaching. These pedons have thick horizons of partly leached, accumulated materials overlying former A or transitional AB horizons. They are usually found on lower concave slopes where sediments are deposited from upslope. Commonly, such pedons can be recognized by their thick Ahe horizons.

Solonetzic Brown

Common horizon sequence: Ah, Ae, Bnjtj, Csa or Ck

These soils have the general properties specified for the Chernozemic order and the Brown great group. They differ from the Orthic Brown soils by having properties indicative of intergrading to the Solonetzic order. Specifically, they have a Bnj, Bnjtj, or Btnj horizon and may have Ae, AB, and saline C horizons. The B horizon usually has prismatic structure and hard consistence. The prisms usually break to blocky secondary structural units having shiny, dark coatings. The eluvial horizon that is found in some Solonetzic Brown soils may be similar to that described for the Eluviated Brown subgroup. Solonetzic Brown soils are usually associated with saline materials, and their B horizons usually have a higher proportion of exchangeable Na or Na and Mg than is characteristic of Orthic Brown soils.

Gleyed Brown

Common horizon sequence: Ah, Bmgj, Ckgj

These soils have the general properties specified for the Chernozemic order and the Brown great group. They differ from the Orthic Brown soils by having faint to distinct mottles indicative of gleying within 50 cm of the surface.

Gleyed Rego Brown

Common horizon sequence: Ah, Ckgj

These soils have the general properties specified for the Chernozemic order and the Brown great group. They differ from the Rego Brown soils by having mottles indicative of gleying. Gleyed Rego Brown soils lack a distinct B horizon at least 5 cm thick and have faint to distinct mottles within 50 cm of the surface.

Gleyed Calcareous Brown

Common horizon sequence: Ah, Bmkgj, Ckgj

These soils have the general properties specified for the Chernozemic order and the Brown great group. They differ from the Calcareous Brown soils by having mottles indicative of gleying. Gleyed Calcareous Brown soils have a Bmk horizon at least 5 cm thick and faint to distinct mottles within 50 cm of the surface.

Gleyed Eluviated Brown

Common horizon sequence: Ah, Aej, Btjgj or Btgj, Ckgj

These soils have the general properties specified for the Chernozemic order and the Brown great group. They differ from the Eluviated Brown soils by having mottles indicative of gleying. Gleyed Eluviated Brown soils have an eluvial horizon and faint to distinct mottles within 50 cm of the surface.

Gleyed Solonetzic Brown

Common horizon sequence: Ah, Ae, Bnjtjgj, Csagj

These soils have the general properties specified for the Chernozemic order and the Brown great group. They differ from the Solonetzic Brown soils by having mottles indicative of gleying. Gleyed Solonetzic Brown soils have a Bnj or a Btnj horizon and faint to distinct mottles within 50 cm of the surface.

DARK BROWN

These Chernozemic soils have A horizons somewhat darker in color than soils of the Brown great group. Dark Brown soils usually occur in association with a native vegetation of mesophytic grasses and forbs in a semiarid climate. In virgin areas the Ah horizon is usually darkest at the surface and becomes progressively lighter in color with depth.

Dark Brown soils have the characteristics specified for the order. The chernozemic A horizon has a color value darker than 3.5 moist and 3.5–4.5 dry; the chroma is usually greater than 1.5 dry. The soil climate of this great group is typically cold, rarely mild, and semiarid.

Orthic Dark Brown

Common horizon sequence: Ah, Bm, Cca or Ck

The Orthic Dark Brown subgroup may be thought of as the central concept of Dark Brown soils. It encompasses the properties specified for the Chernozemic order and the Dark Brown great group. Usually, Orthic Dark Brown soils have brownish-colored, prismatic B horizons, and light-colored horizons of carbonate accumulation similar to those of Orthic Brown soils.

Orthic Dark Brown soils are identified by the following properties:

1. They have a chernozemic A horizon with a color value darker than 3.5 moist and between 3.5–4.5 dry.
2. They have a B horizon (Bm, Btj, Bt) at least 5 cm thick that does not contain alkaline earth carbonates.
3. They lack an Ae horizon at least 2 cm thick.
4. They lack a Bnjtj horizon or a similar horizon characteristic of intergrades to the Solonetzic order.
5. They lack evidence of gleying as indicated by faint to distinct mottling within 50 cm of the surface.

Rego Dark Brown

Common horizon sequence: Ah, C, Cca or Ck

These soils have the general properties specified for the Chernozemic order and the Dark Brown great group. They differ from the Orthic Dark Brown soils either in lacking a B horizon or in having a B horizon (Bm) less than 5 cm thick. Usually Rego Dark Brown soils have an AC profile. They may have grumic or saline features.

Calcareous Dark Brown

Common horizon sequence: Ah, Bmk, Cca or Ck

These soils have the general properties specified for the Chernozemic order and the Dark Brown great group. They differ from the Orthic Dark Brown soils by having a B horizon from which primary alkaline earth carbonates have not been removed completely (Bmk). Otherwise, they have the general properties of Orthic Dark Brown soils.

Eluviated Dark Brown

Common horizon sequence: Ah, Ae, Btj or Bt, Cca, Ck

These soils have the general properties specified for the Chernozemic order and the Dark Brown great group. They differ from the Orthic Dark Brown soils by having an eluvial horizon or horizons (Ahe, Ae, Aej) at least 2 cm thick usually underlain by a weakly to moderately developed illuvial Btj or Bt horizon. Two variations of this subgroup may be recognized. The first has an eluvial horizon developed in a former B horizon, and the other has an eluvial horizon developing in an A horizon subject to periodic deposition of sediment. These variations are described in more detail for the Eluviated Brown subgroup.

Solonetzic Dark Brown

Common horizon sequence: Ah, Ae, Bnjtj, Csa or Ck

These soils have the general properties specified for the Chernozemic order and the Dark Brown great group. They differ from the Orthic Dark Brown soils by having properties indicative of intergrading to the Solonetzic order. Specifically, they have a Bnj, Bnjtj, or Btnj horizon and may have Ae, AB, and saline C horizons. The B horizon usually has prismatic structure with hard consistence. The prisms usually break to blocky secondary structural units having shiny, dark coatings. The eluvial horizon that occurs in some Solonetzic Dark Brown soils may be similar to that described for the Eluviated Dark Brown subgroup. Solonetzic Dark Brown soils are usually associated with saline materials, and their B horizons usually have a higher proportion of exchangeable Na or Na + Mg than is characteristic of Orthic Dark Brown soils.

Gleyed Dark Brown

Common horizon sequence: Ah, Bmgj, Cgj or Ckgj

These soils have the general properties specified for the Chernozemic order and the Dark Brown great group. They differ from the Orthic Dark Brown soils by having faint to distinct mottles indicative of gleying within 50 cm of the surface.

Gleyed Rego Dark Brown

Common horizon sequence: Ah, Ckgj

These soils have the general properties specified for the Chernozemic order and the Dark Brown great group. They differ from the Rego Dark Brown soils by having mottles indicative of gleying. Gleyed Rego Dark Brown soils lack a B horizon at least 5 cm thick and have faint to distinct mottles within 50 cm of the surface.

Gleyed Calcareous Dark Brown

Common horizon sequence: Ah, Bmkgj, Ckgj

These soils have the general properties specified for the Chernozemic order and the Dark Brown great group. They differ from the Calcareous Dark Brown soils by having mottles indicative of gleying. Gleyed Calcareous Dark Brown soils have a Bmk horizon at least 5 cm thick and faint to distinct mottles within 50 cm of the surface.

Gleyed Eluviated Dark Brown

Common horizon sequence: Ah, Aej, Btjgj, Cgj or Ckgj

These soils have the general properties specified for the Chernozemic order and the Dark Brown great group. They differ from the Eluviated Dark Brown soils by having mottles indicative of gleying. Gleyed Eluviated Dark Brown soils have an eluvial horizon and faint to distinct mottles within 50 cm of the surface.

Gleyed Solonetzic Dark Brown

Common horizon sequence: Ah, Ae, Bnjtjgj, Ckgj, Csagj

These soils have the general properties specified for the Chernozemic order and the Dark Brown great group. They differ from the Solonetzic Dark Brown soils by having mottles indicative of gleying. Gleyed Solonetzic Dark Brown soils have a Bnj or a Btnj horizon and faint to distinct mottles within 50 cm of the surface.

BLACK

These Chernozemic soils have A horizons darker in color and commonly thicker than soils of the Brown and Dark Brown great groups. Black soils usually occur in association with a native vegetation of mesophytic grasses and forbs or with mixed grass, forb, and tree cover. Some Black soils occur under alpine grass and shrub vegetation.

Black soils have the characteristics specified for the order, and a chernozemic A horizon with a color value darker than 3.5 dry. The chroma of the chernozemic A is usually 1.5 or less, moist. The soil climate of this great group is typically cold, rarely mild, and subhumid.

Orthic Black

Common horizon sequence: Ah, Bm, Cca or Ck

The Orthic Black subgroup may be thought of as the central concept of Black soils. It encompasses the properties specified for the Chernozemic order and the Black great group. Usually Orthic Black soils have brownish-colored, prismatic B horizons, and light-colored horizons of carbonate accumulation similar to those of Orthic Brown soils.

Orthic Black soils are identified by the following properties:

1. They have a chernozemic A horizon with a color value darker than 3.5 moist and dry.
2. They have a B horizon (Bm, Btj, Bt) at least 5 cm thick that does not contain alkaline earth carbonates.
3. They lack an Ae horizon at least 2 cm thick.
4. They lack a Bnjtj or similar horizon characteristic of intergrades to the Solonetzic order.
5. They lack evidence of gleying as indicated by faint to distinct mottling within 50 cm of the surface.

Rego Black

Common horizon sequence: Ah, Cca or Ck

These soils have the general properties specified for the Chernozemic order and the Black great group. They differ from the Orthic Black soils by lacking a B horizon or having a B horizon (Bm) less than 5 cm thick. Usually Rego Black soils have an AC profile. They may have grumic or saline features.

Calcareous Black

Common horizon sequence: Ah, Bmk, Cca or Ck

These soils have the general properties of the Chernozemic order and the Black great group. They differ from the Orthic Black soils by having a B horizon from which primary alkaline earth carbonates have not been removed completely (Bmk). Otherwise they have the general properties of Orthic Black soils.

Eluviated Black

Common horizon sequence: Ah, Ae, Btj or Bt, Cca or Ck

These soils have the general properties of the Chernozemic order and the Black great group. They differ from the Orthic Black soils by having an eluvial horizon or horizons at least 2 cm thick (Ahe, Ae, Aej) usually underlain by a weakly to moderately developed illuvial Btj or Bt horizon.

Solonetzic Black

Common horizon sequence: Ah, Ae, Bnjtj, Cs or Ck

These soils have the general properties specified for the Chernozemic order and the Black great group. They differ from the Orthic Black soils by having properties indicative of intergrading to the Solonetzic order. Specifically, they have a Bnj, Bnjtj, or Btnj horizon and may have Ae, AB, and saline C horizons. The B horizon usually has prismatic structure and hard consistence. The prisms usually break to blocky secondary structural units with shiny, dark coatings. The eluvial horizon that occurs in some Solonetzic Black soils may be similar to that described for the Eluviated Black subgroup. Solonetzic Black soils are usually associated with saline materials, and their B horizons usually have a higher proportion of exchangeable Na or Na and Mg than is characteristic of Orthic Black soils.

Gleyed Black

Common horizon sequence: Ah, Bmgj, Ckgj

These soils have the general properties specified for the Chernozemic order and the Black great group. They differ from the Orthic Black soils by having faint to distinct mottles indicative of gleying within 50 cm of the surface.

Gleyed Rego Black

Common horizon sequence: Ah, Ckgj

These soils have the general properties specified for the Chernozemic order and the Black great group. They differ from the Rego Black soils by having mottles indicative of gleying. Gleyed Rego Black soils lack a B horizon at least 5 cm thick and have faint to distinct mottles within 50 cm of the surface.

Gleyed Calcareous Black

Common horizon sequence: Ah, Bmkgj, Ckgj

These soils have the general properties specified for the Chernozemic order and the Black great group. They differ from the Calcareous Black soils by having mottles indicative of gleying. Gleyed Calcareous Black soils have a Bmk horizon at least 5 cm thick and faint to distinct mottles within 50 cm of the surface.

Gleyed Eluviated Black

Common horizon sequence: Ah, Aej, Btjgj, Ckgj

These soils have the general properties specified for the Chernozemic order and the Black great group. They differ from the Eluviated Black soils by having mottles indicative of gleying. Gleyed Eluviated Black soils have an eluvial horizon and faint to distinct mottles within 50 cm of the surface.

Gleyed Solonetzic Black

Common horizon sequence: Ah, Ae, Bnjtjgj, Ckgj, Csgj

These soils have the general properties specified for the Chernozemic order and the Black great group. They differ from the Solonetzic Black soils by having mottles indicative of gleying. Gleyed Solonetzic Black soils have a Bnj or a Btnj horizon and faint to distinct mottling within 50 cm of the surface.

DARK GRAY

These Chernozemic soils have chernozemic A horizons with characteristics indicative of eluviation associated with soils developed under forest vegetation. Dark Gray soils usually occur under mixed native vegetation of trees, shrubs, forbs, and grasses in forest-grassland transition zones in areas of cold, subhumid soil climate. Virgin Dark Gray soils usually have leaf mats (L–H horizons) overlying Ah or Ahe horizons. The peds of the A horizons may have dark-colored surfaces, but the crushed peds usually have gray or brownish colors of higher value or chroma. A "salt and pepper" effect, light gray spots, or bands on a darker matrix may be observable in the A horizons, which tend to have platy structure.

Dark Gray soils have the characteristics specified for the order. Virgin soils have a chernozemic A horizon with a color value darker than 3.5 moist and 4.5 dry. An Ap horizon 15 cm thick must have a color value darker than 3.5 moist and 5 dry. Dark Gray soils may have a light-colored Ae horizon 5 cm or less thick provided that the mixed surface horizon (Ap) meets the requirements specified for the great group. Similar soils having a distinct Ae horizon thicker than 5 cm below the chernozemic A horizon and a Bt horizon are classified as Dark Gray Luvisols.

Orthic Dark Gray

Common horizon sequence: Ahe, Ae, Bm or Btj or Bt, Cca or Ck

The Orthic Dark Gray subgroup may be thought of as the central concept of Dark Gray soils. It encompasses the properties specified for the Chernozemic order and the Dark Gray great group. Usually Orthic Dark Gray soils have brownish-colored, prismatic B horizons that commonly meet the requirements of a Bt horizon.

Orthic Dark Gray soils are identified by the following properties:

1. They have a chernozemic A horizon with a color value darker than 3.5 moist and 3.5–4.5 dry for virgin soils (3.5–5 dry for Ap).
2. They have a B horizon (Bm, Btj, Bt) at least 5 cm thick that does not contain alkaline earth carbonates.

3. They lack an Ae horizon more than 5 cm thick.
4. They lack a Bnjtj horizon or a similar horizon characteristic of intergrades to the Solonetzic order.
5. They lack evidence of gleying as indicated by faint to distinct mottling within 50 cm of the surface.

Rego Dark Gray

Common horizon sequence: Ahe, Cca or Ck

These soils have the general properties specified for the Chernozemic order and the Dark Gray great group. They differ from the Orthic Dark Gray soils by lacking a B horizon or having one (Bm) less than 5 cm thick. Usually Rego Dark Gray soils have an AC profile. They may have grumic or saline features.

Calcareous Dark Gray

Common horizon sequence: Ahe, Bmk, Cca or Ck

These soils have the general properties of the Chernozemic order and the Dark Gray great group. They differ from the Orthic Dark Gray soils by having a B horizon from which primary alkaline earth carbonates have not been removed completely (Bmk). Otherwise they have the general properties of Orthic Dark Gray soils.

Solonetzic Dark Gray

Common horizon sequence: Ahe, Ae, Bnjtj, Cs or Ck

These soils have the general properties specified for the Chernozemic order and the Dark Gray great group. They differ from the Orthic Dark Gray soils by having properties indicative of intergrading to the Solonetzic order. Specifically, they have either a Bnj, Bnjtj, or Btnj horizon, and they may have Ae, AB, and saline C horizons. The Ae horizon, if any, is not more than 5 cm thick. The B horizon usually has prismatic structure and hard consistence, and the prisms usually break to blocky secondary structural units with shiny, dark coatings. Solonetzic Dark Gray soils are usually associated with saline materials, and their B horizons usually have a higher proportion of exchangeable Na or Na and Mg than is characteristic of Orthic Dark Gray soils.

Gleyed Dark Gray

Common horizon sequence: Ahe, Bmgj, Ckgj

These soils have the general properties specified for the Chernozemic order and the Dark Gray great group. They differ from the Orthic Dark Gray soils by having faint to distinct mottles indicative of gleying within 50 cm of the surface.

Gleyed Rego Dark Gray

Common horizon sequence: Ahe, Ckgj

These soils have the general properties specified for the Chernozemic order and the Dark Gray great group. They differ from the Rego Dark Gray soils by having mottles indicative of gleying. Gleyed Rego Dark Gray soils lack a B horizon at least 5 cm thick and have faint to distinct mottles within 50 cm of the surface.

Gleyed Calcareous Dark Gray

Common horizon sequence: Ahe, Bmkgj, Ckgj

These soils have the general properties specified for the Chernozemic order and the Dark Gray great group. They differ from the Calcareous Dark Gray soils by having mottles indicative of gleying. Gleyed Calcareous Dark Gray soils have a Bmk horizon at least 5 cm thick and faint to distinct mottles within 50 cm of the surface.

Gleyed Solonetzic Dark Gray

Common horizon sequence: Ahe, Ae, Bnjtjgj, Ckgj, Csgj

These soils have the general properties specified for the Chernozemic order and the Dark Gray great group. They differ from the Solonetzic Dark Gray soils by having mottles indicative of gleying. Gleyed Solonetzic Dark Gray soils have a Bnj or a Btnj horizon and faint to distinct mottles within 50 cm of the surface.

Chapter 6 CRYOSOLIC ORDER

Great Group	Subgroup
Turbic Cryosol	Orthic Turbic Cryosol O.TC
	Brunisolic Turbic Cryosol BR.TC
	Regosolic Turbic Cryosol R.TC
	Gleysolic Turbic Cryosol GL.TC
Static Cryosol	Orthic Static Cryosol O.SC
	Brunisolic Static Cryosol BR.SC
	Regosolic Static Cryosol R.SC
	Gleysolic Static Cryosol GL.SC
Organic Cryosol	Fibric Organic Cryosol FI.OC
	Mesic Organic Cryosol ME.OC
	Humic Organic Cryosol HU.OC
	Terric Fibric Organic Cryosol TFI.OC
	Terric Mesic Organic Cryosol TME.OC
	Terric Humic Organic Cryosol THU.OC
	Glacic Organic Cryosol GC.OC

A diagrammatic representation of profiles of some subgroups of the Cryosolic order is shown in Fig. 28. A common horizon sequence is given for each subgroup; diagnostic horizons are underlined and some other commonly occurring horizons are listed. The subgroups include soils having horizon sequences different from those shown.

Soils of the Cryosolic order occupy much of the northern third of Canada where permafrost remains close to the surface of both mineral and organic deposits. Cryosolic soils predominate north of the tree line, are common in the subarctic forest area in fine textured soils, and extend into the Boreal Forest in some organic materials and into some alpine areas of mountainous regions. Cryoturbation of these soils is common, and it may be indicated by patterned ground features such as sorted and nonsorted nets, circles, polygons, stripes, and earth hummocks.

Cryosolic soils are formed in either mineral or organic materials that have permafrost either within 1 m of the surface or within 2 m if more than one-third of the pedon has been strongly cryoturbated, as indicated by disrupted, mixed, or broken horizons. They have a mean annual temperature below 0°C. Differentiation of Cryosolic soils from soils of other orders involves either determining or estimating the depth to permafrost, which is a difficult task near the southern boundary of permafrost.

The Cryosolic order is divided into three great groups: Turbic Cryosol, Static Cryosol, and Organic Cryosol based on the degree of cryoturbation and the nature of soil material, mineral or organic, as indicated below.

Cryosolic Order

Turbic Cryosol	Static Cryosol	Organic Cryosol
Mineral soil	Mineral soil	Organic soil material
Marked cryoturbation	No marked cryoturbation	Permafrost within 1 m of surface
Usually patterned ground	Permafrost within 1 m of surface	
Permafrost within 2 m of surface		

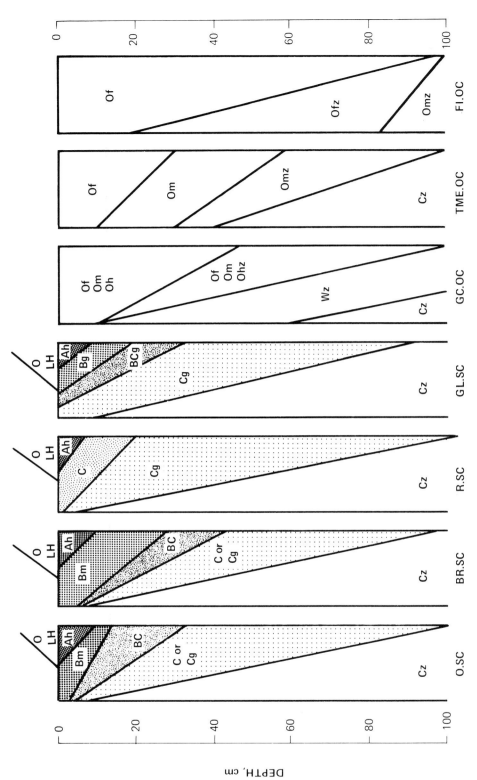

Fig. 28.   Diagrammatic horizon pattern of some subgroups of the Cryosolic order.

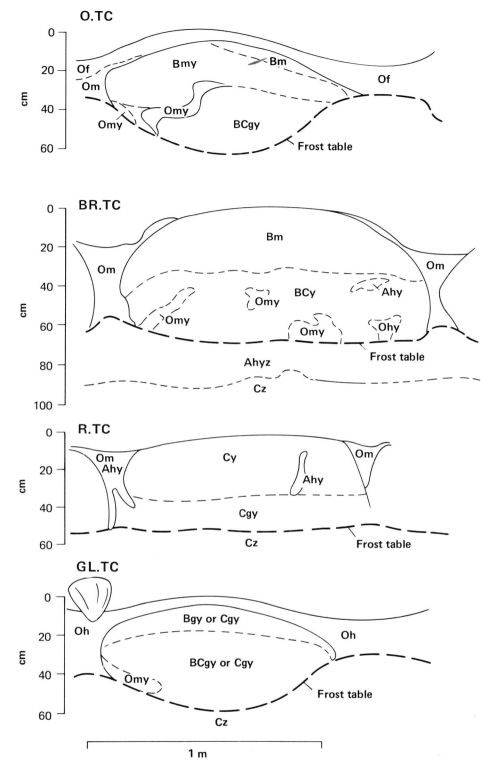

Fig. 28.   Diagrammatic horizon pattern of some subgroups of the Cryosolic order.

TURBIC CRYOSOL

These are Cryosolic soils that have developed primarily in mineral material and have marked evidence of cryoturbation. They generally occur on patterned ground, which includes such cryogenic forms as sorted and nonsorted circles, nets, polygons, stripes, and steps in stony or coarse textured material and nonsorted units such as earth hummocks in medium and fine textured materials. The pedon includes all elements of the microtopography in cycles less than 7 m in width. Processes include sorting of different sized particles and mixing of both mineral and organic material from different horizons. Organic (Oy) or organic-rich, mineral horizons (Ahy) are characteristically present in the region of the permafrost table (upper surface of permafrost layer), and there is generally a buildup of ice in the upper part of the permafrost layer.

Turbic Cryosols are mineral soils having marked evidence of cryoturbation as indicated by broken horizons and displaced material in more than one-third of the pedon and permafrost within 2 m of the surface.

Orthic Turbic Cryosol

Common horizon sequence: Om, <u>Bmy</u>, BCy, Cgy, Omy, <u>Cz</u>

These soils have the general properties specified for soils of the Cryosolic order and the Turbic Cryosol great group. They are identified by the following properties:

1. They have a Bm horizon less than 10 cm thick or a Bmy horizon or both.
2. The horizons are strongly disrupted by cryoturbation. Tongues of mineral and organic horizons, organic and mineral intrusions, and oriented stones occur commonly.
3. The surface horizons are not strongly gleyed, but there is usually a gleyed horizon immediately above the permafrost table.

Orthic Turbic Cryosols usually have a Bmy horizon and subsurface organic (Omy, Ohy) or organic-rich, mineral horizons (Ahy). Peaty surface horizons up to 40 cm thick, moder Ah horizons, and Bm horizons less than 10 cm thick may occur. These soils have been called Upland Tundra and Forest Tundra soils.

Brunisolic Turbic Cryosol

Common horizon sequence: Om, <u>Bm</u>, <u>Bmy</u> or <u>BCy</u>, Cgy, Omy, <u>Cz</u>

These soils have the general properties specified for soils of the Cryosolic order and the Turbic Cryosol great group. They differ from the Orthic Turbic Cryosols by having a Bm horizon more than 10 cm thick and continuous over the imperfectly to well drained part of the pedon that is relatively unaffected by cryoturbation.

Regosolic Turbic Cryosol

Common horizon sequence: Om, <u>Cy</u>, Cgy, <u>Cz</u>

These soils have the general properties specified for the Cryosolic order and the Turbic Cryosol great group. They differ from the Orthic Turbic Cryosols by lacking Bm and Bmy horizons. Usually these soils do not have subsurface Ahy or Oy horizons, or intrusions. Regosolic Turbic Cryosols occur mainly in high Arctic or Alpine sites.

Gleysolic Turbic Cryosol

Common horizon sequence: Om, <u>Bgy</u> or <u>Cgy</u>, <u>Cz</u>

These soils have the general properties specified for the Cryosolic order and the Turbic Cryosol great group. They differ from Orthic Turbic Cryosols by having evidence of gleying in the form of low chromas or mottling to the mineral surface. The surface mineral horizon, Bgy or Cgy, may be overlain by organic layers thinner than 40 cm.

The name Gleysolic rather than Gleyed is used because these soils are not equivalent in degree of gleying to Gleyed subgroups of other orders. Gleysolic subgroups of Cryosolic soils have evidence of gleying similar to soils of the Gleysolic order.

STATIC CRYOSOL

These are Cryosolic soils that have developed primarily in mineral materials and are not strongly cryoturbated. They occur most commonly in coarse textured materials. Patterned ground features such as polygons may or may not occur. They may have organic surface horizons less than 40 cm thick.

Static Cryosols either show no evidence of cryoturbation or have features indicative of cryoturbation in less than one-third of the pedon, and they have permafrost within 1 m of the surface.

Orthic Static Cryosol

Common horizon sequence: Om, Bm, BCgj, Cz

These soils have the general properties specified for the Cryosolic order and the Static Cryosol great group. In addition they have a Bm horizon 10 cm or less thick. The surface horizons (rooting zone) are not strongly gleyed, but gley features occur commonly immediately above the permafrost table.

Brunisolic Static Cryosol

Common horizon sequence: Bm, BCgj, Cz

These soils have the general properties specified for the Cryosolic order and the Static Cryosol great group. They differ from the Orthic Static Cryosols by having a Bm horizon more than 10 cm thick. These soils have been called Arctic Brown soils.

Regosolic Static Cryosol

Common horizon sequence: C, Cz

These soils have the general properties specified for the Cryosolic order and the Static Cryosol great group. They differ from the Orthic Static Cryosols by lacking Bm horizons. They may have thin peaty organic layers and a thin Ah horizon.

Gleysolic Static Cryosol

Common horizon sequence: Om, Bg or Cg, Cz

These soils have the general properties specified for the Cryosolic order and the Static Cryosol great group. They differ from the Orthic Static Cryosols by having evidence of gleying in the form of low chromas or mottling to the mineral surface. The surface mineral horizon, Bg or Cg, may be overlain by organic layers thinner than 40 cm.

ORGANIC CRYOSOL

These are Cryosolic soils that have developed principally from organic material. Landforms associated with Organic Cryosols include palsas, peat polygons, and high center polygons.

An Organic Cryosol has a surface layer that contains more than 17% organic C by weight, about 30% organic matter. It is more than 40 cm thick, or more than 10 cm thick over a lithic contact, or more than 10 cm thick over an ice layer that is at least 30 cm thick. Permafrost occurs within 1 m of the surface.

Fibric Organic Cryosol

Common horizon sequence: Of or Om, Of, Ofz

These soils have the general properties specified for the Cryosolic order and the Organic Cryosol great group. Also, they have organic layers thicker than 1 m, and the material is dominantly fibric in the control section below a depth of 40 cm.

Mesic Organic Cryosol

Common horizon sequence: Of or Om, Om, Omz

These soils have the general properties specified for the Cryosolic order and the Organic Cryosol great group. Also, they have organic layers thicker than 1 m, and the material is dominantly mesic in the control section below a depth of 40 cm.

Humic Organic Cryosol

Common horizon sequence: Om or Oh, Ohz

These soils have the general properties specified for the Cryosolic order and the Organic Cryosol great group. Also, they have organic layers thicker than 1 m, and the material is dominantly humic in the control section below a depth of 40 cm.

Terric Fibric Organic Cryosol

Common horizon sequence: Of, Ofz, Cz

These soils have the general properties specified for the Cryosolic order and the Organic Cryosol great group. Also, they have a mineral contact within 1 m of the surface and are composed dominantly of fibric material above the contact.

Terric Mesic Organic Cryosol

Common horizon sequence: Om, Omz, Cz

These soils have the general properties specified for the Cryosolic order and the Organic Cryosol great group. Also, they have a mineral contact within 1 m of the surface and are composed dominantly of mesic material above the contact.

Terric Humic Organic Cryosol

Common horizon sequence: Oh, Ohz, Cz

These soils have the general properties specified for the Cryosolic order and the Organic Cryosol great group. Also, they have a mineral contact within 1 m of the surface and are composed dominantly of humic material above the contact.

Glacic Organic Cryosol

Common horizon sequence: Of, Om or Oh, Wz

These soils have the general properties specified for the Cryosolic order and the Organic Cryosol great group. Also, they have a layer of ground ice thicker than 30 cm with an upper boundary within 1 m of the surface. The ice layer contains more than 95% ice by volume.

Chapter 7   GLEYSOLIC ORDER

Great Group	*Subgroup*
Humic Gleysol	Orthic Humic Gleysol O.HG
	Rego Humic Gleysol R.HG
	Fera Humic Gleysol FE.HG
Gleysol	Orthic Gleysol O.G.
	Rego Gleysol R.G
	Fera Gleysol FE.G
Luvic Gleysol	Orthic Luvic Gleysol O.LG
	Humic Luvic Gleysol HU.LG
	Fera Luvic Gleysol FE.LG
	Fragic Luvic Gleysol FR.LG

A diagrammatic representation of profiles of some subgroups of the Gleysolic order is shown in Fig. 29. A common horizon sequence is given for each subgroup; diagnostic horizons are underlined and some other commonly occurring horizons are listed. The subgroups include soils with horizon sequences different from those shown.

Soils of the Gleysolic order have features indicative of periodic or prolonged saturation with water and reducing conditions. They occur commonly in association with other soils in the landscape. In areas of subhumid climate Gleysolic soils occur commonly in shallow depressions and on level lowlands that are saturated with water every spring. In more humid areas they occur also on slopes and on undulating terrain. Gleysolic soils are usually associated with either a high groundwater table at some period of the year or temporary saturation above a relatively impermeable layer. Some Gleysolic soils may be submerged under shallow water throughout the year. Commonly the native vegetation associated with Gleysolic soils differs from that of nearby soils of other orders.

Gleysolic soils have within 50 cm of the mineral surface either matrix colors of low chroma or distinct to prominent mottles of high chroma, which are indicative of localized oxidation of ferrous iron and deposition of hydrated ferric oxides. The moist color criteria applied to material within 50 cm of the mineral surface are:

Chromas of 1 or less, with or without mottles, on ped surfaces or in the matrix if peds are lacking; or
Chromas of 2 or less, in hues of 10YR or redder, on ped surfaces or in the matrix if peds are lacking, accompanied by prominent mottles; or

Chromas of 3 or less, in hues yellower than 10YR, on ped surfaces or in the matrix if peds are lacking, accompanied by prominent mottles; or
Hues bluer than 10Y, with or without mottles, on ped surfaces or in the matrix if peds are lacking; or
Prominent gray or brown mottles in materials of reddish color that persists in spite of periodic reduction.

Criteria based on color are used as diagnostic of Gleysolic soils because color is the easiest observable indicator of the overall oxidation-reduction status of a soil. Color in itself is not considered to be important but is a useful indicator of periodic or prolonged reducing conditions in most soil materials.

Some accessory features are useful in the identification of Gleysolic soils.
Saturation to the surface for a month or more while the soil is not frozen could be an adequate diagnostic criterion except for the following:

Information on the duration of saturation is not available for most soils in Canada.
Some soils on slopes are saturated with aerated water. They are wet, but because they are not reduced they are not Gleysolic soils.
Some Podzolic soils are saturated with water for several months each year.
The duration of saturation required to effect reduction depends upon many factors, especially temperature and available energy sources for microbes. Reduction occurs because of the depletion of oxygen by microbial activity. This proceeds very slowly below a temperature of about 5°C.

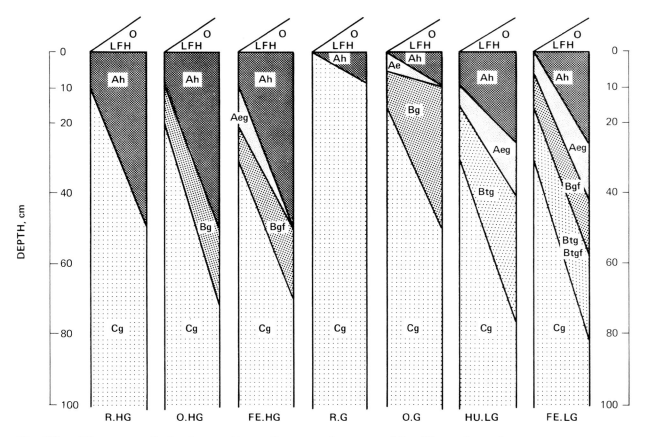

Fig. 29.   Diagrammatic horizon pattern of some subgroups of the Gleysolic order.

Peaty surface layers may be noted, but such layers occur on some soils of other orders and they do not occur on all Gleysolic soils. The position in the landscape is a guide: undrained depressions to level areas in subhumid regions, level to gently sloping areas in humid regions.

Hydrophytic vegetation is a feature, but the key indicator species vary from region to region.

An oxidation-reduction potential, E_{pt}, of less than 100 mV within the upper 50 cm for a period of a week or more is an indicator. Such data are available for only a few soils.

DISTINGUISHING GLEYSOLIC SOILS FROM SOILS OF OTHER ORDERS

Guidelines for the distinction of Gleysolic soils from soils of other orders with which they might be confused are listed below.

Chernozemic. Some soils have a chernozemic A horizon and dull colors or mottling indicative of gleying within the control section. Those having matrix colors of low chromas and distinct to prominent mottles within 50 cm of the mineral surface are classified as Gleysolic. Those with distinct to prominent mottles only below a depth of 50 cm are classified as Chernozemic.

Solonetzic. The soils with both a Bn horizon and evidence of gleying as specified for Gleysolic soils are classified as Gleysolic.

Luvisolic. Some Luvic Gleysols have Ae or Aeg and Btg horizons. They are distinguished from Luvisolic soils on the basis of evidence of the strength of gleying.

Podzolic. Soils having both a podzolic B horizon and evidence of gleying that satisfies the specifications of Gleysolic soils are classified as Podzolic.

Brunisolic. Gleyed subgroups of Brunisolic soils are differentiated from Gleysolic soils on the basis of evidence of gleying too weakly expressed to meet the specifications of Gleysolic soils.

Regosolic. Soils with no horizon differentiation apart from evidence of gleying as specified for Gleysolic soils are classified as Gleysolic.

Organic. Gleysolic soils may have organic surface layers, but they are too thin to meet the minimum limits specified for soils of the Organic order.

Cryosolic. Some Cryosolic soils have matrix colors of low chroma and prominent mottling within 50 cm of the surface like Gleysolic soils. However, Gleysolic soils do not have permafrost within 1 m of the surface or 2 m if the soil is strongly cryoturbated.

Gleysolic soils are divided into three great groups: Humic Gleysol, Gleysol, and Luvic Gleysol, which are separated on the basis of the development of the Ah horizon and the presence or absence of a Bt horizon as shown below.

Gleysolic Order

Humic Gleysol	Gleysol	Luvic Gleysol
Ah, at least 10 cm thick	No Ah or an Ah	A Btg horizon
No Bt horizon	<10 cm thick	Usually an Ahe or
	No Bt horizon	an Aeg horizon

HUMIC GLEYSOL

Soils of this great group have a dark-colored A horizon in addition to the general properties of soils of the Gleysolic order. They occur in poorly drained positions in association with some Chernozemic, Luvisolic, Podzolic, and Brunisolic soils. They may have organic surface horizons derived from grass and sedge, moss, or forest vegetation.

Humic Gleysols have no Bt horizon, and they have either an Ah horizon at least 10 cm thick or a mixed surface horizon (Ap) at least 15 cm thick with all of the following properties:

1. More than 2% organic C.
2. A rubbed color value of 3.5 or less (moist), or 5.0 or less (dry).
3. At least 1.5 units of color value (moist) lower than that of the next underlying horizon if the color value (moist) of that horizon is 4 or more, or 1 unit of color value lower than that of the underlying horizon if its color value is less than 4.

Examples of color values of cultivated Humic Gleysols are:

	Example 1	Example 2
Moist color value of Ap	3.5 or less	2.0 or less
Moist color value of underlying horizon	5.0 or more	3.0 or more

The great group is divided into three subgroups based on the kind and sequence of the horizons. The former subgroup features turbic, placic, saline, carbonated, cryic, and lithic are now recognized taxonomically at either the family or series level. They may be indicated also as phases of subgroups, great groups, or orders.

Orthic Humic Gleysol

Common horizon sequence: LFH or O, Ah, Bg, Cg or C

These soils have the general properties specified for the Gleysolic order and the Humic Gleysol great group. Typically they have a well-developed Ah horizon overlying gleyed B and C horizons. They may have organic surface horizons, an eluvial horizon, and a C horizon that does not have dull colors and mottling indicative of gleying.

Orthic Humic Gleysols are identified by the following properties:

1. They have an Ah horizon at least 10 cm thick as defined for the great group.
2. They have a B horizon, Bg or Bgtj, rarely Bng, at least 5 cm thick.

3. They do not have a Btg horizon or a Bgf at least 5 cm thick.

Rego Humic Gleysol

Common horizon sequence: LFH or O, Ah, Cg

These soils have the general properties specified for the Gleysolic order and the Humic Gleysol great group. They differ from the Orthic Humic Gleysols by lacking a B horizon at least 5 cm thick. Typically they have a well-developed Ah horizon overlying a gleyed C horizon.

Fera Humic Gleysol

Common horizon sequence: LFH or O, Ah, Aeg, Bgf, Cg

These soils have the general properties specified for the Gleysolic order and the Humic Gleysol great group. They differ from the Orthic Humic Gleysols by having a Bgf horizon at least 5 cm thick. The Bgf horizon contains an accumulation of hydrous iron oxide (dithionite extractable) thought to have been deposited as a result of the oxidation of ferrous iron. Usually the Bgf horizon has many prominent mottles of high chroma.

GLEYSOL

Soils of this great group have the general properties specified for soils of the Gleysolic order and they lack a well-developed, mineral-organic surface horizon. They occur widely in poorly drained positions in association with soils of several other orders.

Gleysols lack an Ah and an Ap horizon as specified for Humic Gleysols and a Bt horizon. They may have either an Ah horizon thinner than 10 cm or an Ap horizon with one of the following properties:

1. Less than 2% organic C.
2. A rubbed color value greater than 3.5 (moist) or greater than 5.0 (dry).
3. Little contrast in color value with the underlying layer (less than 1.5 units difference if the value of the underlying layer is 4 or more, or less than 1 unit difference if that value is less than 4).

They have a gleyed B or C horizon and they may have an organic surface horizon.

The great group is divided into three subgroups based on the kind and sequence of the horizons.

Orthic Gleysol

Common horizon sequence: LFH or O, <u>Bg</u>, Cg

These soils have the general properties specified for the Gleysolic order and the Gleysol great group. Typically they have strongly gleyed B and C horizons, and they may have organic surface horizons and an eluvial horizon.

Orthic Gleysols are identified by the following properties:

1. They have a B horizon, Bg or Btjg, rarely Bng, at least 5 cm thick.
2. They may have an Ah or Ap horizon as specified for the Gleysol great group.
3. They do not have a Btg horizon or a Bgf at least 5 cm thick.

Rego Gleysol

Common horizon sequence: LFH or O, <u>Cg</u>

These soils have the general properties specified for the Gleysolic order and the Gleysol great group. They differ from the Orthic Gleysols by lacking a B horizon at least 5 cm thick. Thus they consist of a gleyed C horizon with or without organic surface horizons and a thin Ah or B horizon.

Fera Gleysol

Common horizon sequence: LFH or O, Aeg, <u>Bgf</u>, Cg

These soils have the general properties specified for the Gleysolic order and the Gleysol great group. They differ from the Orthic Gleysols by having a Bgf horizon at least 5 cm thick. The Bgf horizon contains an accumulation of hydrous iron oxide (dithionite extractable), which is thought to have been deposited as a result of the oxidation of ferrous iron. Usually the Bgf horizon has many prominent mottles of high chroma.

LUVIC GLEYSOL

Soils of this great group have the general properties specified for the Gleysolic order and a horizon of clay accumulation. They are similar to Luvisolic soils except that they have dull colors or prominent mottling or both, which are indicative of strong gleying. They may have organic surface horizons and an Ah horizon. Luvic Gleysols occur commonly in poorly drained sites in association with Luvisolic soils and in depressions in areas of Black and Dark Gray Chernozemic soils.

Luvic Gleysols usually have an eluvial horizon (Ahe, Aeg) and a Btg horizon. A Btg horizon is defined on the basis of an increase in silicate clay over that in the A horizon, the presence of clay skins indicating illuvial clay, and colors and mottling indicative of permanent or periodic reduction. Luvic Gleysols may have an organic surface horizon and an Ah horizon. In some cases the A horizon is very dark colored when moist with a value of 2, but its eluvial features usually are evident on drying. Such horizons usually have darker and lighter gray streaks and splotches similar to Ahe horizons of Dark Gray Chernozemic soils. Even if the eluvial horizon is dark in color, the Btg horizon is diagnostic of a Luvic Gleysol.

The great group is divided into four subgroups based on the kind and sequence of the horizons.

Orthic Luvic Gleysol

Common horizon sequence: LFH or O, <u>Aeg</u>, <u>Btg</u>, Cg

These soils have the general properties specified for the Gleysolic order and the Luvic Gleysol great group. Typically they have organic or mineral-organic surface horizons overlying gleyed, eluvial horizons, and a Btg horizon.

Orthic Luvic Gleysols are identified by the following properties:

1. They have an eluvial horizon: Ahe, Ae, Aeg.
2. They have a Btg horizon.
3. They do not have an Ah or Ap horizon as defined for Humic Gleysols and Humic Luvic Gleysols.
4. They lack a Bgf horizon at least 5 cm thick.
5. They lack a fragipan.

Humic Luvic Gleysol

Common horizon sequence: LFH or O, <u>Ah</u>, Aeg, <u>Btg</u>, Cg

These soils have the general properties specified for the Gleysolic order and the Luvic Gleysol great group. They differ from the Orthic Luvic

Gleysols by having a mineral-organic surface horizon that meets the requirements of the Ah or Ap horizon of Humic Gleysols. Thus, the Ah horizon must be at least 10 cm thick and the Ap horizon must contain at least 2% organic C and be darker than the underlying horizon, as specified for Humic Gleysols.

Fera Luvic Gleysol

Common horizon sequence: LFH or O, Ah, <u>Aeg</u>, <u>Bgf</u>, <u>Btg</u>, Cg

These soils have the general properties specified for the Gleysolic order and the Luvic Gleysol great group. They differ from the Orthic Luvic Gleysols by having either a Bgf at least 5 cm thick in addition to a Btg horizon, or a Btgf horizon, and they may have an Ah or Ap horizon that meets the requirements for a Humic Luvic Gleysol. A Bgf or Btgf horizon contains an accumulation of hydrous iron oxide (dithionite extractable), which is thought to have been deposited as a result of the oxidation of ferrous iron. It usually has a high chroma and is commonly a horizon of concentration of rusty mottles.

Fragic Luvic Gleysol

Common horizon sequence: LFH or O, Ah, <u>Aeg</u>, <u>Btgx</u>, Cg

These soils have the general properties specified for the Gleysolic order and the Luvic Gleysol great group. They differ from the Orthic Luvic Gleysols by having a fragipan within or below the Btg horizon. They may also have a dark-colored Ah or Ap horizon as specified for Humic Luvic Gleysols and a Bgf or Btgf horizon as specified for Fera Luvic Gleysols.

Chapter 8   LUVISOLIC ORDER

Great Group	*Subgroup*
Gray Brown Luvisol	Orthic Gray Brown Luvisol O.GBL
	Brunisolic Gray Brown Luvisol BR.GBL
	Podzolic Gray Brown Luvisol PZ.GBL
	Gleyed Gray Brown Luvisol GL.GBL
	Gleyed Brunisolic Gray Brown Luvisol GLBR.GBL
	Gleyed Podzolic Gray Brown Luvisol GLPZ.GBL
Gray Luvisol	Orthic Gray Luvisol O.GL
	Dark Gray Luvisol D.GL
	Brunisolic Gray Luvisol BR.GL
	Podzolic Gray Luvisol PZ.GL
	Solonetzic Gray Luvisol SZ.GL
	Fragic Gray Luvisol FR.GL
	Gleyed Gray Luvisol GL.GL
	Gleyed Dark Gray Luvisol GLD.GL
	Gleyed Brunisolic Gray Luvisol GLBR.GL
	Gleyed Podzolic Gray Luvisol GLPZ.GL
	Gleyed Solonetzic Gray Luvisol GLSZ.GL
	Gleyed Fragic Gray Luvisol GLFR.GL

A diagrammatic representation of profiles of some subgroups of the Luvisolic order is shown in Fig. 30. A common horizon sequence is given for each subgroup; diagnostic horizons are underlined and some other commonly occurring horizons are listed. The subgroups include some soils having horizon sequences different from those shown.

Soils of the Luvisolic order generally have light-colored, eluvial horizons and they have illuvial B horizons in which silicate clay has accumulated. These soils develop characteristically in well to imperfectly drained sites, in sandy loam to clay base-saturated parent materials under forest vegetation in subhumid to humid, mild to very cold climates. Depending on the combination of soil environmental factors, some Luvisolic soils occur under conditions outside the range indicated as characteristic. For example, some Luvisolic soils develop in acid parent materials and some occur in forest-grassland transition zones.

Luvisolic soils occur from the southern extremity of Ontario to the zone of permafrost and from Newfoundland to British Columbia. The largest area of these soils occurs in the central to northern Interior Plains under deciduous, mixed, and coniferous forest. The Gray Luvisols of that area usually have well-developed, platy Ae horizons of low chroma, Bt horizons with moderate to strong prismatic or blocky structures, calcareous C horizons, and sola of high base saturation (neutral salt extraction). Gray Luvisols of the Atlantic Provinces commonly have Bt horizons of weak structure and low to moderate base saturation. The Gray Brown Luvisols of southern Ontario and some valleys of British Columbia characteristically have forest mull Ah horizons, moderate to strong blocky structured Bt horizons, and calcareous C horizons.

Luvisolic soils have an eluvial and Bt horizon as defined. The Bt horizon must have the specified increase in clay over that in the eluvial horizon, clay skins indicative of translocated clay accounting for 1% or more of the area of a section through the horizon, and be at least 5 cm thick. Luvisolic soils may have Ah, Ahe, or dark-colored Ap horizons that satisfy one or more of the following conditions:

1. The dark-colored A horizon does not meet the requirements of a chernozemic A.
2. The dark-colored A horizon is underlain by a thicker, light-colored Ae horizon that extends to a depth 15 cm from the mineral surface.
3. The dark-colored A horizon shows evidence of eluviation (Ahe or Ap) and is underlain by an Ae horizon at least 5 cm thick.
4. If the soil moisture subclass is humid or wetter, the dark-colored A horizon may be of any kind.

Luvisolic soils do not have any of the following: a solonetzic B horizon, a podzolic B horizon if the upper boundary of the Bt horizon is at a depth of more than 50 cm from the mineral surface, evidence of gleying strong enough to meet the

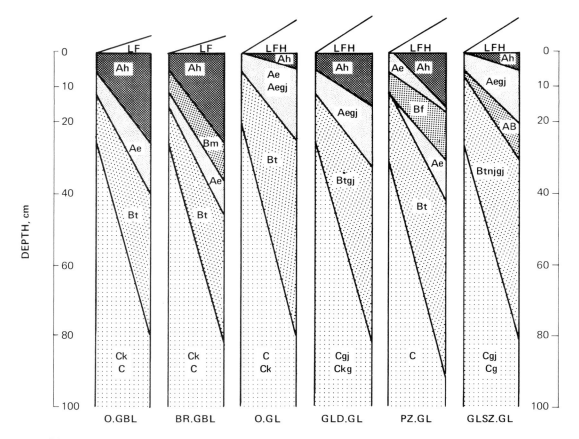

Fig. 30. Diagrammatic horizon pattern of some subgroups of the Luvisolic order.

requirements of the Gleysolic order, organic horizons thick enough to meet the requirements of the Organic order, or permafrost within 1 m of the mineral surface and 2 m if the soils are cryoturbated.

The genesis of Luvisolic soils is thought to involve the suspension of clay in the soil solution near the soil surface, downward movement of the suspended clay with the soil solution, and deposition of the translocated clay at a depth where downward movement of the soil solution ceases or becomes very slow. Commonly, the subhorizon of maximum clay accumulation occurs above a Ck horizon. The eluvial horizon (Ahe, Ae) commonly has platy structure due perhaps to the periodic formation of ice lenses. Any condition that promotes dispersion of clay in the A horizons and deposition of this clay in a discrete subsurface horizon favors the development of Luvisolic soils.

DISTINGUISHING LUVISOLIC SOILS FROM SOILS OF OTHER ORDERS

Guidelines for the distinction of Luvisolic soils from soils of other orders with which they might be confused follow.

Chernozemic. Some Chernozemic soils have Ah, Ae, and Bt horizons as do some Luvisolic soils. A basis of differentiation of these soils is the nature of the Ah and Ae horizons as follows:

1. If the Ah is not a chernozemic A, the soil is Luvisolic.
2. If the soil has a chernozemic A and a light-colored Ae that is thicker than the Ah or Ap and extends to a depth below 15 cm, the soil is Luvisolic.
3. If the soil has an eluviated, dark-colored A horizon (Ahe or Ap) and a distinct Ae horizon thicker than 5 cm or that extends below the Ap, it is Luvisolic.

Solonetzic. Solonetzic soils have a solonetzic B horizon, but Luvisolic soils do not.

Podzolic. Some soils have both a podzolic B and a Bt horizon. The soil is classified as Luvisolic if the upper boundary of the Bt horizon is within 50 cm of the mineral surface and as Podzolic if the boundary is more than 50 cm below the surface.

Brunisolic. Luvisolic soils have a Bt horizon, but Brunisolic soils do not.

Gleysolic. Some Gleysolic soils have Ae and Bt horizons, but unlike Luvisolic soils they also have colors of low chroma or prominent mottling indicative of strong gleying.

Luvisolic soils are divided into two great groups, Gray Brown Luvisol and Gray Luvisol as shown below. The latter accounts for most of the area of Luvisolic soils.

Luvisolic Order

Gray Brown Luvisol	Gray Luvisol
A forest mull Ah	May or may not have an Ah
Eluvial and Bt horizons	Has eluvial and Bt horizons
A mean annual soil temperature >8°C	Usually has a mean annual soil temperature <8°C

Subgroups are separated on the basis of the kind and sequence of the horizons indicating conformity with the central concept of the great group or intergrades to soils of other orders, or additional features. The former subgroup features turbic, cryic, and lithic are now recognized taxonomically at either the family or series level. They may be indicated also as phases of subgroups, great groups, or orders.

GRAY BROWN LUVISOL

Soils of this great group have a forest mull Ah horizon and eluvial and Bt horizons as indicated for the order. They occur typically under deciduous or mixed forest vegetation on calcareous materials in areas of mild, humid climate. Their major area of occurrence is the St. Lawrence Lowland.

Under undisturbed conditions the soils may have thin L, F, and H horizons, but because of high biological activity and the abundance of earthworms the leaf litter is usually quickly incorporated into the soil and humified. A transitional AB or BA horizon having gray coatings on structural aggregates is generally present, particularly in medium and fine textured soils. Although the Bt horizon is generally immediately underlain by calcareous materials, a transitional BC horizon may be present.

Under cultivated conditions the Ah and often part of the Ae are mixed to form an Ap, but the Bt and part of the Ae usually remain intact under the Ap unless cultivation greatly exceeds 15 cm in depth.

Gray Brown Luvisols have either a forest-mull Ah horizon more than 5 cm thick or a dark-colored Ap horizon, an eluvial horizon, and a Bt horizon. The mean annual soil temperature is 8°C or higher and the soil moisture regime is humid or wetter.

The great group is divided into six subgroups on the basis of profile development above the Bt horizon and evidence of gleying.

Orthic Gray Brown Luvisol

Common horizon sequence: Ah, Ae, Bt, Ck

These soils have the properties specified for the Luvisolic order and the Gray Brown Luvisol great group. They have well-developed Ah, eluvial, and Bt horizons, and usually calcareous C horizons. Faint mottling may occur immediately above or within the Bt horizon.

Orthic Gray Brown Luvisols are identified by the following properties:

1. They have either a forest-mull Ah horizon more than 5 cm thick or a dark-colored (moist) Ap horizon.
2. They have an Ae horizon of which the upper 5 cm is light-colored with a chroma of 3 or less. The difference in chroma between the upper and lower part of the Ae is less than 1.
3. They have a Bt horizon and lack a Bf horizon.
4. Distinct mottling indicative of gleying does not occur within 50 cm of the mineral surface, and prominent mottling does not occur at depths of 50–100 cm.

Brunisolic Gray Brown Luvisol

Common horizon sequence: Ah, Ae, Bm or Bf, Ae, Bt, BC, Ck

These soils have the properties specified for the Luvisolic order and the Gray Brown Luvisol great group. They differ from the Orthic Gray Brown Luvisols by having in the upper solum either a Bm horizon at least 5 cm thick with a chroma of 3 or more, or a Bf horizon less than 10 cm thick that does not extend below 15 cm. Such Bm or Bf horizons are thought to have developed in a former Ae horizon. If disturbance results in incorporation of the Bm or Bf horizon into the Ap, the disturbed soil is classified as an Orthic Gray Brown Luvisol.

Podzolic Gray Brown Luvisol

Common horizon sequence: LFH, Ah, Ae, Bf, Ae, Bt, BC, Ck

These soils have the properties specified for the Luvisolic order and the Gray Brown Luvisol great group. They differ from the Orthic Gray Brown Luvisols by having a Bf horizon at least 10 cm thick in the upper solum, and they may or may not have an Ae horizon. The upper boundary of the Bt horizon must be within 50 cm of the mineral soil surface or the soil is classified in the Podzolic order. If disturbance results in incorporation of the Bf horizon into the Ap, the disturbed soil is classified as an Orthic Gray Brown Luvisol.

Gleyed Gray Brown Luvisol

Common horizon sequence: Ah, Aegj, Btgj, Ckg

These soils have the properties specified for the Luvisolic order and the Gray Brown Luvisol great group. They differ from the Orthic Gray Brown Luvisols by having either distinct mottles indicative of gleying within 50 cm of the mineral surface or prominent mottles at depths of 50–100 cm. Commonly the matrix colors are of lower chroma than those of associated, well drained soils. Gleyed Gray Brown Luvisols generally have thicker and darker Ah horizons than the well drained subgroups on similar parent materials. The color and textural differences between the Ae and Bt are generally less marked in the gleyed than in the orthic subgroup.

Gleyed Brunisolic Gray Brown Luvisol

Common horizon sequence: Ah, Bmgj, Aegj, Btgj, Ckg

These soils have the properties specified for the Luvisolic order and the Gray Brown Luvisol great group. They differ from the Brunisolic Gray Brown Luvisols by having either distinct mottles indicative of gleying within 50 cm of the mineral surface or prominent mottles at depths of 50–100 cm.

Gleyed Podzolic Gray Brown Luvisol

Common horizon sequence: Ah, Ae, Bfgj, Aegj, Btgj, Ckg

These soils have the properties specified for the Luvisolic order and the Gray Brown Luvisol great group. They differ from the Podzolic Gray Brown Luvisols by having either distinct mottles indicative of gleying within 50 cm of the mineral surface or prominent mottles at depths of 50–100 cm. In addition to a forest-mull Ah, they have a Bf horizon at least 10 cm thick and a gleyed Bt horizon of which the upper boundary is within 50 cm of the mineral surface.

GRAY LUVISOL

Soils of this great group have eluvial and Bt horizons as specified for the Luvisolic order. They usually have L, F, and H horizons and may have a degraded Ah or Ahe horizon that resembles the upper A horizon of Dark Gray Chernozemic soils. Commonly below the Ae horizon they have an AB or BA horizon in which the ped surfaces are grayer than the interiors of peds. The solum of Gray Luvisols is generally slightly to moderately acid but may be strongly acid. The degree of base saturation (neutral salt extraction) is generally high. The parent materials are usually base saturated and commonly calcareous, but some Gray Luvisols have developed in acid materials.

Gray Luvisols occur typically under boreal or mixed forest vegetation and in forest-grassland transition zones in a wide range of climatic areas. Their main area of occurrence is in the subhumid central to northern part of the Interior Plains, but they occur also in humid and perhumid areas of Eastern Canada. In the latter climatic area, they are found mainly on medium to fine textured parent materials.

Gray Luvisols have eluvial and Bt horizons and their mean annual soil temperature is usually less than 8°C. If the soil moisture regime is subhumid, any dark-colored A horizon must satisfy one or more of the following conditions:

1. It is not a chernozemic A.
2. It is underlain by a thicker Ae horizon that extends to a depth greater than 15 cm below the mineral surface.
3. It shows evidence of degradation (Ahe) and is underlain by an Ae horizon at least 5 cm thick below the Ahe or Ap horizon.

The great group is divided into 12 subgroups on the basis of the kind and sequence of horizons and evidence of gleying.

Orthic Gray Luvisol

Common horizon sequence: LFH, Ae, AB, Bt, C or Ck

These soils have the properties specified for the Luvisolic order and the Gray Luvisol great group. They have well-developed Ae and Bt horizons and usually have organic surface horizons. Faint mottling may occur immediately above or within the Bt horizon.

Orthic Gray Luvisols are identified by the following properties:

1. They have an Ae horizon with a chroma of less than 3 unless the chroma of the parent material is 4 or more.
2. They have a Bt horizon.
3. They lack a Bf horizon.
4. They lack a fragipan.
5. They may have a dark-colored, mineral-organic surface horizon (Ah or Ahe) less than 5 cm thick.
6. They may have an Ap horizon, but its dry color value must be 5 or higher.
7. Distinct mottling indicative of gleying does not occur within 50 cm of the mineral surface, and prominent mottling does not occur at depths of 50–100 cm.

Dark Gray Luvisol

Common horizon sequence: LFH, Ah or Ahe, Ae, Bt, C or Ck

These soils have the properties specified for the Luvisolic order and the Gray Luvisol great group. They differ from the Orthic Gray Luvisols by having an Ah or Ahe horizon more than 5 cm thick. These horizons generally have eluvial features such as gray streaks or splotches when dry, or platy structure. In the case of disturbed soils, the dry color value of the Ap horizon is 3.5–5.0 and some of the Ae horizon remains below the Ap. The differentiation of Dark Gray Luvisols from Dark Gray Chernozemic soils was outlined previously in this chapter. Dark Gray Luvisols have a mean annual soil temperature less than 8°C. They may have a Btnj horizon or a Bm horizon above the Bt.

Brunisolic Gray Luvisol

Common horizon sequence: LFH, Bm or Bf, Ae, Bt, BC, C or Ck

These soils have the properties specified for the Luvisolic order and the Gray Luvisol great group. They differ from the Orthic Gray Luvisols by having in the upper solum either a Bm horizon at least 5 cm thick with a chroma of 3 or more, or a Bf horizon less than 10 cm thick that does not extend below 15 cm. Such Bm or Bf horizons are thought to have developed in a former Ae horizon. These soils do not have a dark-colored Ah or Ahe horizon more than 5 cm thick.

Podzolic Gray Luvisol

Common horizon sequence: LFH, Ae, Bf, Ae, Bt, BC, C or Ck

These soils have the properties specified for the Luvisolic order and the Gray Luvisol great group. They differ from the Orthic Gray Luvisols by having a Bf horizon at least 10 cm thick in the upper solum. They may also have a dark-colored Ah or Ahe horizon more than 5 cm thick. The upper boundary of the Bt horizon must be within 50 cm of the mineral soil surface or the soil is classified in the Podzolic order.

Solonetzic Gray Luvisol

Common horizon sequence: LFH, Ae, AB, Btnj, BC, C or Csk

These soils have the properties specified for the Luvisolic order and the Gray Luvisol great group. They differ from the Orthic Gray Luvisols by having a Btnj horizon indicative of an intergrade to the Solonetzic order. The Btnj horizon usually has a harder consistence, more pronounced coatings on the prismatic or blocky peds, and a lower ratio of exchangeable Ca:Na than the Bt horizons of most Gray Luvisols. This subgroup is associated with saline parent materials. Solonetzic Gray Luvisols do not have an Ah or Ahe horizon thicker than 5 cm, and so the surface horizons do not meet the criteria for Dark Gray Luvisols.

Fragic Gray Luvisol

Common horizon sequence: LFH, Ahe, Ae, Bt, Btx or BCx, C

These soils have the properties specified for the Luvisolic order and the Gray Luvisol great group. They differ from the Orthic Gray Luvisols by having a fragipan either within or below the Bt horizon, and they may have a dark-colored Ah or Ahe horizon more than 5 cm thick, a Btnj, a Bm, or a Bf horizon.

Gleyed Gray Luvisol

Common horizon sequence: LFH, Ae, Btgj, Cg

These soils have the properties specified for the Luvisolic order and the Gray Luvisol great group. They differ from the Orthic Gray Luvisols by having either distinct mottles indicative of gleying within 50 cm of the mineral surface or prominent mottles at depths of 50–100 cm. Commonly the matrix colors are of lower chroma than those of associated, well drained soils.

Gleyed Dark Gray Luvisol

Common horizon sequence: LFH, Ah or Ahe, Ae, Btgj, Cg

These soils have the properties specified for the Luvisolic order and the Gray Luvisol great group. They differ from the Dark Gray Luvisols by having either distinct mottles indicative of gleying within 50 cm of the mineral surface or prominent mottles at depths of 50–100 cm.

Gleyed Brunisolic Gray Luvisol

Common horizon sequence: LFH, Bm or Bf, Aegj, Btgj, BCgj, Cg

These soils have the properties specified for the Luvisolic order and the Gray Luvisol great group. They differ from the Brunisolic Gray Luvisols by having either distinct mottles indicative of gleying within 50 cm of the mineral surface or prominent mottles at depths of 50–100 cm. They do not have Ah or Ahe horizons more than 5 cm thick.

Gleyed Podzolic Gray Luvisol

Common horizon sequence: LFH, Ae, Bf, Aegj, Btgj, BCgj, Cg

These soils have the properties specified for the Luvisolic order and the Gray Luvisol great group. They differ from the Podzolic Gray Luvisols by having either distinct mottles indicative of gleying within 50 cm of the mineral surface or prominent mottles at depths of 50–100 cm. They may have a dark-colored A horizon more than 5 cm thick.

Gleyed Solonetzic Gray Luvisol

Common horizon sequence: LFH, Ae, ABgj, Btnjgj, Cgj or Csag

These soils have the properties specified for the Luvisolic order and the Gray Luvisol great group. They differ from the Solonetzic Gray Luvisols by having either distinct mottles indicative of gleying within 50 cm of the mineral surface or prominent mottles at depths of 50–100 cm. They do not have an Ah or Ahe horizon thicker than 5 cm.

Gleyed Fragic Gray Luvisol

Common horizon sequence: LFH, Ahe, Aegj, Btgj, Btxgj or BCxg, Cg

These soils have the properties specified for the Luvisolic order and the Gray Luvisol great group. They differ from the Fragic Gray Luvisols by having either distinct mottles indicative of gleying within 50 cm of the mineral surface or prominent mottles at depths of 50–100 cm. They may have a dark-colored A horizon more than 5 cm thick, and a Bm, Btnj, or Bf horizon.

Great Group	*Subgroup*
Fibrisol	Typic Fibrisol TY.F
	Mesic Fibrisol ME.F
	Humic Fibrisol HU.F
	Limno Fibrisol LM.F
	Cumulo Fibrisol CU.F
	Terric Fibrisol T.F
	Terric Mesic Fibrisol TME.F
	Terric Humic Fibrisol THU.F
	Hydric Fibrisol HY.F
Mesisol	Typic Mesisol TY.M
	Fibric Mesisol FI.M
	Humic Mesisol HU.M
	Limno Mesisol LM.M
	Cumulo Mesisol CU.M
	Terric Mesisol T.M
	Terric Fibric Mesisol TFI.M
	Terric Humic Mesisol THU.M
	Hydric Mesisol HY.M
Humisol	Typic Humisol TY.H
	Fibric Humisol FI.H
	Mesic Humisol ME.H
	Limno Humisol LM.H
	Cumulo Humisol CU.H
	Terric Humisol T.H
	Terric Fibric Humisol TFI.H
	Terric Mesic Humisol TME.H
	Hydric Humisol HY.H
Folisol	Typic Folisol TY.FO

A diagrammatic representation of the depth relationships of tiers and of Typic and Terric subgroups of Organic soils is shown in Fig. 31. Diagrammatic sketches of profiles of some subgroups of the Organic order are shown in Fig. 32. A common horizon sequence is given for each subgroup; diagnostic horizons or layers are underlined and some other commonly occurring horizons are listed. The subgroups include soils having horizon sequences different from those shown.

Soils of the Organic order are composed largely of organic materials. They include most of the soils commonly known as peat, muck, or bog soils. Most Organic soils are saturated with water for prolonged periods. They occur widely in poorly and very poorly drained depressions and level areas in regions of subhumid to perhumid climate and are derived from vegetation that grows in such sites. However, one group of Organic soils consists of leaf litter overlying rock or fragmental material; soils of this group may occur on steep slopes and rarely be saturated with water.

Organic soils contain 17% or more organic C (30% organic matter) by weight and meet the following specifications.

For organic materials (O) that are commonly saturated with water and consist mainly of mosses, sedges, or other hydrophytic vegetation the specifications are:

1. If the surface layer consists of fibric organic material with or without mesic or humic Op horizons thinner than 15 cm, the organic material must extend to a depth of at least 60 cm.
2. If the surface layer is mesic or humic, the organic material must extend to a depth of at least 40 cm.
3. If a lithic contact occurs at a depth shallower than 40 cm, the organic material must extend to a depth of at least 10 cm. Mineral material less than 10 cm thick may overlie the lithic contact, but the organic material must be more than twice

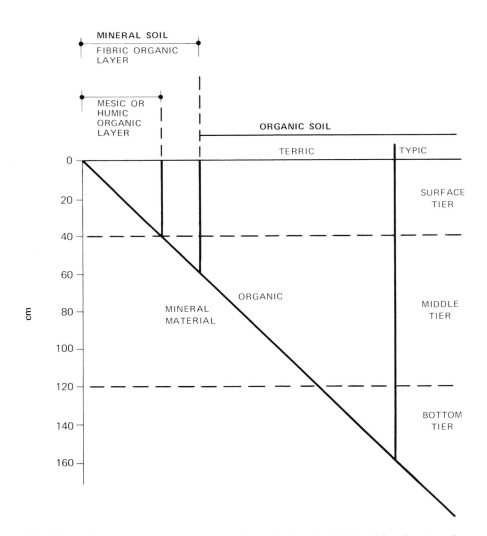

Fig. 31. Diagrammatic representation of depth relationships involved in Organic soil classification.

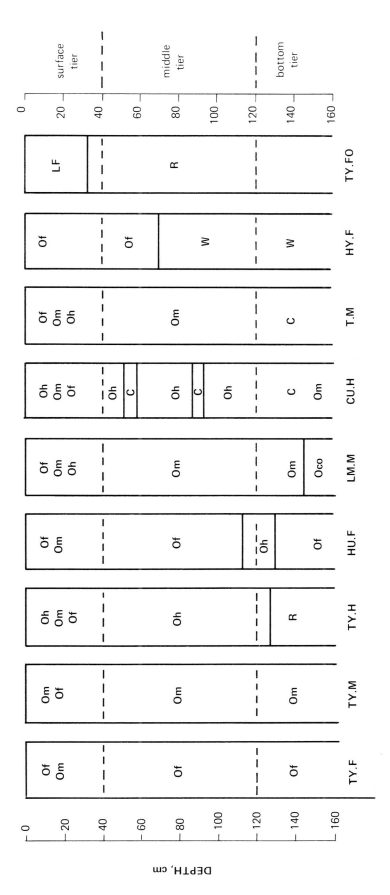

Fig. 32. Diagrammatic horizon pattern of some subgroups of the Organic order.

85

the thickness of the mineral layer.

4. The organic soil may have a mineral layer thinner than 40 cm on the surface provided that the underlying organic material is at least 40 cm thick.
5. Mineral layers thinner than 40 cm that begin within a depth of 40 cm from the surface may occur within an organic soil. A mineral layer or layers with a combined thickness of less than 40 cm may occur within the upper 80 cm.

For organic materials (LFH) that are composed dominantly of forest litter and are not usually saturated with water there must be:

1. Ten centimetres or more of organic material directly overlying a lithic contact or fragmental material.
2. Organic material more than twice the thickness of a mineral soil layer thinner than 10 cm that separates the organic material from the underlying lithic contact or fragmental material.

If more than 10 cm of mineral soil overlies a lithic layer or fragmental material, the soil is classified as a mineral soil regardless of the depth of the LFH horizon at the surface.

LFH of 50 cm over an Ah of 5 cm over R—Organic order.

LFH of 50 cm over an Ah of 5 cm over a Bm of 15 cm over R—Brunisolic order.

The control section (160 cm) for Organic soils is divided into three tiers: surface, 40 cm; middle, 80 cm; and bottom, 40 cm thick (*see* Chapter 2 for detailed definitions). Classification at the great group level is based primarily on properties of the middle tier.

DISTINGUISHING ORGANIC SOILS FROM SOILS OF OTHER ORDERS

Many soils of other orders may have organic horizons at the surface. The distinction between Organic soils and soils of other orders is based on:

1. The thickness and the organic C content of organic-rich surface horizons in the case of soils with O horizons.
2. The thickness of the underlying unconsolidated mineral material in the case of soils with an LFH horizon.
3. The depth to permafrost; organic materials having permafrost at depths of 1 m or less are classified as Cryosolic soils.

Organic soils are divided into four great groups; three of these are based on the degree of decomposition of organic matter commonly saturated with water (O). The other is only briefly saturated forest litter.

Organic Order

Fibrisol	Mesisol	Humisol	Folisol
Fibric middle tier	Mesic middle tier	Humic middle tier	Forest leaf litter over rock or fragmental material, rarely saturated with water

Subgroups are based upon the kinds and sequences of horizons. The former Lithic and Cryic subgroups are now differentiated at the family or series level. They may also be indicated as phases of subgroups, great groups, or orders.

FIBRISOL

Soils of this great group are composed largely of relatively undecomposed fibric organic material. Fibric material usually is classified in the von Post scale of decomposition as classes 1 to 4. Fibrisols occur extensively in Canada, particularly in peat deposits dominated by sphagnum mosses.

Fibrisols have a dominantly fibric middle tier, or middle and surface tiers if a terric, lithic, or hydric contact occurs in the middle tier. Fibric material is the least decomposed type of organic material. It contains large amounts of well-preserved fiber that is retained on a 100-mesh sieve (0.15 mm) and can be identified as to botanical origin. A fibric layer has 40% or more of rubbed fiber by volume and a pyrophosphate index of 5 or more (*see* Chapter 2 for details). If the rubbed fiber volume is 75% or more, the pyrophosphate criterion does not apply. Dominantly fibric means that fibric material is the most abundant type of organic material. If both fibric and mesic layers occur in the middle tier, the tier is dominantly fibric if more than half of its thickness is composed of fibric material. If fibric, mesic, and humic layers are present in the middle tier, it is dominantly fibric if the thickness of fibric layers is greater than that of either mesic or humic layers. Subdominant in the following definitions means next in abundance to the dominant material but not less than 12 cm thickness if sharply contrasting (Of vs Oh), or 25 cm if not sharply contrasting (Om vs Of or Oh).

Typic Fibrisol

Common horizon sequence: Of or Om, Of

Soils of this subgroup have the general properties specified for the Organic order and the Fibrisol great group. They are composed mainly of fibric material that is commonly derived mainly from mosses.

They are identified by the following properties:

1. If present, the middle and bottom tiers are dominantly fibric. A lithic contact may occur.
2. They have neither subdominant humic layers with a total thickness of greater than 12 cm or subdominant mesic layers with a total thickness greater than 25 cm in the middle and bottom tiers.
3. The control section lacks terric, hydric, cumulo, and limno layers.

Mesic Fibrisol

Common horizon sequence: Of or Om, Of, Om, Of

Soils of this subgroup have the general properties specified for the Organic order and the Fibrisol great group. They differ from the Typic Fibrisols by having a subdominant mesic layer (thicker than 25 cm) in the middle or bottom tier. The control section lacks terric, hydric, cumulo, or limno layers.

Humic Fibrisol

Common horizon sequence: Of, Om or Oh, Of, Oh, Of or Om

Soils of this subgroup have the general properties specified for the Organic order and the Fibrisol great group. They differ from the Typic Fibrisols by having a subdominant humic layer thicker than 12 cm in the middle or the bottom tier, and they may also have a subdominant mesic layer. The control section lacks terric, hydric, cumulo, and limno layers.

Limno Fibrisol

Common horizon sequence: Of or Om, Of, Oco

Soils of this subgroup have the general properties specified for the Organic order and the Fibrisol great group. They differ from the Typic Fibrisols by having a limno layer beneath the surface tier. A limno layer is a layer or layers at least 5 cm thick of coprogenous earth (sedimentary peat), diatomaceous earth, or marl. Limno materials include both organic and inorganic materials either deposited in water by precipitation or by the action of aquatic organisms such as algae and including diatoms, or derived from underwater and floating aquatic plants subsequently modified by aquatic animals. Except for some of the coprogenous earths, most of these limno materials are inorganic. Diatomaceous earth is highly siliceous and marl is mainly $CaCO_3$. Limno Fibrisols may have mesic, humic, or cumulo layers, but they do not have terric or hydric layers.

Cumulo Fibrisol

Common horizon sequence: Of or Om, <u>Of</u>, <u>C</u>, Of

   Soils of this subgroup have the general properties specified for the Organic order and the Fibrisol great group. They differ from the Typic Fibrisols by having a cumulo layer beneath the surface tier. They may have mesic or humic layers, but they lack terric, hydric, and limno layers. A cumulo layer consists of multiple layers of mineral material (alluvium) together more than 5 cm thick or one layer 5–30 cm thick.

Terric Fibrisol

Common horizon sequence: Of or Om, <u>Of</u>, <u>C</u>

   Soils of this subgroup have the general properties specified for the Organic order and the Fibrisol great group. They differ from the Typic Fibrisols by having a terric layer (an unconsolidated mineral layer at least 30 cm thick) beneath the surface tier. They may also have cumulo or limno layers, but they do not have mesic, humic, or hydric layers within the control section.

Terric Mesic Fibrisol

Common horizon sequence: Of or Om, <u>Of</u>, <u>Om</u>, <u>C</u>

   Soils of this subgroup have the general properties specified for the Organic order and the Fibrisol great group. They differ from the Typic Fibrisols by having both a terric layer beneath the surface tier and a subdominant mesic layer thicker than 25 cm in the control section. They may also have cumulo layers, but they lack humic and hydric layers.

Terric Humic Fibrisol

Common horizon sequence: Of or Om, <u>Of</u>, <u>Oh</u>, <u>C</u>

   Soils of this subgroup have the general properties specified for the Organic order and the Fibrisol great group. They differ from the Typic Fibrisols by having both a terric layer beneath the surface tier and a subdominant humic layer thicker than 12 cm in the control section. They may also have mesic or cumulo layers, but they lack a hydric layer.

Hydric Fibrisol

Common horizon sequence: Of or Om, <u>Of</u>, <u>W</u>

   Soils of this subgroup have the general properties specified for the Organic order and the Fibrisol great group. They differ from the Typic Fibrisols by having a hydric layer (a layer of water that extends from a depth of not less than 40 cm to a depth of more than 160 cm). They may also have mesic, humic, cumulo, terric, or limno layers.

MESISOL

   Soils of this great group are at a stage of decomposition intermediate between Fibrisols and Humisols. Mesisols have a dominantly mesic middle tier or middle and surface tiers if a terric, lithic, or hydric contact occurs in the middle tier. A mesic layer is an organic layer that fails to meet the requirements of either a fibric or a humic layer. Thus it contains 10–40% rubbed fiber by volume and has a pyrophosphate index of 3–5. Mesic material is usually classified in the von Post scale of decomposition as class 5 or 6.

Typic Mesisol

Common horizon sequence: Of, Om or Oh, <u>Om</u>

   Soils of this subgroup have the general properties specified for the Organic order and the Mesisol great group. They are composed mainly of organic materials at an intermediate stage of decomposition.

   They are identified by the following properties:

1.   If present, the middle and bottom tiers are dominantly mesic. A lithic contact may occur.
2.   These soils do not have terric, hydric, cumulo, or limno layers within the control section.
3.   They lack subdominant humic or fibric layers with a total thickness greater than 25 cm in the middle and bottom tiers.

Fibric Mesisol

Common horizon sequence: Of, Om or Oh, <u>Om</u>, <u>Of</u>, Om

   Soils of this subgroup have the general properties specified for the Organic order and the Mesisol great group. They differ from Typic Mesisols by having a subdominant fibric layer thicker than 25 cm in the middle or bottom tiers.

Humic Mesisol

Common horizon sequence: Of, Om or Oh, <u>Om, Oh,</u> Om

Soils of this subgroup have the general properties specified for the Organic order and the Mesisol great group. They differ from Typic Mesisols by having a subdominant humic layer thicker than 25 cm in the middle or bottom tiers, and they may also have a subdominant fibric layer.

Limno Mesisol

Common horizon sequence: Of, Om or Oh, <u>Om, Oco,</u> Om

Soils of this subgroup have the general properties specified for the Organic order and the Mesisol great group. They differ from Typic Mesisols by having a limno layer beneath the surface tier. Also they may have fibric, humic, and cumulo layers, but they do not have terric or hydric layers.

Cumulo Mesisol

Common horizon sequence: Of, Om or Oh, <u>Om, C,</u> Om

Soils of this subgroup have the general properties specified for the Organic order and the Mesisol great group. They differ from Typic Mesisols by having a cumulo layer beneath the surface tier. They may also have fibric or humic layers, but they lack terric, hydric, and limno layers. A cumulo layer consists of multiple layers of mineral material (alluvium) together more than 5 cm thick or one layer 5–30 cm thick.

Terric Mesisol

Common horizon sequence: Of, Om or Oh, <u>Om, C,</u> Om

Soils of this subgroup have the general properties specified for the Organic order and the Mesisol great group. They differ from Typic Mesisols by having a terric layer (an unconsolidated mineral substratum at least 30 cm thick) beneath the surface tier. They may also have cumulo or limno layers, but they do not have fibric, humic, or hydric layers within the control section.

Terric Fibric Mesisol

Common horizon sequence: Of, Om or Oh, <u>Om, Of, C,</u> Om

Soils of this subgroup have the general properties specified for the Organic order and the Mesisol great group. They differ from Typic Mesisols by having both a terric layer beneath the surface tier and a subdominant fibric layer thicker than 25 cm in the control section.

Terric Humic Mesisol

Common horizon sequence: Of, Om or Oh, <u>Om, Oh, C,</u> Om

Soils of this subgroup have the general properties specified for the Organic order and the Mesisol great group. They differ from Typic Mesisols by having both a terric layer beneath the surface tier and a subdominant humic layer thicker than 25 cm within the control section.

Hydric Mesisol

Common horizon sequence: Of, Om or Oh, <u>Om, W</u>

Soils of this subgroup have the general properties specified for the Organic order and the Mesisol great group. They differ from Typic Mesisols by having a hydric layer and may also have humic, cumulo, terric, or limno layers. A hydric layer is a layer of water that extends from a depth of not less than 40 cm to a depth of more than 160 cm.

HUMISOL

Soils of this great group are at the most advanced stage of decomposition of the great groups of Organic soils. Most of the material is humified, and there are few recognizable fibers. Humisols have a dominantly humic middle tier or middle and surface tiers if a terric, lithic, or hydric contact occurs in the middle tier. A humic layer is an organic layer having less than 10% rubbed fiber by volume and a pyrophosphate index of 3 or less. It has a higher bulk density, usually 0.2 g/cm^3 or greater, and a lower water-holding capacity than fibric or mesic layers. Humic material usually is classified in the von Post scale of decomposition as class 7 or higher and rarely in class 6.

Only minor areas of Humisols are known to occur in Canada.

Typic Humisol

Common horizon sequence: Om or Oh, Oh

Soils of this subgroup have the general properties specified for the Organic order and the Humisol great group. They are composed dominantly of well-decomposed organic materials.

They are identified by the following properties:

1. If present, the middle and bottom tiers are dominantly humic. A lithic contact may occur.
2. They do not have terric, hydric, cumulo, or limno layers within the control section.
3. They have neither subdominant fibric layers with a total thickness greater than 12 cm nor subdominant mesic layers with a total thickness greater than 25 cm in the middle or bottom tiers.

Fibric Humisol

Common horizon sequence: Om or Oh, Oh, Of, Oh

Soils of this subgroup have the general properties specified for the Organic order and Humisol great group. They differ from Typic Humisols by having a subdominant fibric layer thicker than 12 cm in the middle or bottom tiers, and they may also have a subdominant mesic layer.

Mesic Humisol

Common horizon sequence: Om or Oh, Oh, Om, Oh

Soils of this subgroup have the general properties specified for the Organic order and the Humisol great group. They differ from Typic Humisols by having a subdominant mesic layer thicker than 25 cm in the middle or bottom tiers. They lack a subdominant fibric layer below the surface tier.

Limno Humisol

Common horizon sequence: Om or Oh, Oh, Oco, Oh

Soils of this subgroup have the general properties specified for the Organic order and the Humisol great group. They differ from Typic Humisols by having a limno layer beneath the surface tier. They may also have fibric and cumulo layers, but they do not have terric or hydric layers.

Cumulo Humisol

Common horizon sequence: Om or Oh, Oh, C, Oh

Soils of this subgroup have the general properties specified for the Organic order and the Humisol great group. They differ from Typic Humisols by having a cumulo layer beneath the surface tier. Also they may have fibric or mesic layers, but they lack terric, hydric, and limno layers. A cumulo layer consists of multiple layers of mineral material, e.g. alluvium, together more than 5 cm thick or one layer 5–30 cm thick.

Terric Humisol

Common horizon sequence: Om or Oh, Oh, C, Oh

Soils of this subgroup have the general properties specified for the Organic order and the Humisol great group. They differ from Typic Humisols by having a terric layer (an unconsolidated mineral substratum at least 30 cm thick) beneath the surface tier. They may also have cumulo or limno layers, but they do not have fibric, mesic or hydric layers within the control section.

Terric Fibric Humisol

Common horizon sequence: Of or Oh, Oh, Of, C, Oh

Soils of this subgroup have the general properties specified for the Organic order and the Humisol great group. They differ from Typic Humisols by having both a terric layer beneath the surface tier and a subdominant fibric layer thicker than 12 cm within the control section.

Terric Mesic Humisol

Common horizon sequence: Om or Oh, Oh, Om, C, Oh

Soils of this subgroup have the general properties specified for the Organic order and the Humisol great group. They differ from Typic Humisols by having both a terric layer beneath the surface tier and a subdominant mesic layer thicker than 25 cm within the control section.

Hydric Humisol

Common horizon sequence: Om or Oh, <u>Oh</u>, <u>W</u>

Soils of this subgroup have the general properties specified for the Organic order and the Humisol great group. They differ from Typic Humisols by having a hydric layer, and they may also have mesic, humic, cumulo, terric, or limno layers. A hydric layer is a layer of water that extends from a depth of not less than 40 cm to a depth of more than 160 cm.

FOLISOL

Soils of this great group consist typically of thick layers of leaf litter, twigs, branches, and mosses (L, F, and H) overlying rock or fragmental material. Unlike other Organic soils they are not composed dominantly of mosses, sedges, and other aquatic plants. Soils having thick L, F, and H horizons overlying unconsolidated, nonfragmental material are classified as mineral soils.

Folisols consist of an LHF horizon at least 10 cm thick overlying either a lithic contact or fragmental material with interstices filled or partially filled with organic material. A layer of mineral soil thinner than 10 cm may occur above the lithic contact, but the thickness of the organic layers must be more than twice the thickness of the mineral layer.

Only one subgroup of Folisols is identified.

Typic Folisol

Common horizon sequence: <u>LFH</u>, <u>R</u>

Soils of this subgroup have the general properties of the Organic order and the properties of the Folisol great group. They consist of an LFH horizon more than 10 cm thick overlying either fragmental material, or a lithic contact, or a thin layer (<10 cm) of unconsolidated mineral material overlying bedrock or fragmental material.

Chapter 10   PODZOLIC ORDER

Great Group	*Subgroup*
Humic Podzol	Orthic Humic Podzol O.HP
	Ortstein Humic Podzol OT.HP
	Placic Humic Podzol P.HP
	Duric Humic Podzol DU.HP
	Fragic Humic Podzol FR.HP
Ferro-Humic Podzol	Orthic Ferro-Humic Podzol O.FHP
	Ortstein Ferro-Humic Podzol OT.FHP
	Placic Ferro-Humic Podzol P.FHP
	Duric Ferro-Humic Podzol DU.FHP
	Fragic Ferro-Humic Podzol FR.FHP
	Luvisolic Ferro-Humic Podzol LU.FHP
	Sombric Ferro-Humic Podzol SM.FHP
	Gleyed Ferro-Humic Podzol GL.FHP
	Gleyed Ortstein Ferro-Humic Podzol GLOT.FHP
	Gleyed Sombric Ferro-Humic Podzol GLSM.FHP
Humo-Ferric Podzol	Orthic Humo-Ferric Podzol O.HFP
	Ortstein Humo-Ferric Podzol OT.HFP
	Placic Humo-Ferric Podzol P.HFP
	Duric Humo-Ferric Podzol DU.HFP
	Fragic Humo-Ferric Podzol FR.HFP
	Luvisolic Humo-Ferric Podzol LU.HFP
	Sombric Humo-Ferric Podzol SM.HFP
	Gleyed Humo-Ferric Podzol GL.HFP
	Gleyed Ortstein Humo-Ferric Podzol GLOT.HFP
	Gleyed Sombric Humo-Ferric Podzol GLSM.HFP

A diagrammatic representation of profiles of some subgroups of the Podzolic order is shown in Fig. 33. A common horizon sequence is given for each subgroup; diagnostic horizons are underlined and some other commonly occurring horizons are listed. The subgroup includes soils having horizon sequences different from those shown.

Soils of the Podzolic order have B horizons in which the dominant accumulation product is amorphous material composed mainly of humified organic matter combined in varying degrees with Al and Fe. Typically Podzolic soils occur in coarse to medium textured, acid parent materials, under forest or heath vegetation in cool to very cold humid to perhumid climates. However, some occur under soil environmental conditions outside this range. For example, minor areas of Podzolic soils occur in wet sandy sites in areas of subhumid climate and others occur in parent materials that were once calcareous. Podzolic soils can usually be recognized readily in the field. Generally they have organic surface horizons that are commonly L, F, and H but may be Of or Om and a light-colored eluvial horizon, Ae, which may be absent. Most Podzolic soils have a reddish brown to black B horizon with an abrupt upper boundary and lower B or BC horizons with colors progressively yellower in hue and lower in chroma with depth except in reddish-colored parent materials.

Soils of the Podzolic order are defined on the basis of a combination of morphological and chemical criteria of the B horizons. Soils of the order must meet the following limits.

Morphological

1. The podzolic B horizon is at least 10 cm thick and has moist, crushed colors as follows:
    a. The color is black or the hue is either 7.5YR or redder or 10YR near the upper boundary and becomes yellower with depth.
    b. The chroma is higher than 3 or the value is 3 or less.
2. The accumulation of amorphous material in the podzolic B horizon is indicated by:
    a. Brown to black coatings on some mineral grains or brown to black microaggregates.
    b. A silty feel when rubbed wet unless the material is cemented.
3. The texture of the podzolic B horizon is coarser than clay.
4. The soil either has no Bt horizon or the upper boundary of the Bt horizon is at a depth

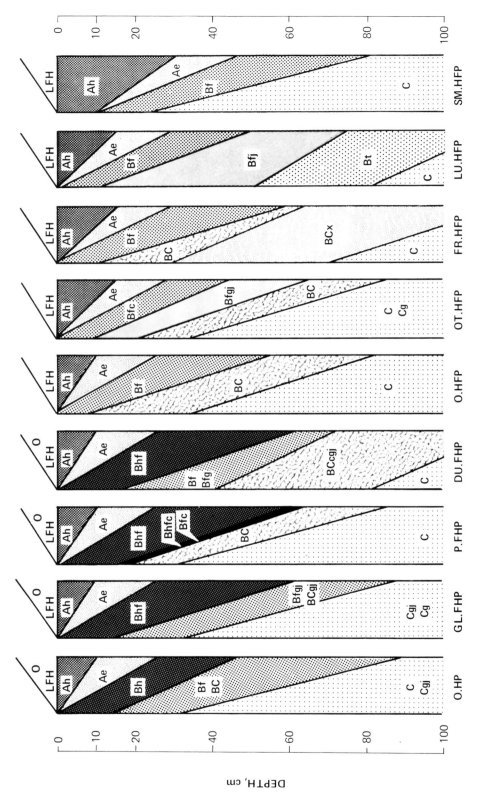

Fig. 33.   Diagrammatic horizon pattern of some subgroups of the Podzolic order.

greater than 50 cm from the mineral soil surface.

Chemical
1. The soils have a B subhorizon (Bh) at least 10 cm thick that contains more than 1% organic C, less than 0.3% pyrophosphate-extractable Fe, and has a ratio of organic C to pyrophosphate-extractable Fe of 20 or more.
2. Alternatively, the soils have a B subhorizon (Bf or Bhf) at least 10 cm thick with the following characteristics:
   a. An organic C content of more than 0.5%.
   b. A pyrophosphate-extractable Al + Fe content of 0.6% or more in textures finer than sand and of 0.4% or more in sands (coarse sand, sand, fine sand, and very fine sand).
   c. A ratio of pyrophosphate-extractable Al + Fe to clay (<2 μm) of more than 0.05.
   d. A ratio of organic C to pyrophosphate-extractable Fe of less than 20, or pyrophosphate-extractable Fe at least 0.3%, or both.

A Bf contains 0.5–5% organic C, and a Bhf contains more than 5% organic C.

Any B horizon that satisfies the specified morphological and chemical requirements is a podzolic B horizon. Some Bh, Bhf, and Bf horizons do not qualify as podzolic B horizons because they are too thin.

Some soils that are not Podzolic will satisfy the minimum morphological limits specified. However, these limits are thought to be useful to exclude from the order certain soils having horizons that satisfy the chemical limits specified but otherwise do not resemble Podzolic soils. To be classified as Podzolic, a borderline soil must meet both the morphological and the chemical limits specified.

Some acid Ah horizons satisfy the morphological and chemical criteria of podzolic B horizons. These are commonly associated with volcanic ash. No specific criteria have been developed to distinguish these horizons from Bhf or Bf horizons. The following guidelines are useful:

1. Such Ah horizons are generally black and underlain by brown or dark brown B horizons. For example, the moist color of the A horizon may be 10YR 2/2 and that of the B 7.5YR 4/4.
2. The ratio of humic to fulvic acid in these Ah horizons is greater than 1:2 (usually 1:1 or higher) and in the underlying B horizon it is less than 1:2.
3. Less than 50% of the total organic C is extracted from these A horizons by alkali pyrophosphate and more than 50% is extracted from the associated B horizons.

Some associated properties of podzolic B horizons

In addition to the properties specified as diagnostic, podzolic B horizons have a number of associated properties that may be useful in distinguishing them from other B horizons. Some of these associated properties are:

1. They have a high pH-dependent cation exchange capacity (CEC). The difference ($\triangle$CEC) between CEC measured at pH 7 and at the pH of the soil is usually at least 8 meq/100 g.
2. The base saturation, as determined by an unbuffered salt, is nearly always below 80% and commonly less than 50%.
3. Unless cemented, they have a high water-holding capacity in relation to their texture.
4. They have a high capacity to fix phosphate.
5. Although they commonly contain appreciably more clay than the overlying Ae horizon (if present), usually very little of the clay occurs as oriented coatings on particles or peds.
6. They give a strongly alkaline reaction in NaF. As a field test a 2% suspension of soil in 1 M NaF gives a pH of 10.3 or more for most podzolic B horizons. Volcanic ash samples also commonly give a high pH with this test, thus the NaF test is not useful for identifying podzolic B horizons in materials containing volcanic ash.

DISTINGUISHING PODZOLIC SOILS FROM SOILS OF OTHER ORDERS

Guidelines for distinguishing Podzolic soils from soils of other orders with which they might be confused are as follows:

Luvisolic. Some Podzolic and some Luvisolic soils have Ae, Bf, and Bt horizons. These soils are classified as Podzolic if the upper boundary of the Bt horizon is at a depth below 50 cm and as Luvisolic if it is at a depth less than 50 cm.

Brunisolic. In the continuum of soils in nature many pedons have properties close to the arbitrary boundary line between Podzolic soils and acid Brunisolic soils. These classification problems are resolved by thorough descriptions and sampling the B horizons of a few pedons having a range of properties thought to be close to the borderline of Podzolic soils. The samples having a B horizon that meets the requirements of a podzolic B are classified as Podzolic. Subsequently in that area, classification decisions are based upon field observations supported by the known relationships between morphology and podzolic B development.

Gleysolic. A podzolic B horizon takes precedence over gley features. Thus a soil having both a podzolic B horizon and gley colors as specified for soils of the Gleysolic order is classified as Podzolic.

Organic. Some soils have podzolic B horizons underlying a thick layer of peat. The soil is classified as Organic if the organic layer is greater than 60 cm thick and fibric with a bulk density <0.1 g/cm³ or 40 cm thick when the bulk density exceeds 0.1 g/cm³.

The Podzolic order is divided into three great groups: Humic Podzol, Fero-Humic Podzol, and Humo-Ferric Podzol on the basis of organic C content and the organic C to pyrophosphate-extractable Fe ratio of the podzolic B horizon as shown below.

Podzolic Order

Humic Podzol	Ferro-Humic Podzol	Humo-Ferric Podzol
Bh at least 10 cm thick with: organic C $>1\%$ pyrophosphate Fe $<0.3\%$ organic C:pyrophosphate Fe $= 20$ or more	Bhf at least 10 cm thick with: organic C $>5\%$ pyrophosphate Fe + Al $= 0.6\%$ or more (0.4% for sands)	Bf, or thin Bhf + Bf at least 10 cm thick with: organic C $= 0.5\text{--}5\%$ pyrophosphate Fe + Al $= 0.6\%$ or more (0.4% for sands)

Subgroups are separated on the basis of the kind and sequence of the horizons indicating conformity with the central concept of the great group, the presence of additional horizons, or intergrading to soils of other orders. Some former subgroup features are now recognized taxonomically at either the family (lithic, some cryic) or series (turbic) level. They may be indicated also as phases of subgroups, great groups, or orders.

HUMIC PODZOL

These soils have a dark-colored podzolic B horizon that contains very little extractable Fe. They occur typically in wet sites so that they are saturated with water during some periods of the year. Characteristically they are found under heath, forest and heath, sphagnum, or western coastal forest vegetation in maritime fringe environments, on some sites at high elevations inland, and in peaty depressions. Under virgin conditions Humic Podzols usually have thick L, F, and H or O horizons underlain by a light-colored eluvial horizon (Ae), an eluvial horizon darkened by humic material, or by a podzolic B horizon, which is usually a Bh. The B horizon may include several kinds of podzolic B subhorizons: Bh, Bhf, and Bf, which may be cemented (ortstein, placic) or friable. The material below the podzolic B horizon may be cemented (duric), compact and brittle (fragipan), or friable.

Humic Podzols have a Bh horizon at least 10 cm thick that usually occurs at the top of the B horizon but may occur below other B horizons. The Bh horizon contains more than 1% organic C and less than 0.3% pyrophosphate-extractable Fe and has a ratio of organic C to pyrophosphate-extractable Fe of 20 or more.

Humic Podzols are generally strongly acid and their B horizons are usually less than 50% base saturated (neutral salt). The pH dependent CEC of the Bh horizon is usually well above 8 meq/100 g.

Under disturbed conditions and where the Bh horizon directly underlies the organic surface layer, the Bh may be confused with an Ah horizon. The guidelines that aid in making this distinction are that more than 50% of the organic C of Bh horizons is extractable by NaOH-Na$_4$P$_2$O$_7$ and more than 50% of the extractable C of Bh horizons is fulvic acid C. Cultivated Humic Podzols are identified by properties of the B horizon below the cultivated layer.

Distinguishing Bh from Bhf horizons may be a problem in the field. Two useful guidelines are:

Bh horizon material usually does not turn redder on ignition because of its low Fe content. Bh horizons are generally almost black. However, some Bhf horizons also have chromas of only 1 or 2.

Humic Podzols are divided into five subgroups based on the kind and sequence of the horizons. No gleyed subgroup has been included because Humic Podzols usually occur in wet sites; thus the great group implies some degree of gleying.

Orthic Humic Podzol

Common horizon sequence: O or LFH, Ae, <u>Bh</u>, Bfgj, BCgj, Cg

These soils have the general properties specified for the Podzolic order and the Humic Podzol great group. They are identified by the following properties:

1. They have a Bh horizon at least 10 cm thick.
2. They do not have an ortstein horizon at least 3 cm thick, a placic horizon, a duric horizon, or a fragipan.

Usually Orthic Humic Podzols have L, F, and H or O horizons and an Ae horizon, and commonly they have a Bhf or Bf horizon underlying the Bh horizons. They may have mottling indicative of gleying at any depth within the control section. Parts of the Bhf or Bf may be cemented, but they do not meet the requirements of an ortstein horizon.

Ortstein Humic Podzol

Common horizon sequence: LFH or O, Ae, <u>Bh</u> or <u>Bhc</u>, <u>Bfc</u>, Cgj

These soils have the general properties specified for the Podzolic order and the Humic Podzol great group. They differ from the Orthic Humic Podzols by having an ortstein horizon at least 3 cm thick. An ortstein horizon is a Bh, Bhf, or Bf horizon that is strongly cemented and occurs in at least one-third of the lateral extent of the pedon. The ortstein horizon is designated as Bhc, Bhfc, or Bfc depending upon its organic C and extractable Fe contents. Ortstein horizons are generally reddish brown to very dark reddish brown in color. Usually Ortstein Humic Podzols have L, F, and H or O horizons and an Ae horizon. They may have mottling indicative of gleying at any depth within the control section and placic or duric horizons or a fragipan.

Placic Humic Podzol

Common horizon sequence: LFH or O, Ae, <u>Bh</u>, <u>Bhfc</u> or <u>Bfc</u>, BCgj, Cgj

These soils have the general properties specified for the Podzolic order and the Humic Podzol great group. They differ from the Orthic Humic Podzols by having a placic horizon within the control section. A placic horizon (Bhfc, Bfc, Bgfc) consists of a single thin layer that is commonly less than 5 mm thick, or a series of thin layers that are irregular or involute, hard, impervious, often vitreous, and dark reddish brown to black. These thin horizons are apparently cemented by Fe-organic complexes, hydrated Fe oxides, or a mixture of Fe and Mn oxides. The placic horizon or thin iron pan may occur in any part of the B horizon except the Bh, and commonly it extends into the BC horizon.

Placic Humic Podzols usually have L, F, and H or O horizons and an Ae horizon. They do not have an ortstein horizon, but they may have a duric horizon or a fragipan. Evidence of gleying in the form of dull colors or mottling is commonly apparent especially above depressions in the placic horizon. These soils occur most commonly in wet sites in maritime regions; frequently the surface is peaty.

Duric Humic Podzol

Common horizon sequence: LFH or O, Ae, <u>Bh</u>, Bhf, <u>BCc</u>, C

These soils have the general properties specified for the Podzolic order and the Humic Podzol great group. They differ from the Orthic Humic Podzols by having a duric horizon within the control section. A duric horizon is a strongly cemented horizon that does not satisfy the criteria of a podzolic B horizon. It usually has an abrupt upper boundary to an overlying podzolic B horizon and a diffuse lower boundary at least 50 cm below. Cementation is usually strongest near the upper boundary, which occurs commonly at a depth of 40–80 cm from the mineral surface. Usually the color of a duric horizon differs little from that of the parent material, and the structure is usually massive or very coarse platy. Moist clods at least 3 cm thick usually cannot be broken in the hands. Air-dry clods of the material do not slake when immersed in water. Some duric horizons may meet the requirements of a Bt horizon (Btc).

Duric Humic Podzols usually have L, F, and H or O horizons. They do not have either an ortstein or a placic horizon, but they may have mottles indicative of gleying in some part of the control section.

Fragic Humic Podzol

Common horizon sequence: LFH or O, Ae, <u>Bh</u>, Bf, <u>BCxgj</u>, C

These soils have the general properties specified for the Podzolic order and the Humic Podzol great group. They differ from the Orthic Humic Podzol subgroup by having a fragipan within the control section. A fragipan (Bx or BCx) is a subsurface horizon of high bulk density that has firm and brittle consistence when moist and hard to extremely hard consistence when dry. Usually it is of medium texture. Commonly it has bleached fracture planes separating very coarse prismatic units and the secondary structure is platy. Usually the fragipan is similar in color to the parent material, but it differs in structure and consistence and sometimes in bulk density. The upper boundary of a fragipan is usually either abrupt or clear, but the lower boundary is usually diffuse. Commonly it is necessary to dig to about 3 m to expose clearly the material beneath the lower boundary of the fragipan. Air-dry clods of fragipans slake in water. A fragipan may have clay skins and meet the limits of a Bt horizon (Btx).

Fragic Humic Podzols usually have L, F, and H or O horizons and an Ae horizon. They do not have ortstein, placic, or duric horizons, but they may have mottles indicative of gleying at some depth within the control section.

FERRO-HUMIC PODZOL

These soils have a dark-colored podzolic B horizon with a high content of organic C and an appreciable amount of extractable Fe and Al. They occur typically in the more humid part of the region of Podzolic soils under forest vegetation, or forest with heath or moss undercover. Under virgin conditions these soils usually have thick L, F, and H or O horizons; they may have an Ah horizon and usually have a light-colored Ae horizon. The podzolic B horizon is usually thick and dark reddish brown in the upper part and grades to lighter colors of higher chroma with depth. Typically the Bhf horizon is of higher chroma (commonly 2, 3, or 4) than the Bh horizon of Humic Podzols (commonly 1 or 2). The material below the podzolic B horizon may be cemented (duric), compact and brittle (fragipan), or friable.

Ferro-Humic Podzols have a Bhf horizon at least 10 cm thick and lack a Bh horizon at least 10 cm thick. The Bhf horizon contains 5% or more organic C and 0.6% or more pyrophosphate-extractable Al + Fe (0.4% for sands). It has a ratio of organic C to pyrophosphate-extractable Fe of less than 20 or more than 0.3% pyrophosphate-extractable Fe or both.

Ferro-Humic Podzols are generally both strongly acid and less than 50% base saturated (neutral salt). The pH-dependent CEC of the Bhf horizon is usually well above 8 meq/100 g and commonly 25 meq or more. The Bhf horizon of these soils usually has a markedly silty feel when rubbed moist, which is presumably because of its high content of amorphous material.

Ferro-Humic Podzols are divided into 10 subgroups based on the kind and sequence of the horizons. Gleyed subgroups are not differentiated for those soils having a relatively impermeable subsoil horizon (placic, duric, fragic, Bt). A Gleyed Ortstein subgroup is included because some ortstein horizons are permeable to water and do not result in temporary gleying.

Orthic Ferro-Humic Podzol

Common horizon sequence: LFH or O, Ae, Bhf, Bf, BC, C

These soils have the general properties specified for the Podzolic order and the Ferro-Humic Podzol great group. They are identified by the following properties:

1. They have a Bhf horizon at least 10 cm thick.
2. They do not have a Bh horizon at least 10 cm thick, an ortstein horizon at least 3 cm thick, a placic horizon, a duric horizon, a fragipan, a Bt horizon, an Ah horizon at least 10 cm thick, or evidence of gleying in the form of distinct mottling within 1 m of the surface.

Usually Orthic Ferro-Humic Podzols have L, F, and H or O horizons and an Ae horizon, and commonly they have a Bf horizon underlying the Bhf. Parts of the Bhf or Bf may be cemented, but they do not meet the requirements of an ortstein horizon.

Ortstein Ferro-Humic Podzol

Common horizon sequence: LFH or O, Ae, Bhf, Bhfc or Bfc, BC, C

These soils have the general properties specified for the Podzolic order and the Ferro-Humic Podzol great group. They differ from the Orthic Ferro-Humic Podzols by having an ortstein horizon at least 3 cm thick. An ortstein horizon is a Bh, Bhf, or Bf horizon that is strongly cemented and occurs in at least one-third of the lateral extent of the pedon. The ortstein horizon in this subgroup is designated as Bhfc or Bfc depending upon its organic C content and is generally reddish brown to very dark reddish brown in color. Usually Ortstein Ferro-Humic Podzols have L, F, and H or O horizons and an Ae horizon. They may have one or more of placic, duric, Ah, or Bt horizons, a fragipan, or faint mottling.

Placic Ferro-Humic Podzol

Common horizon sequence: LFH or O, Ae, <u>Bhf</u>, <u>Bhfc</u> or <u>Bfc</u>, Bf, BC, C

These soils have the general properties specified for the Podzolic order and the Ferro-Humic Podzol great group. They differ from the Orthic Ferro-Humic Podzols by having a placic horizon within the control section. A placic horizon (Bhfc, Bfc, Bgfc) consists of a single thin layer (commonly 5 mm or less thick) or a series of thin layers that are irregular or involute, hard, impervious, often vitreous, and dark reddish brown to black. These thin horizons are apparently cemented by Fe-organic complexes, hydrated Fe oxides, or a mixture of Fe and Mn oxides. The placic horizon or thin iron pan may occur in any part of the B horizon and commonly extends into the BC horizon.

Placic Ferro-Humic Podzols usually have L, F, and H or O horizons and an Ae horizon. They do not have an ortstein horizon, but they may have a duric, Ah, or Bt horizon, or a fragipan. Evidence of gleying in the form of dull colors or mottling is commonly apparent especially above depressions in the placic horizon. These soils occur most commonly in coarse textured deposits in perhumid maritime climates.

Duric Ferro-Humic Podzol

Common horizon sequence: LFH or O, Ae, <u>Bhf</u>, <u>BCc</u>, C

These soils have the general properties specified for the Podzolic order and the Ferro-Humic Podzol great group. They differ from the Orthic Ferro-Humic Podzols by having a duric horizon within the control section. A duric horizon is a strongly cemented horizon that does not satisfy the criteria of a podzolic B horizon. It usually has an abrupt upper boundary to an overlying podzolic B horizon and a diffuse lower boundary at least 50 cm below. Cementation is usually strongest near the upper boundary, which occurs commonly at a depth of 40–80 cm from the mineral surface. Usually the color of a duric horizon differs little from that of the parent material and the structure is massive or very coarse platy. Moist clods at least 3 cm thick usually cannot be broken in the hands. Air-dry clods of the material do not slake when immersed in water. Some duric horizons may meet the requirements of a Bt horizon (Btc).

Duric Ferro-Humic Podzols usually have L, F, and H or O horizons. They do not have an ortstein or a placic horizon, but they may have an Ah horizon and mottles indicative of gleying in some

part of the control section. These soils occur most commonly in coastal southwestern British Columbia.

Fragic Ferro-Humic Podzol

Common horizon sequence: LFH or O, Ae, <u>Bhf</u>, Bf, <u>BCx</u>, C

These soils have the general properties specified for the Podzolic order and the Ferro-Humic Podzol great group. They differ from the Orthic Ferro-Humic Podzols by having a fragipan within the control section. A fragipan (Bx or BCx) is a subsurface horizon of high bulk density that has firm and brittle consistence when moist and hard to extremely hard consistence when dry. Usually it is of medium texture. Commonly it has bleached fracture planes separating very coarse prismatic units and the secondary structure is platy. The fragipan is usually similar in color to the parent material, but it differs in structure and consistence and sometimes in bulk density. The upper boundary of a fragipan is usually either abrupt or clear, but the lower boundary is usually diffuse. It is often necessary to dig to about 3 m to expose clearly the material beneath the lower boundary of the fragipan. Air-dry clods of fragipans slake in water. A fragipan may have clay skins and meet the limits of a Bt horizon (Btx).

Fragic Ferro-Humic Podzols usually have L, F, and H or O horizons and an Ae horizon. They do not have ortstein, placic, or duric horizons, but they may have an Ah horizon and mottles indicative of gleying at some depth within the control section.

Luvisolic Ferro-Humic Podzol

Common horizon sequence: LFH or O, Ae, <u>Bhf</u>, Bf, <u>Bt</u>, C

These soils have the general properties specified for the Podzolic order and the Ferro-Humic Podzol great group. They differ from the Orthic Ferro-Humic Podzols by having a Bt horizon of which the upper boundary is at a depth of at least 50 cm from the mineral surface. If the upper boundary of the Bt horizon is less than 50 cm from the surface, the soil is classified in the Luvisolic order.

Luvisolic Ferro-Humic Podzols usually have L, F, and H or O horizons and an Ae horizon, and they may have an Ah horizon. They do not have ortstein, placic, or duric horizons, or a fragipan, but they may have mottles indicative of gleying at some depth within the control section.

Sombric Ferro-Humic Podzol

Common horizon sequence: LFH or O, Ah, Ae, Bhf, Bf, BC, C

These soils have the general properties specified for the Podzolic order and the Ferro-Humic Podzol great group. They differ from the Orthic Ferro-Humic Podzols by having an Ah horizon at least 10 cm thick.

Usually Sombric Ferro-Humic Podzols have L, F, and H or O horizons and may have an Ae horizon, but they do not have ortstein, placic, duric, or Bt horizons, a fragipan, or distinct mottles indicative of gleying.

Gleyed Ferro-Humic Podzol

Common horizon sequence: LFH or O, Aegj, Bhf, Bfgj, BCg, Cg

These soils have the general properties specified for the Podzolic order and the Ferro-Humic Podzol great group. They differ from the Orthic Ferro-Humic Podzols by having distinct or prominent mottles indicative of gleying within 1 m of the surface. Usually they have thick L, F, and H or O horizons. They do not have ortstein, placic, duric, or Bt horizons, a fragipan, or an Ah horizon at least 10 cm thick.

Gleyed Ortstein Ferro-Humic Podzol

Common horizon sequence: LFH or O, Aegj, Bhf, Bhfc or Bfcg, BCg, Cg

These soils have the general properties specified for the Podzolic order and the Ferro-Humic Podzol great group. They differ from the Ortstein Ferro-Humic Podzols by having distinct to prominent mottles indicative of gleying within 1 m of the surface. Usually they have thick L, F, and H or O horizons. They may have placic, duric, Ah, or Bt horizons, or a fragipan.

Gleyed Sombric Ferro-Humic Podzol

Common horizon sequence: LFH or O, Ah, Aegj, Bhf, Bfgj, BCgj, C

These soils have the general properties specified for the Podzolic order and the Ferro-Humic Podzol great group. They differ from the Sombric Ferro-Humic Podzols by having distinct or prominent

mottles indicative of gleying within 1 m of the surface. Usually they have thick L, F, and H or O horizons, but do not have ortstein, placic, duric, or Bt horizons, or a fragipan.

HUMO-FERRIC PODZOL

These soils have a brownish-colored podzolic B horizon with less organic matter than the B horizon of Ferro-Humic Podzols. They occur widely both in less humid sites of the region of Podzolic soils and in humid sites. Typically they occur under coniferous, mixed, and deciduous forest vegetation, but they may occur under shrub and grass vegetation. Under virgin conditions these soils usually have L, F, and H horizons and they may have an Ah horizon. Usually they have a light-colored Ae horizon with an abrupt lower boundary to a podzolic B horizon in which the reddest hues or highest chromas and lowest color values usually occur near the top of the horizon and fade with depth. Typically the Bf horizon of Humo-Ferric Podzols has higher color values and chromas than the Bhf horizon of Ferro-Humic Podzols. Parts of the Podzolic B horizon may be cemented, and the underlying material may be cemented (duric), compact and brittle (fragipan), or friable.

Humo-Ferric Podzols have a podzolic B horizon at least 10 cm thick but do not have Bh or Bhf horizons at least 10 cm thick. The podzolic B horizon of Humo-Ferric Podzols may include a thin Bhf subhorizon, but usually it is a Bf horizon only. A Bf horizon contains 0.5–5% organic C and 0.6% or more pyrophosphate-extractable Al + Fe (0.4% for sands). Pyrophosphate-extractable Fe is at least 0.3%, or the ratio of organic C to pyrophosphate-extractable Fe is less than 20, or both are true. The ratio of pyrophosphate-extractable Al + Fe to clay is more than 0.05.

Humo-Ferric Podzols are generally strongly acid and less than 50% base saturated (neutral salt). The pH-dependent CEC of the Bf horizon is usually at least 8 meq/100 g. Typically the podzolic B horizon of a Humo-Ferric Podzol contains less amorphous material than is characteristic of a Ferro-Humic Podzol.

Humo-Ferric Podzols are divided into 10 subgroups based on the kind and sequence of the horizons the same as Ferro-Humic Podzols.

Orthic Humo-Ferric Podzol

Common horizon sequence: LFH, Ae, Bf, BC, C

These soils have the general properties specified for the Podzolic order and the Humo-Ferric Podzol great group. They are identified by the following properties:

1. They have a podzolic B horizon at least 10 cm thick (Bf or thin Bhf and Bf).
2. They do not have a Bh horizon at least 10 cm thick, a Bhf horizon at least 10 cm thick, an ortstein horizon at least 3 cm thick, a placic horizon, a duric horizon, a fragipan, a Bt horizon, an Ah horizon at least 10 cm thick, nor evidence of gleying in the form of distinct or prominent mottles within 1 m of the surface.

Usually Orthic Humo-Ferric Podzols have L, F, and H or O horizons and an Ae horizon. Parts of the Bf may be cemented, but they do not meet the requirements of an ortstein horizon.

Ortstein Humo-Ferric Podzol

Common horizon sequence: LFH, Ae, Bfc, Bfj, C

These soils have the general properties specified for the Podzolic order and the Humo-Ferric Podzol great group. They differ from the Orthic Humo-Ferric Podzols by having an ortstein horizon at least 3 cm thick. An ortstein horizon in this subgroup is a Bhf or Bf horizon that is strongly cemented and occurs in at least one-third of the lateral extent of the pedon. Ortstein horizons are generally reddish brown to very dark reddish brown in color. Usually Ortstein Humo-Ferric Podzols have L, F, and H or O horizons and an Ae horizon. They may have faint mottling, and placic, duric, Ah, or Bt horizons, or a fragipan.

Placic Humo-Ferric Podzol

Common horizon sequence: LFH or O, Ae, Bf, Bfc, BC, C

These soils have the general properties specified for the Podzolic order and the Humo-Ferric Podzol great group. They differ from the Orthic Humo-Ferric Podzols by having a placic horizon within the control section. A placic horizon (Bhfc, Bfc, Bgfc) consists of a single thin layer (commonly 5 mm or less thick) or a series of thin layers that are irregular or involute, hard, impervious, often vitreous, and dark reddish brown to black. These thin horizons are apparently cemented by Fe-organic complexes, hydrated Fe oxides, or a mixture of Fe and Mn oxides. The placic horizon or thin iron pan may occur in any part of the B horizon and commonly it extends into the BC horizon.

Placic Humo-Ferric Podzols usually have L, F, and H or O horizons and an Ae horizon. They do not have an ortstein horizon, but they may have a duric horizon or a fragipan. Evidence of gleying in the form of dull colors or mottling is commonly apparent especially above depressions in the placic horizon. These soils occur most commonly in wet sites in maritime regions; frequently the surface is peaty.

Duric Humo-Ferric Podzol

Common horizon sequence: LFH, Ae, Bf, BCc, C

These soils have the general properties specified for the Podzolic order and the Humo-Ferric Podzol great group. They differ from the Orthic Humo-Ferric Podzols by having a duric horizon within the control section. A duric horizon is a strongly cemented horizon that does not satisfy the criteria of a podzolic B horizon. Usually it has an abrupt upper boundary to an overlying podzolic B horizon and a diffuse lower boundary at least 50 cm below. Cementation is usually strongest near the upper boundary, which occurs commonly at a depth of 40–80 cm from the mineral surface. The color of a duric horizon usually differs little from that of the parent material and the structure is usually massive or very coarse platy. Moist clods at least 3 cm thick usually cannot be broken in the hands. Air-dry clods of the material do not slake when immersed in water. Some duric horizons may meet the requirements of a Bt horizon (Btc).

Duric Humo-Ferric Podzols usually have L, F, and H horizons. They do not have either an ortstein or a placic horizon, but they may have an Ah horizon and mottles indicative of gleying in some part of the control section. These soils occur most commonly in coastal southwestern British Columbia.

Fragic Humo-Ferric Podzol

Common horizon sequence: LFH, Ae, Bf, BCx, C

These soils have the general properties specified for the Podzolic order and the Humo-Ferric Podzol great group. They differ from the Orthic Humo-Ferric Podzols by having a fragipan within the control section. A fragipan (Bx or BCx) is a subsurface horizon of high bulk density that is firm and brittle when moist and hard to extremely hard when dry. Usually it is of medium texture. Commonly it has bleached fracture planes separating very coarse prismatic units, and the secondary structure is platy. Usually the fragipan has a color similar to that of the parent material but differs in structure and consistence and sometimes in bulk density. The upper boundary of a fragipan is usually either abrupt or clear, but the lower boundary is usually diffuse. Commonly it is necessary to dig to about 3 m to expose clearly the material beneath the lower boundary of the fragipan. Air-dry clods of fragipans slake in water. A fragipan may have clay skins and meet the limits of a Bt horizon (Btx).

Fragic Humo-Ferric Podzols usually have L, F, and H horizons and an Ae horizon. They do not have ortstein, placic, or duric horizons, but they may have an Ah horizon and mottles indicative of gleying at some depth within the control section.

Luvisolic Humo-Ferric Podzol

Common horizon sequence: LFH, Ae, Bf, Bt, C

These soils have the general properties specified for the Podzolic order and the Humo-Ferric Podzol great group. They differ from the Orthic Humo-Ferric Podzols by having a Bt horizon of which the upper boundary is at a depth of at least 50 cm from the mineral surface. If the upper boundary of the Bt horizon is less than 50 cm from the surface, the soil is classified in the Luvisolic order.

Luvisolic Humo-Ferric Podzols usually have L, F, and H horizons and an Ae horizon, and they may have an Ah horizon. They do not have ortstein, duric, or placic horizons, or a fragipan, but they may have mottles indicative of gleying at some depth within the control section.

Sombric Humo-Ferric Podzol

Common horizon sequence: LFH, Ah, Ae, Bf, BC, C

These soils have the general properties specified for the Podzolic order and the Humo-Ferric Podzol great group. They differ from the Orthic Humo-Ferric Podzols by having an Ah horizon at least 10 cm thick.

Usually Sombric Humo-Ferric Podzols have L, F, and H horizons and may have an Ae horizon. They do not have ortstein, placic, duric, or Bt horizons, or a fragipan, or distinct mottles indicative of gleying.

Gleyed Humo-Ferric Podzol

Common horizon sequence: LFH or O, Aegj, Bfgj, BCg, Cg

These soils have the general properties specified for the Podzolic order and the Humo-Ferric Podzol great group. They differ from the Orthic Humo-Ferric Podzols by having distinct or prominent mottles indicative of gleying within 1 m of the surface. They usually have thick L, F, and H or O horizons and do not have ortstein, placic, duric, or Bt horizons, a fragipan, or an Ah horizon at least 10 cm thick.

Gleyed Ortstein Humo-Ferric Podzol

Common horizon sequence: LFH or O, Aegj, Bfcgj, Bfcjcjgj, Cg

These soils have the general properties specified for the Podzolic order and the Humo-Ferric Podzol great group. They differ from the Ortstein Humo-Ferric Podzols by having distinct or prominent mottles indicative of gleying within 1 m of the surface. They usually have thick L, F, and H or O horizons, and they may have Ah, Ae, Bt, placic, or duric horizons, or a fragipan.

Gleyed Sombric Humo-Ferric Podzol

Common horizon sequence: LFH or O, Ah, Aegj, Bfgj, BCg, Cg

These soils have the general properties specified for the Podzolic order and the Humo-Ferric Podzol great group. They differ from the Sombric Humo-Ferric Podzols by having distinct or prominent mottles indicative of gleying within 1 m of the surface. They usually have thick L, F, and H or O horizons and may have an Ae horizon. They do not have ortstein, placic, duric, or Bt horizons, or a fragipan.

Chapter 11   REGOSOLIC ORDER

Great Group	Subgroup
Regosol	Orthic Regosol O.R.
	Cumulic Regosol CU.R
	Gleyed Regosol GL.R
	Gleyed Cumulic Regosol GLCU.R
Humic Regosol	Orthic Humic Regosol O.HR
	Cumulic Humic Regosol CU.HR
	Gleyed Humic Regosol GL.HR
	Gleyed Cumulic Humic Regosol GLCU.HR

A diagrammatic representation of profiles of some subgroups of the Regosolic order is shown in Fig. 34. A common horizon sequence is given for each subgroup; diagnostic horizons are underlined and some other commonly occurring horizons are listed. The subgroup includes soils having horizon sequences different from those shown.

Regosolic soils are weakly developed. The lack of development of genetic horizons may be due to any of a number of factors: youthfulness of the material, recent alluvium; instability of the material, colluvium on slopes subject to mass wasting; nature of the material, nearly pure quartz sand; climate, dry cold conditions. Regosolic soils are generally rapidly to imperfectly drained. They occur under a wide range of vegetation and climates.

Regosolic soils have too weak a horizon development to meet the requirements of any other order. They have none of the following: solonetzic B, Bt, podzolic B, Bm at least 5 cm thick, evidence of gleying strong enough to meet the requirements of Gleysolic soils, organic surface horizons thick enough to meet the requirements of Organic soils, or permafrost within 1 or 2 m if the soils are strongly cryoturbated. They may have L, F, and H or O horizons. Also they may have an Ah horizon less than 10 cm thick or of any thickness if there is no underlying B horizon at least 5 cm thick and the Ah horizon does not satisfy the criteria of a chernozemic A.

DISTINGUISHING REGOSOLIC SOILS FROM OTHERS

Guidelines for distinguishing Regosolic soils from soils of other orders with which they might be confused follow:

Chernozemic. Some Humic Regosols might be confused with Rego subgroups of Chernozemic soils. Such soils (usually Ah, C profiles) are classified as Humic Regosols if the Ah horizon fails to satisfy the requirements of a chernozemic A because of any of the following:

1. It is a moder rather than a mull Ah.
2. It lacks structure.
3. The soil climate is outside the range specified for a chernozemic A.
4. Low base saturation or any other reason.

Brunisolic. Brunisolic soils must have a B horizon (Bm, Btj, Bfj) at least 5 cm thick. Regosolic soils usually do not have a B horizon and in those that do it is less than 5 cm thick.

Gleysolic. Some Gleysolic soils resemble Regosolic soils by having very weakly developed horizons. However, Gleysolic soils must have dull colors or mottles indicative of strong gleying; Regosolic soils do not.

Cryosolic. Cryosolic soils have permafrost within 1 m of the surface or 2 m if strongly cryoturbated; Regosolic soils do not.

The Regosolic order is divided into two great groups based on the presence or absence of a significant development of an Ah horizon as shown below.

Regosolic Order

Regosol	Humic Regosol
Ah <10 cm	Ah at least 10 cm thick
Bm, absent or <5 cm	Bm, absent or <5 cm

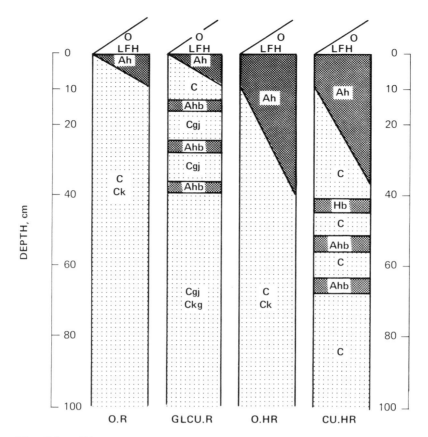

Fig. 34.   Diagrammatic horizon pattern of some subgroups of the Regosolic order.

Subgroups are based upon evidence of either relative stability of the material or periodic deposition of material and of gleying. Regosols with saline, cryic, turbic, and lithic features are differentiated taxonomically either at the family (lithic, some cryic) or the series (saline, turbic) levels. These features may also be indicated as phases of a subgroup, great group, or order.

REGOSOL

These are Regosolic soils that do not have an Ah horizon at least 10 cm thick at the mineral soil surface. They may have buried mineral-organic layers and organic surface horizons, but no B horizon at least 5 cm thick.

Orthic Regosol

Common horizon sequence: C

These soils have the properties specified for the Regosolic order and the Regosol great group. They are identified by the following properties:

1. If they have an A horizon, it is less than 10 cm thick.
2. The B horizon is less than 5 cm thick or absent.
3. They have a small amount of organic matter in the control section, which is indicated by a uniform color so that the color value difference between layers is less than one Munsell unit.
4. They are well drained and lack any evidence of gleying within the upper 50 cm.

Cumulic Regosol

Common horizon sequence: C, Ahb, C

These soils have the properties specified for the Regosolic order and the Regosol great group. They differ from the Orthic Regosols by having from the surface, or below any thin Ah horizon, layers that vary in color value by 1 or more units, or organic matter contents that vary irregularly with depth. They lack evidence of gleying within 50 cm of the mineral surface. Commonly these soils result from intermittent flooding and deposition of material.

Gleyed Regosol

Common horizon sequence: Cgj

These soils have the properties specified for the Regosolic order and the Regosol great group. They differ from the Orthic Regosols by having faint to distinct mottles indicative of gleying within 50 cm of the mineral surface.

Gleyed Cumulic Regosol

Common horizon sequence: Cgj, Ahb, Cgj

These soils have the properties specified for the Regosolic order and the Regosol great group. They differ from the Cumulic Regosols by having faint to distinct mottles indicative of gleying within 50 cm of the mineral surface.

HUMIC REGOSOL

These are Regosolic soils that have an Ah horizon at least 10 cm thick at the mineral soil surface. They may have organic surface horizons and buried mineral-organic horizons. They do not have a B horizon at least 5 cm thick.

Orthic Humic Regosol

Common horizon sequence: Ah, C

These soils have the properties specified for the Regosolic order and the Humic Regosol great group. They are identified by the following properties:

1. They have an Ah horizon at least 10 cm thick.
2. They have no B horizon or the B horizon is less than 5 cm thick.
3. They have a low content of organic matter throughout the control section below the A horizon; this is reflected in a uniform color with differences of Munsell color value of less than one unit between layers.
4. They lack faint to distinct mottling indicative of gleying within the upper 50 cm.

Cumulic Humic Regosol

Common horizon sequence: Ah, C, Ahb, C

These soils have the properties specified for the Regosolic order and the Humic Regosol great group. They differ from the Orthic Humic Regosols by having layers below the Ah horizon that vary in color value by one or more units, or organic matter contents that vary irregularly with depth. They do not have faint to distinct mottles indicative of gleying within 50 cm of the mineral surface. Commonly these soils result from either mass wasting of soil downslope or intermittent flooding and deposition of material.

Gleyed Humic Regosol

Common horizon sequence: Ah, Cgj

These soils have the properties specified for the Regosolic order and the Humic Regosol great group. They differ from the Orthic Humic Regosols by having faint to distinct mottles indicative of gleying within 50 cm of the mineral surface.

Gleyed Cumulic Humic Regosol

Common horizon sequence: Ah, Cgj, Ahb, Cgj

These soils have the properties specified for the Regosolic order and the Humic Regosol great group. They differ from the Cumulic Humic Regosols by having faint to distinct mottles indicative of gleying within 50 cm of the mineral surface.

Chapter 12   SOLONETZIC ORDER

Great Group	*Subgroup*
Solonetz	Brown Solonetz B.SZ
	Dark Brown Solonetz DB. SZ
	Black Solonetz BL.SZ
	Alkaline Solonetz A.SZ
	Gleyed Brown Solonetz GLB.SZ
	Gleyed Dark Brown Solonetz GLDB.SZ
	Gleyed Black Solonetz GLBL.SZ
Solodized Solonetz	Brown Solodized Solonetz B.SS
	Dark Brown Solodized Solonetz DB.SS
	Black Solodized Solonetz BL.SS
	Dark Gray Solodized Solonetz DG.SS
	Gray Solodized Solonetz G.SS
	Gleyed Brown Solodized Solonetz GLB.SS
	Gleyed Dark Brown Solodized Solonetz GLDB.SS
	Gleyed Black Solodized Solonetz GLBL.SS
	Gleyed Dark Gray Solodized Solonetz GLDG.SS
	Gleyed Gray Solodized Solonetz GLG.SS
Solod	Brown Solod B.SO
	Dark Brown Solod DB.SO
	Black Solod BL.SO
	Dark Gray Solod DG.SO
	Gray Solod G.SO
	Gleyed Brown Solod GLB.SO
	Gleyed Dark Brown Solod GLDB.SO
	Gleyed Black Solod GLBL.SO
	Gleyed Dark Gray Solod GDG.SO
	Gleyed Gray Solod GLG.SO

A diagrammatic representation of profiles of some subgroups of the Solonetzic order is shown in Fig. 35. A common horizon sequence is given for each subgroup; diagnostic horizons are underlined and some other commonly occurring horizons are listed. The subgroup includes soils having horizon sequences different from those shown.

Soils of the Solonetzic order have B horizons that are very hard when dry and swell to a sticky mass of very low permeability when wet. Typically the solonetzic B horizon has prismatic or columnar macrostructure that breaks to hard to extremely hard, blocky peds with dark coatings. They occur on saline parent materials in some areas of the semiarid to subhumid Interior Plains in association with Chernozemic soils and to a lesser extent with Luvisolic and Gleysolic soils. Most Solonetzic soils are associated with a vegetative cover of grasses and forbs. Although some occur under tree cover, it is thought that the trees did not become established until solodization was well under way.

Solonetzic soils are thought to have developed from parent materials that were more or less uniformly salinized with salts high in sodium. Leaching of salts by descending rainwater presumably results in deflocculation of the sodium-saturated colloids. The peptized colloids are apparently carried downward and deposited in the B horizon. Further leaching results in depletion of alkali cations in the A horizon, which becomes acidic and a platy Ae horizon usually develops. The underlying B horizon usually consists of darkly stained, fused, intact columnar peds. Structural breakdown of the upper part of the B horizon apparently occurs at an advanced stage of development as exchangeable sodium is leached downward. At this stage the solonetzic B usually breaks readily to blocky peds coated with white silicious powder. Complete destruction of the solonetzic B horizon is the most advanced stage of solodization. The rate of evolution through the stages of development depends on the salt content and hydraulic conductivity of the parent material and the climate.

Most Solonetzic soils in Canada have a neutral to acidic A horizon indicating that some solodization has occurred. Soils with strongly alkaline A horizons, an early stage of Solonetzic soil formation,

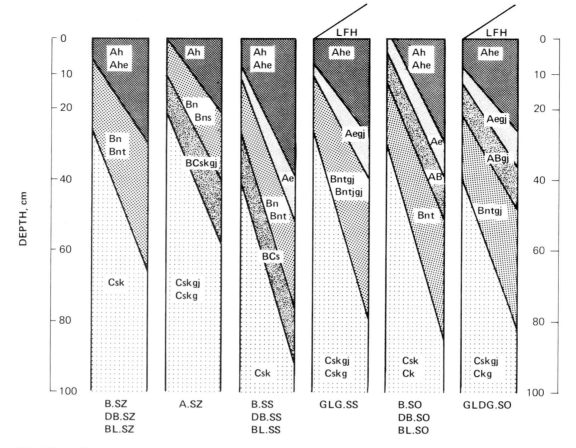

Fig. 35.   Diagrammatic horizon pattern of some subgroups of the Solonetzic order.

are uncommon in Canada. As solodization proceeds the horizons of salt and lime accumulation move downward from the B to the C horizon. In most Solonetzic soils the saturation extract of the C horizon has a conductivity of more than 4 mS/cm. Solodization is arrested where saline groundwater is within capillary reach of the solum, and resalinization may occur in groundwater discharge areas.

Soils of the Solonetzic order have a solonetzic B horizon (Bn or Bnt). This horizon has columnar or prismatic structure, is hard to extremely hard when dry, and has a ratio of exchangeable Ca to Na of 10 or less. The macrostructural units usually break to form hard to extremely hard blocky peds with dark coatings. Solonetzic soils do not have permafrost within 1 m of the surface, a surface organic layer thicker than 60 cm if fibric or 40 cm if mesic or humic, a podzolic B horizon, or evidence of gleying strong enough to meet the criteria for Gleysolic soils.

DISTINGUISHING SOLONETZIC SOILS FROM SOILS OF OTHER ORDERS

Chernozemic. Soils having a chernozemic A horizon and a solonetzic B horizon are classified as Solonetzic. However, some Bnt horizons of Solonetzic soils are similar to the Btnj horizons of some Solonetzic subgroups of Chernozemic soils. In borderline cases the ratio of exchangeable Ca to Na determines the classification.

Luvisolic. Some Luvisolic soils are similar to Gray and Dark Gray Solods. The soils having a Bnt horizon rather than a Btnj are classified as Solonetzic.

Gleysolic. Some soils have solonetzic B horizons, dull colors, and mottling indicative of strong gleying. These soils are classified as Gleysolic.

The Solonetzic order includes three great groups: Solonetz, Solodized Solonetz, and Solod. They are separated on the basis of the degree of expression of the Ae horizon and the breakdown of the upper part of the B horizon.

Solonetz	Solodized Solonetz	Solod
No continuous Ae at least 2 cm thick	An Ae horizon at least 2 cm thick An intact, columnar Bnt or Bn	An Ae horizon at least 2 cm thick A distinct AB or BA horizon (disintegrating Bnt)

Subgroups are separated on the basis of features indicating different climatic zones as reflected in the color of the A horizon and on the presence or absence of gleying. Lithic features are now recognized taxonomically at the family level or as a phase of subgroups, great groups, or orders.

SOLONETZ

The soils of this great group usually have an Ah, Ahe, or Ap horizon overlying the solonetzic B horizon; any Ae horizon is thin and usually discontinuous. The boundary between the A and B horizons is abrupt and usually occurs within 20 cm of the surface. The solonetzic B horizon, Bn or Bnt, is hard, commonly massive breaking to angular blocky, and has a low hydraulic conductivity. Dark stainings occur commonly on ped surfaces in the B horizon, which usually has a neutral to strongly alkaline reaction and may contain carbonates. The C horizon is saline and usually calcareous.

Solonetz soils occur throughout the area of Solonetzic soils. The great group is usually associated with parent materials of high salinity and low hydraulic conductivity or with relatively arid sites.

Solonetz soils have a solonetzic B horizon, Bn or Bnt, and lack a continuous Ae horizon at least 2 cm thick. The Solonetz great group is divided into seven subgroups.

Brown Solonetz

Common horizon sequence: Ah, Bn or Bnt, Csk

Soils of this subgroup have a solonetzic B horizon as defined for the Solonetzic order and the properties specified for the Solonetz great group. They are associated with grass and forb vegetation and a subarid to semiarid climate. Areas of these soils often have patchy microrelief due to differential erosion, and the B horizon is exposed in some eroded pits. Plant growth in the eroded pits is usually very sparse.

Brown Solonetz soils have either an Ah, Ahe, or Ap horizon with color values higher than 4.5 dry

and chromas usually higher than 1.5 dry, or an exposed solonetzic B horizon. They do not have a strongly alkaline (pH of 8.5 or more) A horizon nor distinct mottles indicative of gleying within the upper 50 cm.

Dark Brown Solonetz

Common horizon sequence: Ah, Bn or Bnt, Csk

Soils of this subgroup have a solonetzic B horizon as defined for the Solonetzic order and the properties specified for the Solonetz great group. They are associated with mesophytic grasses and forbs in a semiarid climate. Areas of Dark Brown Solonetz soils often have patchy microrelief due to differential erosion of the A horizon, but bare eroded pits are not as common as in areas of Brown Solonetz soils.

Dark Brown Solonetz soils have either an Ah, Ahe, or Ap horizon with color values lower than 3.5 moist and 3.5–4.5 dry, or an exposed solonetzic B horizon. Chromas of the surface horizon are usually higher than 1.5. The soils do not have strongly alkaline (pH of 8.5 or more) A horizons nor distinct mottles indicative of gleying within the upper 50 cm.

Black Solonetz

Common horizon sequence: Ah, Bnt, Csk

Soils of this subgroup have a solonetzic B horizon as defined for the Solonetzic order and the properties specified for the Solonetz great group. They are associated mainly with the growth of mesophytic grasses and forbs in a subhumid climate, but occur also in areas of discontinuous shrub and tree cover with a ground cover of forbs and grasses. The microrelief associated with differential erosion of the A horizon in areas of Brown and Dark Brown Solonetz soils occurs rarely in areas of Black Solonetz soils.

Black Solonetz soils have an Ah, Ahe, or Ap horizon with color values lower than 3.5 moist and dry and chromas usually less than 2. They do not have a strongly alkaline (pH of 8.5 or more) A horizon nor faint to distinct mottles indicative of gleying within the upper 50 cm.

Alkaline Solonetz

Common horizon sequence: Ah, Bn, Csk

Soils of this subgroup have a solonetzic B horizon as defined for the Solonetzic order and the properties specified for the Solonetz great group. They are associated with highly saline materials and with mesophytic grasses and forbs that include alkali-tolerant species. The alkaline A horizon may be of any color including brown, black, and gray. Alkaline Solonetz soils occupy a minor area and commonly occur in groundwater discharge sites.

Alkaline Solonetz soils have a strongly alkaline A horizon (pH of 8.5 or more) and a solonetzic B horizon. They may have mottles indicative of gleying within the upper 50 cm.

Gleyed Brown Solonetz

Common horizon sequence: Ah, Bngj, Cskgj

Soils of this subgroup have a solonetzic B horizon as defined for the Solonetzic order and the properties specified for the Solonetz great group. They differ from the Brown Solonetz soils by having faint to distinct mottles indicative of gleying within 50 cm of the surface.

Gleyed Dark Brown Solonetz

Common horizon sequence: Ah, Bngj, Cskgj

Soils of this subgroup have a solonetzic B horizon as defined for the Solonetzic order and the properties specified for the Solonetz great group. They differ from the Dark Brown Solonetz soils by having faint to distinct mottles indicative of gleying within 50 cm of the surface.

Gleyed Black Solonetz

Common horizon sequence: Ah, Bntgj, Cskgj

Soils of this subgroup have a solonetzic B horizon as defined for the Solonetzic order and the properties specified for the Solonetz great group.

They differ from the Black Solonetz soils by having faint to distinct mottles indicative of gleying within 50 cm of the surface.

SOLODIZED SOLONETZ

The soils of this great group have an Ae horizon and a hard columnar or prismatic solonetzic B horizon. The Ae horizon usually has well-developed platy structure and its reaction is acid to neutral. The Bnt or Bn horizon is hard to extremely hard when dry and usually has a columnar macrostructure with white-capped, coherent columns that break to blocky peds with dark coatings. Usually the Bnt horizon has many clay skins. The C horizon is saline and commonly calcareous.

Solodized Solonetz soils have a distinct Ae horizon at least 2 cm thick with an abrupt boundary to a strongly expressed, intact, solonetzic B horizon. The Solodized Solonetz great group is divided into eight subgroups.

Brown Solodized Solonetz

Common horizon sequence: Ah, Ae, Bn or Bnt, Csk

Soils of this subgroup have a solonetzic B horizon as defined for the Solonetzic order and the properties specified for the Solodized Solonetz great group. They are associated with grass and forb vegetation and a subarid to semiarid climate. Areas of this subgroup often have irregular microrelief due to differential erosion of the A horizons. The eroded pits usually support only a very sparse plant cover.

Brown Solodized Solonetz soils have an Ah, Ahe, or Ap horizon with color values higher than 4.5 dry and chromas usually higher than 1.5 dry. They have Ae and solonetzic B horizons as specified for the great group. They do not have faint to distinct mottles indicative of gleying within the upper 50 cm.

Dark Brown Solodized Solonetz

Common horizon sequence: Ah, Ae, Bn or Bnt, Csk

Soils of this subgroup have a solonetzic B horizon as defined for the Solonetzic order and the properties specified for the Solodized Solonetz great group. They are associated with mesophytic grasses and forbs in a semiarid climate. Areas of Dark Brown Solodized Solonetz soils commonly have irregular microrelief due to differential erosion of the A horizons.

Dark Brown Solodized Solonetz soils have an Ah, Ahe, or Ap horizon with color values lower than 3.5 moist and 3.5–4.5 dry and chromas usually higher than 1.5. They have Ae and solonetzic B horizons as specified for the great group. They do not have faint to distinct mottles indicative of gleying within the upper 50 cm.

Black Solodized Solonetz

Common horizon sequence: Ah, Ae, Bnt or Bn, Csk

Soils of this subgroup have a solonetzic B horizon as defined for the Solonetzic order and the properties specified for the Solodized Solonetz great group. They are associated mainly with mesophytic grass and forb vegetation and a subhumid climate, but they occur also in areas of discontinuous shrub and tree vegetation with a ground cover of forbs and grasses. Differential erosion of the A horizon, which is common in areas of Brown and Dark Brown Solodized Solonetz soils, seldom occurs in these soils.

Black Solodized Solonetz soils have an Ah, Ahe, or Ap horizon with color values lower than 3.5 dry and chromas usually lower than 2 dry. They have Ae and solonetzic B horizons as specified for the great group. They do not have faint to distinct mottles indicative of gleying within the upper 50 cm.

Dark Gray Solodized Solonetz

Common horizon sequence: Ahe, Ae, Bnt, Csk

Soils of this subgroup have a solonetzic B horizon as defined for the Solonetzic order and the properties specified for the Solodized Solonetz great group. They are associated mainly with sparse forest vegetation, a ground cover of forbs and grasses, a subhumid climate, and saline parent material.

Dark Gray Solodized Solonetz soils have an Ahe or Ap horizon with color values of 3.5–4.5 dry and chromas usually lower than 2. They have Ae and solonetzic B horizons as specified for the great group. They lack faint to distinct mottles indicative of gleying within the upper 50 cm.

Gray Solodized Solonetz

Common horizon sequence: Ahe, Ae, Bnt, Csk

Soils of this subgroup have a solonetzic B horizon as defined for the Solonetzic order and the properties specified for the Solodized Solonetz great group. They are associated usually with sparse forest vegetation, a subhumid climate, and Eluviated Black or Dark Gray Luvisol soils developed from parent materials of lower salinity.

Gray Solodized Solonetz soils have an Ahe, Ae, or Ap horizon with color values higher than 4.5 dry and chromas usually lower than 2. They have Ae and solonetzic B horizons as specified for the great group. They do not have faint to distinct mottles indicative of gleying within the upper 50 cm.

Gleyed Brown Solodized Solonetz

Common horizon sequence: Ah, Aegj, Bngj, Cskgj

Soils of this subgroup have a solonetzic B horizon as defined for the Solonetzic order and the properties specified for the Solodized Solonetz great group. They differ from the Brown Solodized Solonetz soils by having faint to distinct mottles indicative of gleying within 50 cm of the surface.

Gleyed Dark Brown Solodized Solonetz

Common horizon sequence: Ah, Aegj, Bngj or Bntgj, Cskgj

Soils of this subgroup have a solonetzic B horizon as defined for the Solonetzic order and the properties specified for the Solodized Solonetz great group. They differ from the Dark Brown Solodized Solonetz soils by having faint to distinct mottles indicative of gleying within 50 cm of the surface.

Gleyed Black Solodized Solonetz

Common horizon sequence: Ah, Aegj, Bntgj, Cskgj

Soils of this subgroup have a solonetzic B horizon as defined for the Solonetzic order and the properties specified for the Solodized Solonetz great group. They differ from the Black Solodized Solonetz soils by having faint to distinct mottling indicative of gleying within 50 cm of the surface.

Gleyed Dark Gray Solodized Solonetz

Common horizon sequence: Ahe, Aegj, Bntgj, Cskg

Soils of this subgroup have a solonetzic B horizon as defined for the Solonetzic order and the properties specified for the Solodized Solonetz great group. They differ from the Dark Gray Solodized Solonetz soils by having faint to distinct mottles indicative of gleying within 50 cm of the surface.

Gleyed Gray Solodized Solonetz

Common horizon sequence: Ahe, Aegj, Bntgj, Cskg

Soils of this subgroup have a solonetzic B horizon as defined for the Solonetzic order and the properties specified for the Solodized Solonetz great group. They differ from the Gray Solodized Solonetz soils by having faint to distinct mottles indicative of gleying within 50 cm of the surface.

SOLOD

In addition to an Ae horizon, the soils of this great group have an AB or BA horizon, which appears to have developed through degradation of the upper part of a former solonetzic B horizon. Both the Ae and AB horizons are usually platy. The upper boundary of the solonetzic B horizon is gradual and usually at greater depth than the B horizon of the associated Solonetz and Solodized Solonetz soils. The solonetzic B horizon commonly does not have strong columnar structure and usually breaks to blocky peds that are hard to very hard when dry. Clay skins are common to frequent in the B horizon. The Cs or Csa horizon commonly occurs below a Cca or Ck horizon.

Solods have a distinct Ae horizon at least 2 cm thick, an AB or BA horizon at least 5 cm thick, and a solonetzic B horizon. The great group is divided into eight subgroups.

Brown Solod

Common horizon sequence: Ah, Ae, AB, Bnt, Ck, Csk

Soils of this subgroup have a solonetzic B horizon as defined for the Solonetzic order and the properties specified for the Solod great group. They are associated with grass and forb vegetation and a subarid to semiarid climate. In areas of these soils there is commonly evidence of previously eroded pits, but they are usually shallow and grass covered.

Brown Solods have an Ah, Ahe, or Ap horizon with color values higher than 4.5 dry and chromas usually higher than 1.5 dry. They have Ae, AB or BA, and solonetzic B horizons as specified for the great group. They do not have faint to distinct mottles indicative of gleying within the upper 50 cm.

Dark Brown Solod

Common horizon sequence: Ahe, Ae, AB, Bnt, Ck, Csk

Soils of this subgroup have a solonetzic B horizon as defined for the Solonetzic order and the properties specified for the Solod great group. They are associated with mesophytic grasses and forbs in a semiarid to subhumid climate. Evidence of former eroded pits is common in areas of these soils, but the depressions are shallow and grass covered.

Dark Brown Solods have an Ah, Ahe or Ap horizon with color values lower than 3.5 moist and 3.5–4.5 dry and chromas usually higher than 1.5. They have Ae, AB or BA, and solonetzic B horizons as specified for the great group. They do not have faint to distinct mottles indicative of gleying within the upper 50 cm.

Black Solod

Common horizon sequence: Ahe, Ae, AB, Bnt, Ck, Csk

Soils of this subgroup have a solonetzic B horizon as defined for the Solonetzic order and the properties specified for the Solod great group. They are associated mainly with mesophytic grasses and forbs in a subhumid climate, but they occur also in areas of thin or discontinuous shrub and tree cover.

Black Solods have an Ah, Ahe, or Ap horizon with color values lower than 3.5 dry and chromas usually higher than 1.5. They have Ae, AB or BA, and solonetzic B horizons as specified for the great group. They do not have faint to distinct mottles indicative of gleying within the upper 50 cm.

Dark Gray Solod

Common horizon sequence: Ahe, Ae, AB, Bnt, Ck, Csk

Soils of this subgroup have a solonetzic B horizon as defined for the Solonetzic order and the properties specified for the Solod great group. They are associated with forest, shrub, and grass vegetation, a subhumid climate, and Eluviated Black or Dark Gray Luvisol soils in materials of lower salinity.

Dark Gray Solods have an Ah, Ahe or Ap horizon with color values of 3.5–4.5 dry and chromas usually lower than 2. They have Ae, AB, and solonetzic B horizons as specified for the great group. They do not have faint to distinct mottles indicative of gleying within the upper 50 cm.

Gray Solod

Common horizon sequence: Ahe, <u>Ae</u>, <u>AB</u>, <u>Bnt</u>, Ck, Csk

Soils of this subgroup have a solonetzic B horizon as defined for the Solonetzic order and the properties specified for the Solod great group. They are associated with forest vegetation, a subhumid climate, and Dark Gray Luvisols developed in materials of lower salinity.

Gray Solods have an Ahe, Ae or Ap horizon with color values higher than 4.5 dry and chromas usually lower than 2 dry. They have Ae, AB or BA, and solonetzic B horizons as specified for the great group. They do not have faint to distinct mottles indicative of gleying within the upper 50 cm.

Gleyed Brown Solod

Common horizon sequence: <u>Ah</u>, <u>Aegj</u>, <u>ABgj</u>, <u>Bntgj</u>, Cskg

Soils of this subgroup have a solonetzic B horizon as defined for the Solonetzic order and the properties specified for the Solod great group. They differ from the Brown Solods by having faint to distinct mottles indicative of gleying within 50 cm of the surface.

Gleyed Dark Brown Solod

Common horizon sequence: <u>Ah</u>, <u>Aegj</u>, <u>ABgj</u>, <u>Bntgj</u>, Cskg

Soils of this subgroup have a solonetzic B horizon as defined for the Solonetzic order and the properties specified for the Solod great group. They differ from the Dark Brown Solods by having faint to distinct mottles indicative of gleying within 50 cm of the surface.

Gleyed Black Solod

Common horizon sequence: <u>Ah</u>, <u>Aegj</u>, <u>ABgj</u>, <u>Bntgj</u>, Cskg

Soils of this subgroup have a solonetzic B horizon as defined for the Solonetzic order and the properties specified for the Solod great group. They differ from the Black Solods by having faint to distinct mottles indicative of gleying within 50 cm of the surface.

Gleyed Dark Gray Solod

Common horizon sequence: <u>Ahe</u>, <u>Aegj</u>, <u>ABgj</u>, <u>Bntgj</u>, Cskg

Soils of this subgroup have a solonetzic B horizon as defined for the Solonetzic order and the properties specified for the Solod great group. They differ from the Dark Gray Solods by having faint to distinct mottles indicative of gleying within 50 cm of the surface.

Gleyed Gray Solod

Common horizon sequence: <u>Ahe</u>, <u>Aegj</u>, <u>ABgj</u>, <u>Bntgj</u>, Cskg

Soils of this subgroup have a solonetzic B horizon as defined for the Solonetzic order and the properties specified for the Solod great group. They differ from the Gray Solods by having faint to distinct mottles indicative of gleying within 50 cm of the surface.

The criteria and guidelines used in differentiating classes in the family and series categories are outlined in this chapter, but the numerous classes are not defined.

The family is a category of the system of soil taxonomy in the same sense as an order, great group, and subgroup. The family was developed relatively recently in the Canadian system of soil taxonomy, thus it is not yet used as much as the long-established categories such as the great group and the series. However, it has great potential application both as a basis of use interpretations of soils and as a basis of naming units on soil maps. Although the series category has been used throughout the history of soil survey in Canada, it has evolved to an increasingly specific category. Some of the series of a few decades ago would now be divided among several families.

Subgroups are divided into families on the basis of certain chemical, physical, and other properties of the soil that reflect environmental factors. The family differentiae are uniform throughout the eight orders of mineral soils and another set of differentiae is used uniformly for soils of the Organic order. The differentiating criteria for families of mineral soils are: particle size, mineralogy, reaction, depth, and soil climate. Those for families of Organic subgroups are: kind of surface tier, reaction, soil climate, particle size of terric layer, and the kind of limno layer. Many of these properties are major ones with respect to the suitability of the soil for various uses. An Orthic Regosol might occur in gravel, clay, or material of some intermediate, particle-size class. Particle size, which affects many uses, is not diagnostic of soil classes above the family category. A Rego Black soil might have a lithic contact at 15 cm or it might occur in deep unconsolidated material. This important difference is not recognized taxonomically above the family level.

FAMILY CRITERIA AND GUIDELINES FOR MINERAL SOILS

The diagnostic criteria are applicable to the control section as defined in Chapter 2.

Particle size

The term "particle size" refers to the grain size distribution of the whole soil including the coarse fraction. It differs from texture, which refers to the fine earth (<2 mm) fraction only. In addition, textural classes are usually assigned to specific horizons whereas family particle-size classes indicate a composite particle size of a part of the control section that may include several horizons. These particle-size classes may be regarded as a compromise between engineering and pedological classifications. The limit between sand and silt is 74 μm in the engineering classifications and either 50 or 20 μm in pedological classifications. The engineering classifications are based on weight percentages of the fraction less than 74 mm, whereas textural classes are based on the less than 2 mm fraction.

The very fine sand fraction, 0.05–0.1 mm, is split in the engineering classifications. The particle-size classes make much the same split but in a different manner. A fine sand or loamy fine sand normally has an appreciable content of very fine sand, but most of the very fine sand fraction is coarser than 74 μm. A silty sediment, such as loess, also has an appreciable amount of very fine sand, but most of it is finer than 74 μm. In particle-size classes the very fine sand is allowed to "float." It is assigned to sand if the texture is fine sand, loamy fine sand or coarser, and to silt if the texture is very fine sand, loamy very fine sand, sandy loam, silt loam, or finer.

The particle-size classes defined herein permit a choice of either 7 or 11 classes depending upon the degree of refinement desired. The broad class "clayey" indicating 35% clay or more in the fine earth of defined horizons may be subdivided into fine-clayey (35–60% clay) and very-fine-clayey (60% or more clay) classes (Fig. 36.).

The particle-size classes for family groupings are as follows:

Fragmental. Stones, cobbles and gravel, with too little fine earth to fill interstices larger than 1 mm.

Sandy-skeletal. Particles coarser than 2 mm occupy 35% or more by volume with enough fine earth to fill interstices larger than 1 mm; the fraction finer than 2 mm is that defined for the sandy particle-size class.

Loamy-skeletal. Particles 2 mm–25 cm occupy 35% or more by volume with enough fine earth to fill interstices larger than 1 mm; the fraction finer than 2 mm is that defined for the loamy particle-size class.

Clayey-skeletal. Particles 2 mm–25 cm occupy 35% or more by volume with enough fine earth to fill interstices larger than 1 mm; the fraction finer than 2 mm is that defined for the clayey particle-size class.

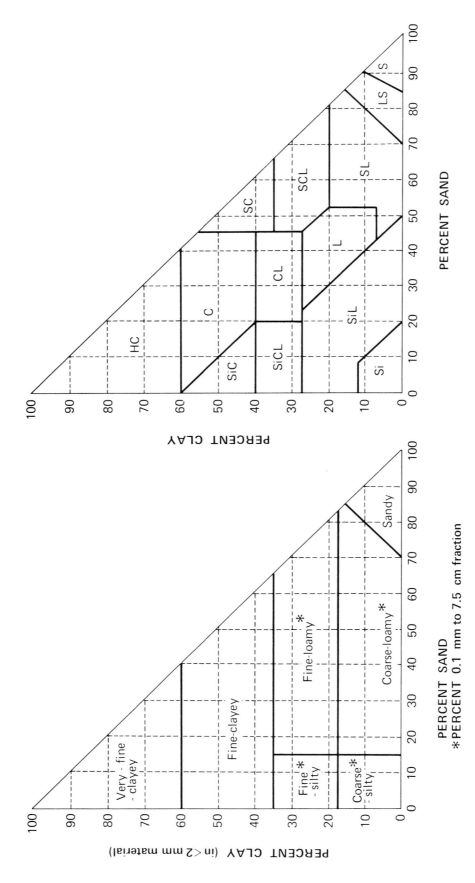

Fig. 36. Family particle-size classes and texture classes.

Sandy. The texture of the fine earth includes sands and loamy sands, exclusive of loamy very fine sand and very fine sand textures; particles 2 mm–25 cm occupy less than 35% by volume.

Loamy. The texture of the fine earth includes loamy very fine sand, very fine sand, and finer textures with less than 35% clay; particles 2 mm–25 cm occupy less than 35% by volume.

Coarse-loamy. A loamy particle size that has 15% or more by weight of fine sand (0.25–0.1 mm) or coarser particles, including fragments up to 7.5 cm, and has less than 18% clay* in the fine earth fraction.

Fine-loamy. A loamy particle size that has 15% or more by weight of fine sand (0.25–0.1 mm) or coarser particles, including fragments up to 7.5 cm, and has 18–35% clay* in the fine earth fraction.

Coarse-silty. A loamy particle size that has less than 15% of fine sand (0.25–0.1 mm) or coarser particles, including fragments up to 7.5 cm, and has less than 18% clay* in the fine earth fraction.

Fine-silty. A loamy particle size that has less than 15% of fine sand (0.25–0.1 mm) or coarser particles, including fragments up to 7.5 cm, and has 18–35% clay* in the fine earth fraction.

Clayey. The fine earth contains 35% or more clay* by weight and particles 2 mm–25 cm occupy less than 35% by volume.

Fine-clayey. A clayey particle size that has 35–60% clay* in the fine earth fraction.

Very-fine-clayey. A clayey particle size that has 60% or more clay* in the fine earth fraction.

Substitute classes

Special terms are used for some soils in which particular combinations of texture and mineralogy require special emphasis. At present these include soils containing large amounts of volcanic ash and cinders, thixotropic soils, and soils formerly differentiated as grumic subgroups. The terms cindery and ashy apply to some soils differentiated formerly as Andic subgroups of Brunisolic soils. The term "grumic" substitutes for "very fine textured, montmorillonitic." These terms replace both particle-size and mineralogy family class terms.

Cindery. At least 60% of the whole soil by weight consists of volcanic ash and cinders; 35% or more by volume of cinders have a diameter of 2 mm and larger.

Ashy. At least 60% of the whole soil by weight consists of volcanic ash and cinders; less than 35% by volume has a diameter of 2 mm and larger.

Thixotropic. Less than 35% by volume has a diameter of 2 mm or larger; the fine earth is thixotropic and the exchange complex is dominated by amorphous materials.

Ashy-skeletal. Rock fragments other than cinders occupy 35% or more by volume; the matrix is ashy as defined above.

Thixotropic-skeletal. Rock fragments other than cinders occupy 35% or more by volume; the fine earth is thixotropic as defined above.

Grumic. Very fine textured soils with transitional A and B self-mulching horizons and a granular, mulched layer at the surface. Grumic families of soils of the Chernozemic, Solonetzic, and Regosolic orders are known to occur.

Application of particle-size classes, including substitute classes

To apply particle-size classes use the weighted average particle size of the control section or segment of it listed below. The weighted average can usually be estimated, but in marginal cases it may be necessary to calculate the weighted average percentage of one or more size fractions. This is done by summing the products of fraction percentage times horizon depth for the whole control section or applicable segment of it and dividing by the total thickness.

If there are strongly contrasting particle sizes, as shown in Table 1, both are used, e.g. fine-loamy over sandy.

In assigning particle-size classes only a segment of the control section is commonly used. Surface layers are generally excluded and Bn and Bt horizons are given special emphasis. The following guidelines indicate the segment of the control section used for establishing soil family particle-size classes:

1. In soils having a lithic contact within 36 cm of the surface, particle size is assessed in all of the material above the lithic contact.
2. In other soils lacking a significant** Bt or Bn horizon particle size is assessed in the part of the control section between 25 and 100 cm.
3. In other soils that have a significant Bt or Bn horizon extending deeper than 25 cm the particle size is assessed:
   a. In the upper 50 cm of the Bt or Bn horizons (or the entire horizon if thinner), if

---

* Carbonates of clay size are not considered to be clay but are treated as silt.

** For this purpose a significant Bt or Bn horizon is at least 15 cm thick and has an upper boundary within a depth of 50 cm.

there are no strongly contrasting classes in or below these horizons.

    b. In that part of the control section between the top of the Bt or Bn horizon and 1 m depth, if it contains strongly contrasting classes.

    c. In the 25 cm–1 m depth, if there are no strongly contrasting classes in or below the Bt or Bn horizon, but there is a strongly contrasting A horizon more than 50 cm thick.

4. If the base of a significant Bt or Bn horizon or the control section in which it occurs is shallower than 25 cm, particle size is assessed either on that part of the control section below the top of the Bt or Bn or below the base of the Ap, whichever is shallower.

Strongly contrasting particle-size classes

These identify major variations within the control section that affect properties such as water movement and retention. They emphasize features that may not have been identified at higher taxonomic levels.

The minimum significant thickness of a strongly contrasting layer is 15 cm. The particle-size classes in Table 1 are strongly contrasting if the transition is less than 12 cm thick. For ashy-skeletal and thixotropic-skeletal classes, enter the table at clayey-skeletal.

Where three strongly contrasting layers occur within the control section, the lowest layer and the thicker of the overlying layers are used to establish contrasting classes.

Strongly contrasting particle-size classes are written as follows: sandy over clayey, fragmental over sandy, etc.

Mineralogy

Mineralogy classes are based on the mineralogical composition of selected particle-size fractions in the control section or segment of it used for the designation of the particle-size class. If contrasting classes are recognized, the mineralogy of only the upper contrasting layer defines the family mineralogy. Soils are placed in the first mineralogy class listed in Table 2 that accommodates them, even though they may meet the requirements of other classes. Thus a soil that had a $CaCO_3$ equivalent of 50% or more throughout the control section combined with a mixture of quartz, feldspar, illite, and vermiculite would be designated as a carbonatic family mineralogy class.

In the absence of data the placement of soils will commonly depend on judgment. Many of the classes are rare in Canada and relate to specific parent materials. Most Canadian soils have mixed mineralogy; notable exceptions are montmorillonitic, clayey soils of the Interior Plains.

TABLE 1. STRONGLY CONTRASTING PARTICLE SIZES

Recognized permutations are designated by an X at the intersect.

	Fragmental	Sandy-skeletal	Loamy-skeletal	Clayey-skeletal	Sandy	Loamy — Coarse-loamy	Loamy — Coarse-silty	Loamy — Fine-loamy	Loamy — Fine-silty	Clayey — Fine-clayey	Clayey — Very-fine-clayey	Cindery	Ashy	Thixotropic
						Over								
Fragmental			X	X		X	X	X	X	X	X			X
Sandy-skeletal				X		X	X	X	X	X	X	X		X
Loamy-skeletal	X									X	X		X	X
Clayey-skeletal	X	X			X									
Sandy	X			X			X	X	X	X	X	X		X
Loamy	X	X			X					X	X	X	X	X
Clayey	X	X	X		X	X	X	X	X					
Cindery													X	

The underscore indicates that the broader term (loamy) can be used if desired.

TABLE 2. KEY TO MINERALOGY CLASSES

Class	Definition	Determinant size fraction
	Classes applied to soils of any particle-size class	
Carbonatic	More than 40% by weight carbonates (expressed as $CaCO_3$) plus gypsum, and the carbonates are >65% of the sum of carbonates and gypsum.	Whole soil, particles <2 mm in diameter, or whole soil <20 mm, whichever has higher percentages of carbonates plus gypsum.
Serpentinitic	More than 40% by weight serpentine minerals (antigorite, chrysotile, fibrolite, and talc).	Whole soil, particles <2 mm in diameter.
Gypsic	More than 40% by weight of carbonates (expressed as $CaCO_3$) plus gypsum, and the gypsum is >35% of the sum of carbonates and gypsum.	Whole soil, particles <2 mm in diameter, or whole soil <20 mm, whichever has higher percentages of carbonates plus gypsum.
Sulfurous	Soils containing either iron sulfates, commonly jarosite, if the pH after oxidation is less than 3.5; or more than 0.75% sulfur in the form of polysulfides if the soil contains less than three times as much carbonate ($CaCO_3$ equivalent) as sulfur.	Whole soil, particles <2 mm in diameter.
	Classes applied to soils having a sandy, sandy-skeletal, loamy, or loamy-skeletal particle-size class	
Micaceous	More than 40% mica by weight.*	0.05–2 mm
Siliceous	More than 90% by weight* of silica minerals (quartz, chalcedony, or opal) and other extremely durable minerals that are resistant to weathering.	0.05–2 mm
Mixed	All others that have <40% of any one mineral other than quartz or feldspars.	0.05–2 mm
	Classes applied to soils having a clayey particle-size class	
Kaolinitic	More than half kaolinite, tabular halloysite, dickite, and nacrite by weight and smaller amounts of other 1:1 or nonexpanding 2:1 layer minerals or gibbsite.	<0.002 mm
Montmorillonitic	More than half montmorillonite and nontronite by weight or a mixture that has more montmorillonite than any other clay mineral.	<0.002 mm
Illitic	More than half illite (hydrous mica) by weight and commonly 4% K_2O.	<0.002 mm
Vermiculitic	More than half vermiculite by weight or more vermiculite than any other clay mineral.	<0.002 mm
Chloritic	More than half chlorite by weight or more chlorite than any other clay mineral.	<0.002 mm
Mixed	Other soils.	<0.002 mm

* Percentages by weight are estimated from grain counts. Usually a count of one or two of the dominant size fractions of a conventional mechanical analysis is sufficient for placement of the soil.

Soil depth

Depth classes are applicable only in soils having a lithic contact or permafrost within a depth of 1 m. In the following classes for mineral soils, depth is measured from the surface to the contact:

extremely shallow lithic	20 cm deep or less
very shallow lithic	20–50 cm deep
shallow lithic	50–100 cm deep
extremely shallow cryic	20 cm deep or less
very shallow cryic	20–50 cm deep

Reaction classes

It is assumed that the range of pH in the solum is sufficiently well characterized in the subgroup classification of most soils and requires no special recognition at the family level. Important differences in reaction in subgroups of Gleysols and Gray Luvisols can be accommodated at the series level. Family reaction classes are applicable only to the C horizons of mineral soils. They are used in all subgroups except where they would be redundant as in the Chernozemic and Solonetzic orders, Gray Brown Luvisol, Melanic Brunisol, and Eutric Brunisol great groups, and soils of sulfurous families.

Classes are based on the average pH in 0.01 M $CaCl_2$ of the C horizon (C, Ck, Cs, Cg) including IIC, etc., but excluding Csa and Cca. In the absence of a C horizon, the horizon overlying the lithic contact is used.

The classes are:

acid	pH of 5.5 or lower
neutral	pH 5.5–7.4
alkaline	pH of 7.4 and higher

Calcareous classes

It is assumed that $CaCO_3$ levels in the solum are sufficiently well understood from the subgroup classification of most soils and require no special recognition at the family level. Important differences in $CaCO_3$ content in subgroups of Gleysols and Gray Luvisols can be accommodated at the series level. Family calcareous classes are therefore applicable only to C horizons or the horizon overlying a lithic contact as described under reaction classes. They are used in all soils with Ck or Cca horizons.

The classes are:

weakly calcareous	1–6% $CaCO_3$ equivalent
strongly calcareous	6–40% $CaCO_3$ equivalent
extremely calcareous	over 40% $CaCO_3$ equivalent

The class extremely calcareous is redundant in soils with carbonatic mineralogy.

Soil climate

The soil climate classes are applicable to all soils and the criteria used are those of the map *Soil Climates of Canada*. In this system soils can be grouped according to their temperature and moisture regimes into classes (Tables 3 and 4).

Rather than relying upon the map designations for a given area, soil sites need to be individually assessed on the basis of observations of local climatic and microclimatic variations. Extrapolation from local meteorological station data should allow for any unrepresentative site features such as vegetation and exposure. A useful estimate of mean summer soil temperature can be obtained by averaging the three midmonthly readings of soil temperature at 50 cm taken in July, August, and September.

FAMILY CRITERIA AND GUIDELINES FOR ORGANIC SOILS

Characteristics of surface tier

Organic surface tier: fennic, silvic, sphagnic (each used only for fibric surface tiers), mesic, humic.

Mineral surface tier, 15–40 cm thick: sandy, coarse-loamy, coarse-silty, fine-loamy, fine-silty, clayey.

Reaction

Euic: pH >4.5 (0.01 M $CaCl_2$) in some part of the organic materials of the control section.

Dysic: pH <4.5 (0.01 M $CaCl_2$) in all parts of the organic materials of the control section.

Soil climate

The soil climate classes are applicable to all soils and the criteria used are those of the map *Soil*

Climates of Canada. In this system soils can be grouped according to their temperature and moisture regimes into the classes given in Tables 3 and 4. These classes were designed for well drained mineral soils in temperate areas. Therefore, Organic soils in mild regimes may have temperatures equivalent to the associated mineral soils, but the other Organic soils probably are at least one temperature class colder than associated imperfectly to well drained mineral soils.

TABLE 3.   SOIL TEMPERATURE CLASSES

EXTREMELY COLD

MAST $< -7°C$.
Continuous permafrost usually occurs below the active layer within 1 m of the surface.
No significant growing season, <15 days $>5°C$.
Remains frozen within the lower part of the control section.
Cold to very cool summer, MSST $<5°C$.
No warm thermal period $>15°C$.

VERY COLD

MAST $-7-2°C$.
Discontinuous permafrost may occur below the active layer.
Soils with Aquic regimes usually remain frozen within part of the control section.
Short growing season, <120 days $>5°C$.
Degree-days $>5°C$ are <550.
Moderately cool summer, MSST $5-8°C$.
No warm thermal period $>15°C$.

COLD

MAST $2-8°C$.
No permafrost.
Undisturbed soils are usually frozen in some part of the control section for a part of the dormant season.
Soils with Aquic regimes may remain frozen for part of the growing season.
Moderately short to moderately long growing season, $140-220$ days $>5°C$.
Degree-days $>5°C$ are $550-1250$.
Mild summer, MSST $8-15°C$.
An insignificant or very short, warm thermal period, $0-50$ days $>15°C$.
Degree-days $>15°C$ are <30.

COOL

MAST $5-8°C$.
Undisturbed soils may or may not be frozen in part of the control section for a short part of the dormant season.
Moderately short to moderately long growing season, $170-220$ days $>5°C$.
Degree-days $>5°C$ are $1250-1700$.
Mild to moderately warm summer, MSST $15-18°C$.
Significant very short to short warm thermal period, >60 days $>15°C$.
Degree-days $>15°C$ are $30-220$.

MILD

MAST $8-15°C$.
Undisturbed soils are rarely frozen during the dormant season.
Moderately long to nearly continuous growing season, $200-365$ days $>5°C$.
Degree-days $>5°C$ are $1700-2800$.
Moderately warm to warm summer, MSST $15-22°C$.
Short to moderately warm thermal period, $90-180$ days $>15°C$.
Degree-days $>15°C$ are $170-670$.

MAST: mean annual soil temperature
MSST: mean summer soil temperature

TABLE 4.   SOIL MOISTURE SUBCLASSES

The term Climatic Moisture Index (CMI) expresses the growing season precipitation as a percentage of the potential water used by annual crops when water is readily available from the soil.

$$CMI = \frac{P}{P + SM + IR} \times 100$$

P   = growing season precipitation
SM = water available to crops that is stored in the soil at the beginning of the growing season
IR = irrigation requirements or water deficit for the growing season

AQUEOUS REGIME
Free water standing continuously on the soil surface.

AQUIC REGIME
Soil is saturated for significant periods of the growing season.
Peraquic
Soil saturated for very long periods.
Ground water level at or within capillary reach of the surface.
Aquic
Soil saturated for moderately long periods.
Subaquic
Soil saturated for short periods.

MOIST UNSATURATED REGIME
Varying periods and intensities of water deficits during the growing season.
Perhumid
No significant water deficits in the growing season.
Water deficits <2.5 cm. CMI >84.
Humid
Very slight deficits in the growing season.
Water deficits 2.5–6.5 cm. CMI 74–84.
Subhumid
Significant deficits within the growing season.
Water deficits 6.5–13 cm. CMI 59–73.
Semiarid
Moderately severe deficits in growing season.
Water deficits 13–19 cm. CMI 46–58.
Subarid
Severe deficits in growing season. Water deficits 19–38 cm in cool and cold regimes; 19–51 cm in mild regimes. CMI 25–45.
Arid
Very severe deficits in growing season.
Water deficits >38 cm in cool regimes and >51 cm in mild regimes. CMI <25.

The moisture subclasses in Table 4 are defined imprecisely on the basis of the degree and duration of saturation. Table 5 gives guidelines for the selection of the appropriate moisture subclass in organic soils. These criteria apply to the surface tier.

Particle size of terric layer

The particle-size classes that are to be recognized at the family level for mineral material in Terric subgroups of Organic soils are fragmental, sandy, sandy-skeletal, loamy, loamy-skeletal, clayey, and clayey-skeletal.

Limno materials

Limno classes apply only to the Limno subgroups and are marl, diatomaceous, and coprogenous. The definitions of these materials may be found in Chapter 2 where horizons and tiers are described. Note the exclusion from the Organic order of soils in which mineral sediment, marl, or diatomaceous earth layers thicker than 40 cm occur at the surface or that have mineral sediment, marl, or diatomaceous earth layers thicker than 40 cm within the upper 80 cm of the profile.

Depth to lithic contact

Shallow is less than 100 cm deep and moderately deep is 100–160 cm deep.

TABLE 5. MOISTURE SUBCLASSES AS APPLIED TO ORGANIC SOILS

Moisture Regime	Aqueous	Aquic			Moist Soils	
Classification	Aqueous	Peraquic	Aquic	Subaquic	Perhumid	Humid
Descriptive Condition	Free surface water	Saturated for very long periods Very poorly drained	Saturated for moderately long periods Poorly drained	Saturated for short periods Imperfectly drained	Moist with no significant seasonal deficit Imperfectly to moderately well drained	Moist with no significant seasonal deficit Moderately well drained
Suggested Criteria Saturation period (months)	Continuous 11.5–12	Very long >10	Long to moderately short 4–10	Short to very short <4	Very short <2	Very short to insignificant <0.5
Moist period (months)	Insignificant <0.5	Very short <2	Short to moderately long 2–8	Long to very long 8–11.5	Long to very long 8–11.5	Very long >11.5
Associated Native Vegetation	Hydrophytic Nymphaea Potamogeton Scirpus Typha, Phragmites Drepanocladus	Hydrophytic Scirpus Typha Carex Drepanocladus Feather mosses Tamarack	Hydrophytic to mesophytic Wet forest black spruce, mixed feather and sphagnum mosses Ericaceous shrubs	Hydrophytic to mesophytic Wet to very moist forest black spruce, sphagnum Ericaceous shrubs	Mesophytic Moist forest black spruce, mixed sphagnum and feather mosses Ericaceous shrubs, lichens	Mesophytic Disturbed species Cultivated species
Associated Peat Landform	Wetlands, marsh, floating fen, collapse scars	Flat fens, patterned fens, spring fens, swamps	Blanket bogs, transitional bogs	Domed bogs, plateaus	Frozen plateaus, frozen palsas, frozen peat polygons	Drained peat land Folisols

NOMENCLATURE FOR SOIL FAMILIES

The soil family name consists of the subgroup name followed by a series of adjectives designating the family classes in the following order:

Mineral soils: particle size, mineralogy, depth, reaction, calcareousness, soil climate.
Organic soils: surface tier, reaction, soil climate, particle size of terric layer, limno material.

Some of the modifiers are not necessary for some subgroups; for example, the reaction class should not be indicated for Alkaline Solonetz soils. Some examples of family names are:

Orthic Humo-Ferric Podzol, coarse-loamy, mixed, acid, cool perhumid.
Orthic Eutric Brunisol, coarse-silty over sandy, mixed, shallow, strongly calcareous, cold humid.
Terric Mesisol, humic, dysic, cool aquic, loamy-skeletal.
Limno Humisol, humic, euic, mild aquic, co-progenous.

A family thus described is a taxonomic entity within which from one to a large number of series may be established. Like the series, its suitability as a basis for naming pure or complex mapping units varies from region to region and according to the scale of mapping.

In some instances it is useful to indicate phases of families. This is done by adding "family" after the modifiers in the family name followed by the appropriate phase terms and "phase." An example is:

Orthic Humo-Ferric Podzol, coarse-loamy, mixed, acid, cool perhumid family; peaty, level phase.

For convenience and brevity the name of a common series may be used to designate a family. For example, it is acceptable to refer to "Breton family" to indicate the family Orthic Gray Luvisol, fine-loamy, mixed, neutral, cold, subhumid.

SOIL SERIES

The concept of the soil series has changed greatly since the beginning of the century when a series was somewhat analogous to a geological formation. Now the series is a category in the system of soil taxonomy in the same way that order and great group are categories. A soil series is a conceptual class that has, or should have, defined limits in the same way as a great group. The link between the conceptual entity, soil series, and real bodies of soil is the pedon. Any pedon may be classified as a unique soil series, but series have been named for only a very small proportion of the kinds of pedons that occur.

Soil series are subdivisions of soil families based upon relatively detailed properties of the pedon within the depth of the control section. They cannot transgress climatic, particle-size, or other boundaries recognized in family separations. The significance of differences in properties of the kinds of pedons that fall within a soil family depends on the combinations of these properties. No specific property or group of properties has been assigned limits and used consistently from family to family and within families to define series. Each potential soil series is treated as an individual case and the decision on whether or not it should be recognized as a separate taxon involves a judgment based on the following guidelines:

1. The properties that distinguish a particular series from other series must be sufficiently recognizable that qualified field pedologists can identify the series consistently.
2. The properties used to differentiate series must be within the control section (*see* 4 and 5 below).
3. Soils of a series must occupy at least a few hundred hectares. The establishment of a series to classify a few pedons occupying a few hectares is not justified even if the pedons have unique properties.
4. Soil series within families of mineral soils are usually differentiated on the basis of the following properties:

   a. Color, including mottling
   b. Texture
   c. Structure
   d. Consistence
   e. Thickness and degree of expression of horizons and of the solum
   f. Abundance of coarse fragments
   g. Depth to bedrock, permafrost, or contrasting material to a finer degree than used in higher taxa
   h. Depth to free carbonates
   i. Depth to and concentration of soluble salts
   j. pH
   k. Lithology.
5. Soil series within families of soils of the Organic order may be differentiated on the basis of the following properties:

   a. Parent material: botanical origin of fibers and nature of terric layer, if any
   b. Abundance of logs and stumps
   c. Calcareousness
   d. Bulk density
   e. Mineral content of organic material
   f. Soil development in the terric layer
   g. Mineralogy of terric or cumulo layers
   h. Texture of cumulo layers.

Few series of Organic soils have been established and it is likely that other series criteria will emerge.

Pedons classified as a given soil series have a similar number and arrangement of horizons whose color, texture, structure, consistence, thickness, reaction, or some combinations of these properties are within a defined range. In the case of soils without genetic horizons, the above statement applies to the C horizons to the depth of the control section.

The concept of the soil series has been refined progressively in Canada throughout the last half century. Many "series" established 20, 30, or more years ago might include pedons that belong to several subgroups today. Years ago soil taxonomy was focused on the series and the great group; much less attention was given to other categories. Series were differentiated without reference to family criteria, which were not developed until recently. Thus many of the "series" used today still include, to a degree, the attributes of the more generalized series of several years ago. In the process of establishing new series and refining old series today the pedologist should work downward in soil taxonomy considering the differentiation of soil properties at the order, great group, subgroup, and family levels before subdividing the family into series. Taxonomy will probably not be extended to the series level in many medium- to small-scale soil surveys. For more detailed work, the series is a category of paramount importance because it is the most specific level in soil taxonomy and the one used for most interpretations. Sound judgments, based upon the guidelines stated, on the part of soil mappers and correlators are essential in decisions on the establishment of series. The definition of a series implies a statement of the limits of its properties.

A soil phase is a unit of soil outside the system of soil taxonomy. It is a functional unit that may be designed according to the purpose of the survey. Phases of taxa at any categorical level from order to series may be defined. In addition, areas not classified in soil taxonomy such as rockland and steep slopes may be designated as phases on soil maps. The two general reasons for differentiation of soil phases are:

To recognize and to name soil and landscape properties that are not used as criteria in soil taxonomy, for example, slope or erosion.

To recognize and to name at a relatively high categorical level soil properties that are used as differentiae at a lower categorical level. For example, depth to a lithic layer is a family criterion, but it can be used as a phase criterion at the order, great group, and subgroup levels. It may be useful at a generalized level to refer to Brunisolic soils, very shallow lithic phase.

The properties recognized above must be associated with areas of soil or nonsoil as mapped. The major phase differentiae are listed below.

SLOPE

The slope classes are defined as follows:

Slope class	Percent slope	Approximate degrees	Terminology
1	0–0.5	0	level
2	0.5–2.5	0.3–1.5	nearly level
3	2–5	1–3	very gentle slopes
4	6–9	3.5–5	gentle slopes
5	10–15	6–8.5	moderate slopes
6	16–30	9–17	strong slopes
7	31–45	17–24	very strong slopes
8	46–70	25–35	extreme slopes
9	71–100	35–45	steep slopes
10	>100	>45	very steep slopes

For example, Dystric Brunisol and rock outcrop, moderate slopes.

WATER EROSION

The following water-erosion classes as defined in the *Soil Survey Manual* of the U.S. Department of Agriculture, pp. 261–264 (Soil Survey Staff 1951) are used as phases.

Class W1, slightly eroded phase

Up to about 25% of the original A horizon may have been removed from most of the area. In most cases the soils eroded to this degree are not significantly different in use capabilities and management requirements from uneroded soils.

Class W2, moderately eroded phase

Approximately 25–75% of the original A horizon may have been lost from most of the area. The present Ap horizon consists of a mixture of underlying horizon material with the original A horizon material. Shallow gullies may be present.

Class W3, severely eroded phase

More than about 75% of the original A horizon and commonly part of the B horizon have been lost from most of the area. Shallow gullies are common and a few deep ones may occur.

Class W4, gullied land phase

The land is dissected by moderately deep to deep gullies with small areas of intact soil between the gullies. The area is unsuitable for crop production without reclamation.

WIND EROSION

The following wind erosion classes, as defined in the *Soil Survey Manual*, p. 267 (Soil Survey Staff 1951), are used as soil phases.

Class D1, wind-eroded phase

Wind has removed about 25–75% of the original A horizon and tillage results in mixing of subsurface horizon material with the remnants of the original surface layer.

Class D2, severely wind-eroded phase

Wind has removed more than 75% of the original A horizon and commonly part of the B or other underlying horizon.

Class D3, blown-out land phase

Wind has removed most of the solum and numerous blowout holes are carved into the parent material. Some areas between blowouts are deeply buried by soil material from the blowouts. The area is unsuitable for crop production without extensive reclamation.

SOIL DEPOSITION

The phases for deposition as described in the *Soil Survey Manual,* pp. 295–296 (Soil Survey Staff 1951), are being used currently in Canada. Two phases are defined as follows:

Overblown phase

The deposit of wind-removed materials on the soil is great enough to influence management but is not great enough to destroy the essential characteristics of the soil series.

Overwash phase

Deposits from water erosion lie thick enough on the soil to influence management requirements significantly but are not deep enough to destroy the essential characteristics of the soil series.

STONINESS

Six phases of stoniness are defined on the basis of the percentage of the land surface occupied by fragments coarser than 15 cm in diameter.

Nonstony phase

There are very few stones (<0.01% of surface, stones more than 30 m apart).

Slightly stony phase

Some stones are present that hinder cultivation slightly or not at all (0.01–0.1% of surface, stones 10–30 m apart).

Moderately stony phase

Enough stones are present to cause some interference with cultivation (0.1–3% of surface, stones 2–10 m apart).

Very stony phase

There are sufficient stones to handicap cultivation seriously; some clearing is required (3–15% of surface, stones 1–2 m apart).

Exceedingly stony phase

The stones prevent cultivation until considerable clearing is done (15–50% of surface, stones 0.1–0.5 m apart).

Excessively stony phase

The land surface is too stony to permit cultivation; it is boulder or stone pavement (more than 50% of surface, stones less than 0.1 m apart).

ROCK OUTCROP

Six phases of rockiness (bedrock exposure) are defined.

Nonrocky phase

Bedrock exposures do not interfere seriously with tillage. Exposures are generally more than 75 m apart and cover less than 2% of the surface.

Slightly rocky phase

The bedrock exposures interfere with tillage but not enough to make intertilled crops impracticable. Depending on how the pattern affects tillage, rock exposures are roughly 25–75 m apart and cover about 2–10% of the surface.

Moderately rocky phase

The bedrock exposures make tillage of inter-tilled crops impracticable, but the soil can be worked for hay crops or improved pasture if other soil characteristics are favorable. Rock exposures are roughly 10–25 m apart and cover about 10–25% of the surface depending on the pattern.

Very rocky phase

The rock outcrops make all use of machinery impracticable, except for light machinery where other soil characteristics are especially favorable for improved pasture. The land may have some use for wild pasture or forests depending on the other soil characteristics. Rock exposures or patches of soil too thin over rock for use are roughly 2–10 m apart and cover about 25–50% of the surface depending on the pattern.

Exceedingly rocky phase

There is sufficient rock outcrop or insufficient depth of soil over rock to make all use of machinery impracticable. The land may have some value for poor pasture or forestry. Rock outcrops are about 2 m or less apart and cover 50–90% of the area.

Excessively rocky phase

Over 90% of the surface of the land is exposed bedrock (rock outcrop).

PEATY

Any mineral soil having a surface horizon of 15–60 cm of fibric moss peat or 15–40 cm of other kinds of peat may be designated as a peaty phase.

OTHER DIFFERENTIAE

Other differentiae that are used taxonomically at lower categorical levels are principally family and some series criteria. These may be used as phase criteria at the order, great group, and subgroup levels.

Family criteria

Definitions are given in Chapter 13.

Particle size. e.g. Humo-Ferric Podzols, fragmental phase. Particle size of the mineral surface layer of a soil series may be indicated as a phase, e.g. Breton silt loam.

Mineralogy. e.g. Black, montmorillonitic phase.

Substitute classes (particle size and mineralogy). e.g. Dystric Brunisols, cindery phase or Gleyed Brown, grumic phase.

Depth. e.g. Regosols, shallow lithic phase (lithic contact 50–100 cm from surface); Organic Cryosols, very shallow cryic phase (permafrost at 20 cm or less).

Reaction. e.g. Regosols, alkaline phase.

Calcareous. e.g. Rego Dark Brown, extremely calcareous phase.

Soil climate. e.g. Podzolic, cold perhumid phase.

Other family criteria for Organic soils that may be used as phases of higher categories are characteristics of the surface tier, e.g. Mesisols, fine loamy phase; reaction, e.g. Typic Fibrisols, dysic phase; and kind of limno material, e.g. Limno Mesisol, diatomaceous phase.

Series criteria

Physical disruption. e.g. Humo-Ferric Podzols, turbic phase (*see* Chapter 2 for a definition of turbic).

Salinity. e.g. Orthic Brown, saline.

Influence of volcanic ash. e.g. Orthic Dystric Brunisol, andic.

Secondary carbonates in the A horizon. e.g. Orthic Brown, carbonated.

Other series differentiae may also be named as phases of higher categories.

In addition subgroup differentiae may be used to indicate phases of classes at the order level, e.g. Podzolic soils, gleyed phase.

Chapter 15

CORRELATION OF CANADIAN SOIL TAXONOMY WITH OTHER SYSTEMS

The approximate equivalents of the soil horizons and taxa in the Canadian system are given for the U.S. system (Soil Survey Staff 1975) and in the terminology of the FAO-Unesco soil map of the world (FAO 1974). The horizon designations and terms are rarely exactly equivalent. The definitions of soil horizons and of soil taxa differ from one system to another. The U.S. system includes a category, suborder, that is not in the Canadian system and the FAO soil units are arranged into only two categories. Thus the categorical levels of the related taxa are generally not equivalent. The closest approximation to equivalence of taxa is in the case of Organic soils (Canadian) and Histosols (U.S.). Great groups and subgroups of Organic soils are very nearly equivalent to the corresponding suborder and great groups of Histosols. This correspondence is the result of the United States and Canadian pedologists working together on the development of taxonomy for Organic soils. Even in this case there are differences, for example, the organic matter content required for Histosols differs somewhat from that required for soils of the Organic order.

In other orders differences in the approximately equivalent taxa are greater. For example, most Chernozemic soils are Mollisols, but some are Vertisols and others Aridisols. Many Mollisols are Chernozemic soils, but some are Gleysolic soils, others are Solonetzic, and still others are Melanic Brunisols. Similarly there are basic differences between Podzolic soils and Spodosols. Most Podzolic soils are Spodosols, but a significant proportion are Inceptisols because a spodic horizon must be dominated more by amorphous material than a podzolic B horizon. Conversely, a few Podzolic Luvisols are Spodosols. At lower levels in the systems the differences become progressively greater. The tables that follow are not adequate for correlating either the horizon designations or the taxonomy of a given pedon as expressed in one system with those of another system. Adequate correlation requires a knowledge of the criteria and definitions in the systems involved.

However, Tables 6, 7, and 8 provide some idea of the relation of soil horizon designations and soil taxa at the upper levels in the three systems. The tables have been revised from those prepared by J. S. Clayton for previous issues of the Canadian system. Revisions were required because of some changes in horizon designations and in the definitions of horizons and taxa in both the Canadian and U.S. systems. Correlation at the subgroup level is not presented.

TABLE 6. CORRELATION OF HORIZON DEFINITIONS AND DESIGNATIONS

1. Canadian	2. U.S.	3. FAO	Comments
O	O	H	1. Can. limits, organic horizon (O) >17% organic C.* 2,3. U.S. and FAO limits, lower limit of organic horizons ranges proportionately from 20% OM with 0% clay to 30% OM with >50% clay.
Of	Oi	H	
Om	Oe	H	
Oh	Oa	—	
Oco	Lco	H	Coprogenous limno material.
—	Lca	—	Marl.
—	Ldi	—	Diatomaceous earth.
—	cn	—	Ferrihumic material in Histosols.
L-F	H	O	Generally not saturated with water for prolonged periods.
L-H	H	O	
F-H	H	O	
A	A	A	1. Limit, <17% organic C. 2,3. Upper limit of OM ranges proportionately from 20% OM with 0% clay to 30% OM with clay >50%.
Ah	Ah	Ah	
Ahe	AE	(Ah-E)	
Ae	E	E	
Ap	Ap	Ap	
AB	AB or EB	AB or EB	Transitional horizons.
BA	BA or BE	BA or BE	

* 17% organic C equals about 30% organic matter.

TABLE 6. (cont'd)

1. Canadian	2. U.S.	3. FAO	Comments
A & B	A & B	A/B	Interfingered horizons.
AC	AC	A/C	
B	B	B	
Bt	Bt	Bt	
Bf	Bhir or Bir	Bs	1. Has specific limits, 2 & 3 do not.
Bhf	Bhir	Bhs	1. >5% organic C.
Bgf	Birg	Bgs	
Bh	Bh	Bh	
Bn	B2 (natric)	Bn	
Bm	Bs	Bu	
C	C	C	
ΠC	ΠC	ΠC	
R	R	R	
Other suffixes			May be used with A, B, or C horizons.
b	b	b	1 and 2, buried; 3, buried or bisequal.
c	m	m	
ca	ca	k	
—	cs	—	Accumulation of gypsum.
cc	cn	c	
g	g	g or r	3. g indicates mottling and r strong reduction.
j	—	—	
k	—	—	
—	pn	—	Plinthite.
—	—	q	Silica accumulation.
s	—	—	Visible salts.
sa	sa	—	1. Includes gypsum, 2. does not.
—	si	—	Silica cementation.
—	sq	—	Residual sesquioxide concentration.
u	—	—	Turbic.
—	u	u	Unspecified.
x	x	x	
y	—	—	Cryoturbation.
—	—	y	Accumulation of gypsum.
z	f	—	Permanently frozen.

TABLE 7. CORRELATION OF UNITED STATES AND FAO DIAGNOSTIC HORIZONS WITH NEAREST CANADIAN EQUIVALENTS

1. U.S.	2. FAO	3. Canadian	Comments
Mollic Epipedon	Mollic A	Chernozemic A	With the high base status.
Anthropic A	Mollic A	Ap	
Umbric Epipedon	Umbric A	Ah	With low base status.
Histic Epipedon	Histic H	Of, Om, Oh	
Ochric Epipedon	Ochric A	light-colored A	
Plaggen	—	Ap	
Albic horizon	Albic E	Ae	
Argillic horizon	Argillic B	Bt	
Agric horizon	Argillic B	Illuvial B	Formed under cultivation.
Natric horizon	Natric B horizon	Bn or Bnt	
Spodic horizon	Spodic B horizon	podzolic B	
Cambic horizon	Cambic B horizon	Bm, Bg, Btj	
Oxic horizon	Oxic B horizon		
Duripan	m	c	
Durinodes	—	cc	
Fragipan	x	Fragipan	
Calcic horizon	Calcic horizon	Bca or Cca	
Petrocalcic	Bkm	Bcac or Ccac	
Gypsic	Gypsic	Asa, Bsa, Csa	3. Only if sa horizon is dominantly CaSO$_4$.

TABLE 7.   (cont'd)

1. U.S.	2. FAO	3. Canadian	Comments
Salic	—	Asa, Bsa, Csa	
Placic	Thin iron pan	Placic	
Plinthite	Plinthite	—	
Lithic contact	—	Lithic contact	
Paralithic contact	—	IICc	
g	Gleyic horizon	g	
—	sulfuric horizon	—	Low pH, jarosite mottles.

TABLE 8.   TAXONOMIC CORRELATION AT THE CANADIAN ORDER AND GREAT GROUP LEVELS
(ONLY THE NEAREST EQUIVALENTS ARE INDICATED)

Canadian	U.S.	FAO
Chernozemic	Boroll, some Vertisols	Kastanozem, Chernozem, Rendzina, Phaeozem
Brown	Aridic Boroll subgroups	Kastanozem (aridic)
Dark Brown	Typic Boroll subgroups	Kastanozem (typic)
Black	Udic Boroll subgroups, Rendoll	Chernozem, Rendzina
Dark Gray	Boralfic Boroll subgroups, Alboll	Greyzem
Solonetzic	Natric great groups, Mollisol & Alfisol	Solonetz
Solonetz	Natric great groups, Mollisol & Alfisol	Mollic, Orthic, or Gleyic Solonetz
Solodized Solonetz	Natric great groups, Mollisol & Alfisol	Mollic, Orthic, or Gleyic Solonetz
Solod	Glossic Natriboroll, Natralboll	Solodic Planosol
Luvisolic	Boralf & Udalf	Luvisol
Gray Brown Luvisol	Hapludalf or Glossudalf	Albic Luvisol
Gray Luvisol	Boralf	Albic Luvisol, Podzoluvisol
Podzolic	Spodosol, some Inceptisols	Podzol
Humic Podzol	Cryaquod, Humod	Humic Podzol
Ferro-Humic Podzol	Humic Cryorthod, Humic Haplorthod	Orthic Podzol
Humo-Ferric Podzol	Cryorthod, Haplorthod	Orthic Podzol

TABLE 8. (cont'd)

Canadian	U.S.	FAO
Brunisolic	Inceptisol, some Psamments	Cambisol
Melanic Brunisol	Cryochrept, Eutrochrept, Hapludoll	Cambisol, Eutric Cambisol
Eutric Brunisol	Cryochrept, Eutrochrept	Eutric Cambisol
Sombric Brunisol	Umbric Dystrochrept	Dystric Cambisol
Dystric Brunisol	Dystrochrept, Cryochrept	Dystric Cambisol
Regosolic	Entisol	Fluvisol, Regosol
Regosol	Entisol	Regosol
Humic Regosol	Entisol	Fluvisol, Regosol
Gleysolic	Aqu-suborders	Gleysol, Planosol
Humic Gleysol	Aquoll, Humaquept	Mollic, Humic, Calcaric Gleysol
Gleysol	Aquent, Fluvent, Aquept	Eutric, Dystric Gleysol
Luvic Gleysol	Argialboll, Argiaquoll, Aqualf	Planosol
Organic	Histosol	Histosol
Fibrisol	Fibrist	Histosol
Mesisol	Hemist	Histosol
Humisol	Saprist	Histosol
Folisol	Folist	Histosol
Cryosolic	Pergelic subgroups	Gelic
Turbic Cryosol	Pergelic Ruptic subgroups	Cambisol, Regosol, Fluvisol, etc.
Static Cryosol	Pergelic subgroups	
Organic Cryosol	Pergelic Histosol or Pergelic Histic subgroups of other orders	Gelic Histosol

This chapter provides a very brief summary of the main terminology used in describing soils at the scales of the landscape and the pedon. It refers to the section of the *CanSIS Manual for Describing Soils in the Field* (Working Group on Soil Survey Data 1975) in which detailed definitions of the terminology and methods of coding descriptive data may be found.

1. Landform and relief. *See* 8B in the Manual and Chapter 17 in this publication.
2. Erosion. *See* 8H in the Manual and Chapter 14 in this publication for definitions of water and wind erosion classes.
3. Stoniness. *See* 8J in the Manual and Chapter 14 herein for definitions of stoniness classes. Terminology for coarse fragments is given in Table 9.
4. Rockiness (bedrock exposure). *See* 8K in the Manual and Chapter 14 herein for definitions of rockiness classes.
5. Soil water regime. *See* 8D, E, F, and G in the Manual. The soil drainage classes have been under revision for several years, but no final decision has been reached on the characterization of the various aspects of the soil water regime. The current position is to classify the following aspects of the soil water regime:

> Regional regime, soil family moisture regime subclass.
> Site water regime, which depends upon position and relief.
> Water-holding capacity of the control section or pore size distribution.
> Capacity to transmit water, transmissibility.
> Zone of saturation and duration of saturation.
> Seepage and surface runoff.

While the more comprehensive system is being developed, the accepted drainage classes are used: rapidly, well, moderately well, imperfectly, poorly, and very poorly drained. Recent developments in the classification of the soil water regime can be found in the proceedings of the latest meetings of the Canada Soil Survey Committee and in the current issue of the Manual.

6. Soil color. *See* 10C in the Manual. Munsell notations, e.g. 10YR 5/3, (hue, value, and chroma) as well as the appropriate color name (brown for the notation given) are used to indicate the colors of individual horizons of the pedon. Preferably record both moist (10YR 3/3 m) and dry (10YR 5/3 d) soil colors and indicate whether the sample is moist (m) or dry (d) if color is recorded at only one moisture state.
7. Soil texture. *See* 10K in the Manual. Textural classes are defined in terms of the size distribution of primary particles as estimated by sieve and sedimentation analysis. The textural classes are indicated in Fig. 37; named size classes of primary particles and their dimensions are as follows:

Name of separate	Diameter, mm
very coarse sand	2.0 –1.0
coarse sand	1.0 –0.5
medium sand	0.5 –0.25
fine sand	0.25–0.10
very fine sand	0.10–0.05
silt	0.05–0.002
clay	<0.002
fine clay	<0.0002

8. Mottles. *See* 10L in the Manual. Mottles are spots or blotches of different color or shade of color interspersed with the dominant soil color. Note the color of the matrix and the principal mottles, and the pattern of mottling. The latter is indicated in terms of abundance (few, common, many), size (fine, medium, coarse), and contrast with the matrix (faint, distinct, prominent).
9. Soil structure. *See* 10M in the Manual. Soil structure refers to the aggregation of primary soil particles into compound particles that are separated from adjoining aggregates by surfaces of weakness. Soil structure is classified in terms of grade or distinctness (weak, moderate, strong), class or size (fine, medium, coarse, very coarse), and type (granular, platy, prismatic, blocky). See Table 10 and Fig. 38.
10. Consistence. *See* 10N in the Manual. Soil consistence refers to its resistance to deformation or rupture and its degree of cohesion and adhesion. Consistence of wet soil is classified in terms of stickiness (nonsticky, slightly sticky, sticky, very sticky) and plasticity (nonplastic, slightly plastic, plastic, very plastic). Consistence is classified for moist soil as: loose, very friable, friable, firm, or very firm and for dry soil as: loose, soft, slightly hard, hard, very hard, and extremely hard. Cementation refers to brittle, hard consistence due to some cementing substance. The classes of cementation are: weakly cemented, strongly cemented, and indurated.
11. Roots. *See* 10T in the Manual. Abundance, size, orientation, distribution, and depth of root penetration are noted.
12. Pores. *See* 10U in the Manual. Abundance, size, orientation, distribution, continuity, morphology, and type of pore are estimated and noted.
13. Clay films (argillans). *See* 10S in the Manual. Clay films are described in terms of: frequency, thickness, location, and color.

TABLE 9. TERMINOLOGY FOR VARIOUS SHAPES AND SIZES OF COARSE FRAGMENTS

Shape and kind of fragments	Size and name of fragments		
	Up to 8 cm in diameter	*8–25 cm in diameter*	*25 + cm in diameter*
Rounded and subrounded fragments (all kinds of rocks)	Gravelly	Cobbly	Stony (or bouldery)*
Irregularly shaped angular fragments			
Chert	Cherty	Coarse cherty	Stony
Other than chert	Angular gravelly	Angular cobbly	Stony
	Up to 15 cm in length	*15–38 cm in length*	*38 + cm in length*
Thin flat fragments			
Thin flat sandstone, limestone, and schist	Channery	Flaggy	Stony
Slate	Slaty	Flaggy	Stony
Shale	Shaly	Flaggy	Stony

* Bouldery is sometimes used where stones are larger than 60 cm.

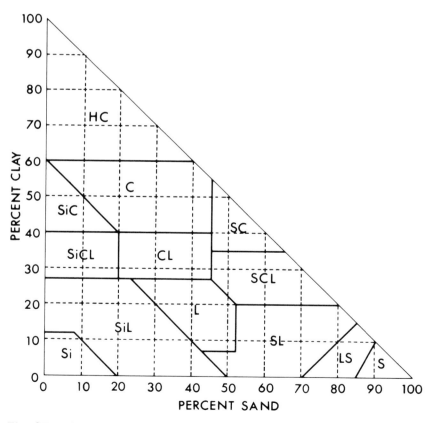

Fig. 37. Soil texture classes. Percentages of clay and sand in the main textural classes of soil; the remainder of each class is silt.

TABLE 10.   TYPES AND CLASSES OF SOIL STRUCTURE

Type	Kind	Class	Size mm
1. Structureless: no observable aggregation or no definite orderly arrangement around natural lines of weakness.	A. Single grain structure: loose, incoherent mass of individual particles as in sands.		
	B. Amorphous (massive) structure: a coherent mass showing no evidence of any distinct arrangement of soil particles.		
2. Blocklike: soil particles are arranged around a point and bounded by flat or rounded surfaces.	A. Blocky (angular blocky): faces rectangular and flattened, vertices sharply angular.	Fine blocky Medium blocky Coarse blocky Very coarse blocky	<10 10–20 20–50 >50
	B. Subangular blocky: faces subrectangular, vertices mostly oblique, or subrounded.	Fine subangular blocky Medium subangular blocky Coarse subangular blocky Very coarse subangular blocky	<10 10–20 20–50 >50
	C. Granular: spheroidal and characterized by rounded vertices.	Fine granular Medium granular Coarse granular	<2 2–5 5–10
3. Platelike: soil particles are arranged around a horizontal plane and generally bounded by relatively flat horizontal surfaces.	A. Platy structure: horizontal planes more or less developed.	Fine platy Medium platy Coarse platy	<2 2–5 >5
4. Prismlike: soil particles are arranged around a vertical axis and bounded by relatively flat vertical surfaces.	A. Prismatic structure: vertical faces well-defined, and edges sharp.	Fine prismatic Medium prismatic Coarse prismatic Very coarse prismatic	<20 20–50 50–100 >100
	B. Columnar structure: vertical edges near top of columns are not sharp. (Columns may be flat-topped, round-topped, or irregular).	Fine columnar Medium columnar Coarse columnar Very coarse columnar	<20 20–50 50–100 >100

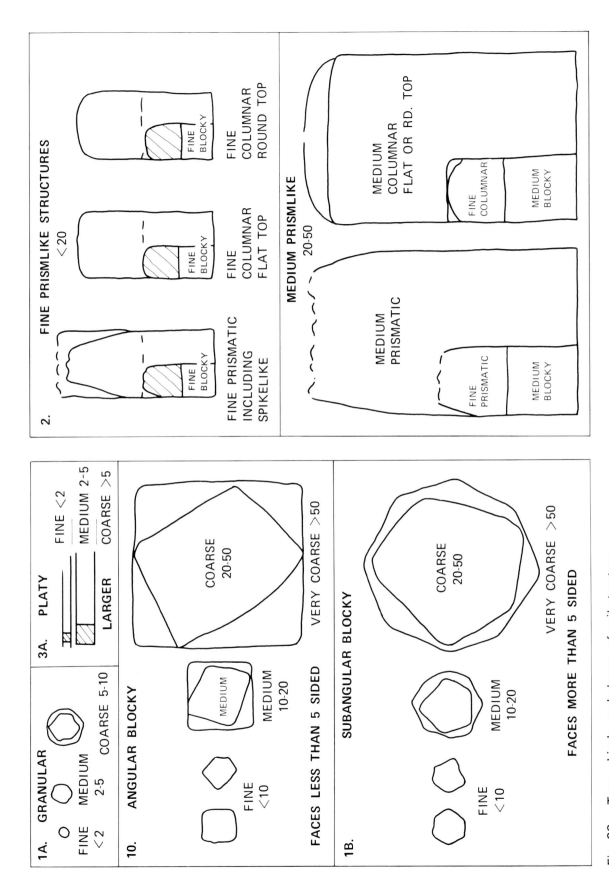

Fig. 38. Types, kinds, and classes of soil structure.

14. Horizon boundary. *See* 10P in the Manual. The lower boundary of each horizon is described in terms of distinctness (abrupt, clear, gradual, diffuse) and form (smooth, wavy, irregular, broken).

15. Ice. *See* Pihlainen and Johnston (1963) and Brown and Kupsch (1974) for terminology for describing ice and other features of permafrost soils.

16. Other features. *See* 8 and 10 in the Manual. Some of the other features of soils and sites that may be described are: humus form, permafrost, land use, concretions, nodules, carbonate content, salinity, coarse fragments, and reaction.

EXAMPLE OF A PEDON DESCRIPTION

Descriptive data for soils are commonly entered on CanSIS forms, but conventional descriptions are necessary for some purposes. The following order of listing properties is recommended: color, texture, mottles, structure, consistence, roots, pores, clay films, concretions, carbonates, salts, stones, horizon boundary, thickness range, and reaction. A description of a Gleyed Humo-Ferric Podzol follows:

Horizon	Depth cm	Description
L-H	7.5–0	Black (10YR 2/1 m), dark grayish brown (10YR 4/1 d); semidecomposed organic matter; fibrous, abundant, fine and medium roots; abrupt, smooth boundary; 5–10 cm thick; acid.
Ae	0–10	Gray (5YR 6/1 m), light gray (5YR 7/1 d); sandy loam; single grain; loose, friable; few, fine and medium roots; few, fine, vesicular pores; clear, wavy boundary with some fine tongues into underlying horizon; 5–12 cm thick; acid.
Bfgj	10–30	Reddish brown (5YR 4/4 m, 5/4 d); sandy loam; common, medium, distinct strong brown (7.5YR 5/6) mottles; amorphous; friable; few, fine and very fine roots; few, medium and fine pores; some gravel; clear, smooth boundary; 15–25 cm thick; acid.
Bfg	30–61	Reddish brown (5YR 4/3 m, 5/3 d); sandy loam; many, medium to coarse, prominent strong brown (7.5YR 5/6) mottles; amorphous; firm, few stones; clear, smooth boundary; 20–38 cm thick; acid.
C	61 +	Reddish brown (2.5YR 4/4 m, 5/4 d) sandy loam; amorphous; firm; slightly plastic; some stones; acid.

Chapter 17   LANDFORM CLASSIFICATION

This chapter was prepared by the Landform Mapping Systems Subcommittee of the Canada Soil Survey Committee: D. F. Acton (chairman), N. F. Alley, R. Baril, A. T. Boydell, J. H. Day, R. J. Fulton, P. K. Heringa, T. M. Lord, J. I. MacDougall, J. L. Nowland, W. W. Pettapiece, E. W. Presant, B. Rochefort, J. A. Shields, R. E. Smith, and M. D. Sudom.

HISTORY

A system of landform classification for soil mapping has been desired by soil scientists in Canada for a long time. The Canada Soil Survey Committee adopted a system at a meeting held at the University of Guelph in February 1976. Many aspects of the system came from mapping schemes used by the Geological Survey of Canada for surficial geological mapping. The system also embodies concepts developed initially by R. J. Fulton and later by N. F. Alley while doing terrain mapping in British Columbia. However, the needs of the soil scientist for a terrain or landform classification system are not necessarily compatible with those of the geologist. A national system without any constraints that might be inherent in the system developed for British Columbia was required. Consequently, the Landform Classification Subcommittee of the CSSC wanted to ensure that the system devised to meet the soil survey requirements in British Columbia (*Terrain Classification System* 1976) was acceptable for soil surveys throughout Canada.

SCOPE

The landform classification system under consideration is categorical in nature but does not involve any rigid hierarchy. It is intended to be a field classification system rather than a theoretical taxonomic one.

Landforms in this system are considered to include materials and form. Emphasis is placed on objectivity whereby the two basic attributes are recognized in terms of their inherent properties rather than on inferred genesis. Genetic terms are frequently used to denote materials and in some instances a knowledge of the genesis of a material or form may be required to classify it accurately. The system also attempts to map comprehensively all landforms rather than stress prominent features of importance to the interpretation of glacial history as is sometimes the case in surficial geological mapping.

The system is considered to apply to "local" landforms that are readily represented on maps at scales of 1:50 000 to 1:500 000. These local forms contrast to "regional" landforms that would be represented at scales of 1:1 000 000 or smaller.

In many respects the system is still conceptual in scope and is not parametric because it generally lacks precise limits on the boundaries between classes. It is anticipated that with further development parameters can be applied to provide a more rigid definition of classes.

The Material category recognizes four groups of materials: unconsolidated mineral, organic, consolidated, and ice. A number of classes of unconsolidated mineral and organic materials have been established, but classes of consolidated materials (bedrock) and ice have not been recognized. Textures of unconsolidated mineral and fiber content of organics are recognized in a category called Material Qualifiers.

Surface Expression, or form, associated with a material or deposit is considered in the first instance on the basis of the primary depositional form. Post depositional forms, essentially erosional, as well as processes are recognized by a category called Modifying Processes.

Finally, a category named Qualifying Descriptors makes possible further qualification of the kinds of materials and the current state of processes as to whether they are active or inactive.

OBJECTIVES

1.   To provide a standard glossary of local landform terminology for the needs of a soil survey. Definitions of other geological terms may be found in the references cited (American Geological Institute 1960*a* and *b*).
2.   To provide a system for field collection of landform information in soil surveys involving scales of 1:50 000 and smaller.
3.   To provide a system for cataloging local landform information (on-file maps, data banks).
4.   To provide a system for the recognition of the landform component of the mapping unit used by soil surveys.

GENETIC MATERIALS

Materials are classified according to their essential properties within a general framework of their mode of formation. Four groups (components) of materials have been recognized to facilitate further characterization of the texture and the surface expression of the materials. These groups and the classes established within them are presented below.

Unconsolidated mineral component

The unconsolidated mineral component consists of clastic sediments that may or may not be stratified, but whose particles are not cemented together. They are essentially of glacial or post-glacial origin but include poorly consolidated and weathered bedrock.

The classes and their definitions follow:

A—Anthropogenic L—Lacustrine W—Marine
C—Colluvial   M—Morainal   U—Undifferent-
E—Eolian   S—Saprolite   iated
F—Fluvial   V—Volcanic

Anthropogenic: Man-made or man-modified materials, including those associated with mineral exploitation and waste disposal.

They include materials constructed by man or geological materials modified by man so that their physical properties (structure, cohesion, compaction) have been drastically altered. These materials will commonly possess a wide range of textures. The assumed process status is active.

Examples: areas of landfill, spoil heaps, and open-pit mines.

On site symbols will be used for anthropogenic sites where the zone of disturbance is too small to be mapped as an areal unit.

Colluvial: Massive to moderately well stratified, nonsorted to poorly sorted sediments with any range of particle sizes from clay to boulders and blocks that have reached their present position by direct, gravity-induced movement.

They are restricted to products of mass-wasting whereby the debris is not carried by wind, water, or ice (excepting snow avalanches). The assumed process status is active.

Processes include slow displacements such as creep and solifluction and rapid movements such as earth flows, rockslides, avalanches, and falls. Where colluvial materials are derived from an unconsolidated deposit but overlie a different unit or form a discrete surface expression, they will be mapped as colluvial. Colluvial material, which is derived from unconsolidated Quaternary sediments, that overlies and resembles its parent unit will be mapped as the parent unit. Colluvial materials exclude those materials deposited at the base of steep slopes by unconcentrated surface runoff or sheet erosion.

Eolian: Sediment, generally consisting of medium to fine sand and coarse silt particle sizes, that is well sorted, poorly compacted, and may show internal structures such as cross bedding or ripple laminae, or may be massive. Individual grains may be rounded and show signs of frosting.

These materials have been transported and deposited by wind action. The assumed process status is inactive.

Examples: dunes, veneers and blankets of sand and coarse silt, and loess but not tuffs.

Fluvial: Sediment generally consisting of gravel and sand with a minor fraction of silt and rarely clay. The gravels are typically rounded and contain interstitial sand. Fluvial sediments are commonly moderately to well sorted and display stratification, but massive, nonsorted fluvial gravels do occur. These materials have been transported and deposited by streams and rivers.

The assumed process status is inactive.

Examples: channel deposits, overbank deposits, terraces, alluvial fans, and deltas.

Lacustrine: Sediment generally consisting of either stratified fine sand, silt, and clay deposited on the lake bed; or moderately well sorted and stratified sand and coarser materials that are beach and other nearshore sediments transported and deposited by wave action.

These are materials that either have settled from suspension in bodies of standing fresh water or have accumulated at their margins through wave action. The assumed process status is inactive.

Examples: lake sediments and beaches.

Morainal: Sediment generally consisting of well-compacted material that is nonstratified and contains a heterogeneous mixture of particle sizes, often in a mixture of sand, silt, and clay that has been transported beneath, beside, on, within, and in front of a glacier and not modified by any intermediate agent.

Examples: basal till (ground moraine), lateral and terminal moraines, rubbly moraines of cirque glaciers, hummocky ice-disintegration moraines, and preexisting, unconsolidated sediments reworked by a glacier so that their original character is largely or completely destroyed.

Saprolite: Rock containing a high proportion of residual silts and clays formed by alteration, chiefly by chemical weathering.

The rock remains in a coherent state, interstitial grain relationships are undisturbed, and no downhill movement due to gravity has occurred. The assumed process status is active.

Examples: rotten rock containing corestones.

Volcanic: Unconsolidated pyroclastic sediments.

The assumed process status is inactive.

Examples: volcanic dust, ash, cinders, and pumice.

Marine: Unconsolidated deposits of clay, silt, sand, or gravel that are well to moderately well sorted and well stratified to moderately stratified (in some places containing shells). They have settled from suspension in salt or brackish water bodies or have accumulated at their margins through shoreline processes such as wave action and longshore drift.

Nonfossiliferous deposits may be judged marine, if they are located in an area that might reasonably be considered to have contained salt water at the time the deposits were formed.

The assumed process status is inactive.

Undifferentiated: A layered sequence of more than three types of genetic material outcropping on a steep erosional escarpment.

This complex class is to be used where units relating to individual genetic materials cannot be delimited separately at the scale of mapping. It may include colluvium derived from the various genetic materials and resting upon the scarp slope.

Organic component

The organic component consists of peat deposits containing >30% organic matter by weight that may be as thin as 10 cm if they overlie bedrock but are otherwise greater than 40 cm and generally greater than 60 cm thick. The classes and their definitions follow.

B—Bog (sphagnum peat)
N—Fen (fen or sedge peat)
O—Organic, undifferentiated
S—Swamp (forest peat)

Bog: Sphagnum or forest peat materials formed in an ombrotrophic environment due to the slightly elevated nature of the bog tending to be disassociated from nutrient-rich ground water or surrounding mineral soils.

Near the surface the materials are usually undecomposed (fibric), yellowish to pale brown in color, loose and spongy in consistence, and entire sphagnum plants are readily identified. These materials are extremely acid (pH <4.5), and have low bulk density (<0.1 g/cm^3) and very high fiber content (>85% unrubbed and 50% rubbed). At depths they become darker in color, compacted, and somewhat layered. Bogs are associated with slopes or depressions with a water table at or near the surface in the spring and slightly below it during the remainder of the year. They are usually covered with sphagnum, but sedges may also grow on them. Bogs may be treed or treeless and are frequently characterized by a layer of ericaceous shrubs.

Fen: Sedge peat materials derived primarily from sedges with inclusions of partially decayed stems of shrubs formed in a eutrophic environment due to the close association of the material with mineral-rich waters.

It is usually moderately well to well decomposed, dark brown in color, with fine- to medium-sized fibers but may be well decomposed and black with fine fibers. Decomposition often becomes greater at lower depths. Fen materials are medium acid to neutral (pH 5.5–7.5), relatively low in fiber (20–80% unrubbed and 2–25% rubbed), and relatively dense (0.1–0.2 g/cm^3). They are associated with relatively open peat lands with a mineral-rich water table that persists seasonally at or very near the surface. The materials are covered with a dominant component of sedges, but grasses and reeds may be associated in local pools. Sphagnum is usually subordinate or absent and the more exacting mosses are common. Often there is much low to medium height shrub cover and sometimes a sparse layer of trees.

Swamp: A peat-covered or peat-filled area with the water table at or above the peat surface. The dominant peat materials are shallow to deep mesic to humic forest and fen peat formed in a eutrophic environment resulting from strong water movement from the margins or other mineral sources.

It is usually moderately well to well decomposed and has a dark brown to reddish brown matrix; the more decomposed materials are black in color. It has an amorphous or very fine fibered structure and somewhat layered macrostructure and contains a random distribution of coarse- to medium-sized woody fragments. There may be layers of larger woody particles of stems, roots, and trunks of coniferous tree species. Forest peat materials are usually base saturated and medium acid to neutral (pH 5.5–7.5); the matrix material is relatively dense (>0.1 g/cm^3) and density increases with depth. The fiber content is intermediate between sphagnum and fen peats (approximately 55% unrubbed and 10% rubbed). These materials are associated with stream courses, lake edges, subsurface drainage, glacial depressions, and bog margins. Standing to gently flowing waters occur seasonally or persist for long periods on the surface. The substrate is usually continually waterlogged. The vegetation cover may consist of coniferous or deciduous trees, tall shrubs, herbs, and mosses. In some regions sphagnum mosses may be abundant.

Consolidated component

The consolidated component consists of tightly packed, indurated materials of bedrock origin. The materials include igneous, metamorphic, sedimentary, and consolidated volcanic rocks. The only class is bedrock (R), which is undifferentiated.

Ice component

The ice component includes areas of snow and ice where evidence of active glacier movement is present within the boundary of the defined unit area. This movement will be indicated by features such as crevasses, supraglacial moraines, icefalls, and ogives. The assumed process status is active.

Examples: cirque glaciers, mountain icefields, valley and piedmont glaciers.

Ice (I) is the only class and it is undifferentiated.

MATERIAL MODIFIERS

Material modifiers are used to qualify unconsolidated mineral and organic deposits. Particle-size classes serve to indicate the size, roundness, and sorting of unconsolidated mineral deposits. Fiber classes indicate the degree of decomposition and fiber size of organic materials.

Particle-size classes for unconsolidated materials

a—blocky	l—loamy
b—bouldery	p—pebbly
c—clayey	r—rubbly
k—cobbly	s—sandy
g—gravelly	si—silty

Blocky:	An accumulation of angular particles greater than 256 mm in size.
Bouldery:	An accumulation of rounded particles greater than 256 mm in size.
Clayey:	An accumulation of particles where the fine earth fraction contains 35% or more clay (<0.002 mm) by weight and particles greater than 2 mm are less than 35% by volume.
Cobbly:	An accumulation of rounded particles having a diameter of 64–256 mm.
Gravelly:	An accumulation of rounded particles ranging in size from pebbles to boulders.
Loamy:	An accumulation of particles of which fine earth fraction contains 35% or more clay (<0.002 mm) by weight and particles greater than 2 mm are less than 35% by volume.
Pebbly:	An accumulation of rounded particles having a diameter of 2–64 mm.
Rubbly:	An accumulation of angular fragments having a diameter of 2–256 mm.
Sandy:	An accumulation of particles of which the fine earth fraction contains more than 70% by weight of fine sand or coarser particles. Particles greater than 2 mm occupy less than 35% by volume.
Silty:	An accumulation of particles of which the fine earth fraction contains less than 15% of fine sand or coarser particles and has less than 35% clay. Particles greater than 2 mm occupy less than 35% by volume.

Well-sorted materials will generally be described by the use of a single particle-size term; less well sorted and poorly sorted materials will be described by using two particle-size terms. A subordinate textural component will not generally be shown if it constitutes less than 35% of the total volume of the deposit.

Fiber classes for organic materials

The amount of fiber and its durability are important characterizing features of organic deposits in that they reflect on the degree of decomposition of the material. The prevalence of woody materials in peats is also of prime importance.

f—Fibric
m—Mesic
h—Humic
w—Woody

Fibric:	The least decomposed of all organic materials; there is a large amount of well-preserved fiber that is readily identifiable as to botanical origin. Fibers retain their character upon rubbing.

Mesic: Organic material in an intermediate stage of decomposition; intermediate amounts of fiber are present that can be identified as to their botanical origin.

Humic: Highly decomposed organic material; small amounts of fiber are present that can be identified as to their botanical origin. Fibers can be easily destroyed by rubbing.

Woody: Organic material containing more than 50% of woody fibers.

SURFACE EXPRESSION

The surface expression of genetic materials is their form (assemblage of slopes) and pattern of forms. Form as applied to unconsolidated deposits refers specifically to the product of the initial mode of origin of the materials. When applied to consolidated materials, form refers to the product of their modification by geological processes. Surface expression also indicates the manner in which unconsolidated genetic materials relate to the underlying unit.

Classes for unconsolidated and consolidated mineral components

a—Apron	m—Rolling
b—Blanket	r—Ridged
f—Fan	s—Steep
h—Hummocky	t—Terraced
i—Inclined	u—Undulating
l—Level	v—Veneer

Apron: A relatively gentle slope at the foot of a steeper slope and formed by materials from the steeper, upper slope.

Examples: two or more coalescing fans, a simple slope.

Blanket: A mantle of unconsolidated materials thick enough to mask minor irregularities in the underlying unit but still conforming to the general underlying topography.

Examples: lacustrine blanket overlying hummocky moraine.

Fan: A fan-shaped form similar to the segment of a cone and having a perceptible gradient from the apex to the toe.

Examples: alluvial fans, talus cones, some deltas.

Hummocky: A very complex sequence of slopes extending from somewhat rounded depressions or kettles of various sizes to irregular to conical knolls or knobs. There is a general lack of concordance between knolls or depressions. Slopes are generally 9–70% (5–35°).

Examples: hummocky moraine, hummocky glaciofluvial.

Inclined: A sloping, unidirectional surface with a generally constant slope not broken by marked irregularities. Slopes are 2–70% (1–35°). The form of inclined slopes is not related to the initial mode of origin of the underlying material.

Examples: terrace scarps, river banks.

Level: A flat or very gently sloping, unidirectional surface with a generally constant slope not broken by marked elevations and depressions. Slopes are generally less than 2% (1°).

Examples: floodplain, lake plain, some deltas.

Rolling: A very regular sequence of moderate slopes extending from rounded, sometimes confined concave depressions to broad, rounded convexities producing a wavelike pattern of moderate relief. Slope length is often 1.6 km or greater and gradients are greater than 5% (3°).

Examples: bedrock controlled ground moraine, some drumlins.

Ridged: A long, narrow elevation of the surface, usually sharp crested with steep sides. The ridges may be parallel, subparallel, or intersecting.

Examples: eskers, crevasse fillings, washboard moraines, some drumlins.

Steep: Erosional slopes, greater than 70% (35°), on both consolidated and unconsolidated materials. The form of a steep erosional slope on unconsolidated materials is not related to the initial mode of origin of the underlying material.

Examples: escarpments, river banks, and lakeshore bluffs.

Terraced: Scarp face and the horizontal or gently inclined surface (tread) above it.

Example: alluvial terrace.

Undulating: A very regular sequence of gentle slopes that extends from rounded, sometimes confined concavities to broad rounded convexities producing a wavelike pattern of low local relief. Slope length is generally less than 0.8 km and the dominant gradient of slopes is 2–5% (1–3°).

Examples: some drumlins, some ground moraine, lacustrine veneers and blanket over morainal deposits.

Veneer: Unconsolidated materials too thin to mask the minor irregularities of the underlying unit surface. A veneer will range from 10 cm to 1 m in thickness and will possess no form typical of the material's genesis.

Examples: shallow lacustrine deposits overlying glacial till, loess cap, etc.

Classes for organic component

b—Blanket   h—Horizontal
o—Bowl   p—Plateau
d—Domed   r—Ribbed
f—Floating   s—Sloping

Blanket: A mantle of organic materials that is thick enough to mask minor irregularities in the underlying unit but still conforms to the general underlying topography.

Example: blanket bog.

Bowl: A bog or fen occupying concave-shaped depressions.

Example: bowl bog.

Domed: A bog with an elevated, convex, central area much higher than the margin. Domes may be abrupt (with or without a frozen core) or gently sloping or have a stepped surface.

Examples: palsa, peat mound, raised bog.

Floating: A level organic surface associated with a pond or lake and not anchored to the lake bottom.

Example: floating fen.

Horizontal: A flat peat surface not broken by marked elevations and depressions.

Examples: flat bog, horizontal fen.

Plateau: A bog with an elevated, flat, central area only slightly higher than the margin.

Examples: peat plateau, bog plateau, polygonal peat plateau.

Ribbed: A pattern of parallel or reticulate low ridges associated with fens.

Examples: string fen, net fen.

Sloping: A peat surface with a generally constant slope not broken by marked irregularities.

Example: sloping fen.

Some examples of materials and surface expression are shown in Figs. 39–66. The photographs were made available through the courtesy of: C. J. Acton (53, 58); D. F. Acton (40, 42, 44, 45, 47, 48, 52, 57); N. F. Alley (39, 41, 59); P. Baurdeau (43); R. Marcoux (51, 62); K. Michalica (61); J. L. Nowland (46); B. Rochefort (60); J. A. Shields (49, 54, 55, 56); C. Tarnocai (63, 64, 65, 66); C. Wang (50).

SLOPE

A set of slope classes has been provided to make possible a quantification of the dominant but not necessarily most abundant slopes within a mapped unit of a local landform. There are 10 slope classes and each one is defined in terms of percent and degrees. Measurements are to the nearest tenth in the two lowest classes.

Slope class	Percent slope	Approximate degrees	Terminology
1	0–0.5	0	level
2	0.5–2.5	0.3–1.5	nearly level
3	2–5	1–3	very gentle slopes
4	6–9	3.5–5	gentle slopes
5	10–15	6–8.5	moderate slopes
6	16–30	9–17	strong slopes
7	31–45	17–24	very strong slopes
8	46–70	25–35	extreme slopes
9	71–100	35–45	steep slopes
10	>100	>45	very steep slopes

Figs. 39–44.   Examples of unconsolidated materials.

Fig. 39.   Colluvial material.

Fig. 40.   Eolian material.

Fig. 41.   Fluvial material.

Fig. 42.   Lacustrine material.

Fig. 43. Thin marine sands over marine clays in the background have been deranged by progressive rotational flow slides in the foreground.

Fig. 44. Morainal material.

Figs. 45–50. Surface expressions of colluvial, eolian, and fluvial materials.

Fig. 45. Colluvial apron at the base of Nahanni Butte, N.W.T.

Fig. 46. Hummocky eolian material, active and stabilized sand dunes in Prince Edward Island.

Fig. 47.   Fluvial fan in the foreground, Carcajou Lake, N.W.T.

Fig. 48.   Fluvial apron in the midground, Carcajou Canyon, N.W.T.

Fig. 49.   Ridged and hummocky glaciofluvial material, Kamloops, B.C.

Fig. 50.   Undulating glaciofluvial material, eastern New Brunswick.

Figs. 51–56. Surface expressions of morainal materials.

Fig. 51. Morainal blanket over undulating bedrock, eastern Quebec.

Fig. 52. Hummocky and ridged morainal material in the midground and background, Kamloops, B.C.

Fig. 53. Ridged morainal material. The lines of trees mark the swales between parallel ridges, southern Ontario.

Fig. 54. Rolling morainal material, southeastern Alberta.

Fig. 55.   Undulating morainal material, southern Saskatchewan.

Fig. 56.   Morainal veneer over rolling bedrock, Vancouver Island, B.C.

Figs. 57–62.   Surface expressions of lacustrine and marine materials.

Fig. 57.   Hummocky glaciolacustrine material, Biggar, Sask.

Fig. 58.   Level lacustrine material, southwestern Ontario.

Fig. 59.   A lacustrine terrace dissected by streams, between a river and hills, Kamloops, B.C.

Fig. 60.   Undulating marine landform marks the remnants of ancient clay flow slides, Pontiac County, Que.

Fig. 61.   Thin marine veneer over level bedrock, Grande-Anse, N.B.

Fig. 62.   Marine veneer and blanket over hummocky bedrock, Montmagny, Que.

Figs. 63–66.   Surface expressions of bogs and fens.

Fig. 63.   The domed bog in the midground has mainly sphagnum vegetation, Sibbeston Lake, N.W.T.

Fig. 64.   Plateaus in this bog are marked by the light brown vegetation with sparse tree cover. The flat, reddish brown areas are sedge-covered fens, Norman Wells, N.W.T.

Fig. 65.   The horizontal fen in the foreground is dominated by sedge vegetation, Manitoba.

Fig. 66.   The ribbed fen has sedge vegetation broken by low ridges where spruce trees grow, Fort Simpson, N.W.T.

MODIFYING PROCESSES

Terms that describe the geological processes that have modified or are currently modifying genetic materials and their surface expression are considered within the modifying processes category of the system.

These modifiers are to be used where a relatively large part of the map unit is modified. On-site symbols can be used to indicate modification of a relatively small part of a map unit.

The assumed common process status (active, inactive) is specified in the definition of each modifier. Where this status varies from the assumed state, it must be qualified in the description.

A—Avalanched K—Karst modified
B—Beveled N—Nivated
C—Cryoturbated P—Piping
D—Deflated S—Soliflucted
E—Eroded (channeled) V—Gullied
F—Failing W—Washed
H—Kettled

Avalanched: Slopes modified by frequent avalanche activity.

An avalanche is a large mass of snow, ice, soil, or rock, or mixtures of these materials, falling or sliding very rapidly under the force of gravity. The assumed process status is active.

Examples: avalanche cones, avalanche tracks or chutes.

Cryoturbated: Surface modified by processes of frost action.

It includes the stirring, churning modification and other disturbances of soil that result from frost action. This involves frost heaving and differential and mass movements, which produce patterned ground. The assumed process status is active. Processes involving downslope movements of material overlying a frozen layer are excluded from this modifier and considered more specifically as soliflucted.

Examples: sorted nets, stripes, unsorted circles, earth hummocks.

Beveled: Surface cut or planed by running water but not underlain by fluvial materials.

Beveled applies to river-cut terraces in bedrock and river terraces cut into till or lacustrine silts. The assumed process status is inactive.

Example: river cut terrace in bedrock.

Deflated: Modified by the sorting out, lifting, and removal of loose, dry, fine-grained particles (clay and silt sizes) by the turbulent, eddy action of the wind.

The assumed process is inactive.

Example: deflated lacustrine terrace.

Eroded (channeled): Surface crossed by a series of abandoned channels.

The term applies to fluvial plains, terraces, and fans. The assumed process status is inactive.

Example: abandoned channels on alluvial terrace.

Failing: Modification of surfaces by the formation of tension fractures or by large consolidated or unconsolidated masses moving slowly downslope.

Colluvial processes resulting in shallow surface movements are not described as failing. The process status is only active.

Example: slumps.

Kettled: Deposit or feature modified by depressions left by melting ice blocks.

Depressions can be formed by the melting blocks of ice buried in glaciofluvial, glaciolacustrine, or glacial till materials. Kettle depressions usually have steep sides and are bound by an abrupt convex break of slope. They occur in a variety of shapes and sizes from round basins to branching valleys. The assumed process status is inactive.

Examples: pitted outwash and lacustrine, knob and kettle topography.

Karst modified: Modification of carbonate and other rocks by processes of solution and of overlying unconsolidated materials by collapse resulting from that solution.

This type of modifier applies to carbonate and other rocks whose surfaces are marked by features of collapse and solution and also where the rocks are overlain by unconsolidated materials that show posthumous collapse depressions. The assumed process status is active.

Examples: sinkholes, dolines, uvalas.

Nivated: Surface modified by frost action, erosion, and mass wasting beneath and around a snowbank so as to produce transverse, longitudinal, and circular hollows.

Examples: nivation terraces in colluvium, nivation hollow.

Piping: Surface modified by small hollows, commonly aligned along routes of subsurface drainage, and resulting from the subsurface removal of particulate matter in unconsolidated materials.

It occurs most commonly in lake silts but may also affect alluvium, loess, and volcanic ash. The assumed process status is active.

Example: piping in silty lacustrine terrace.

Soliflucted: Surface modified by the process of slow gravitational downslope movement of saturated, nonfrozen earth material behaving apparently as a viscous mass over a surface of frozen ground.

These are commonly associated with processes of cryoturbation and nivation occurring in alpine and subalpine areas. The assumed process status is active.

Examples: lobes, stripes, sheets, terracettes.

Gullied: The modification of surface by fluvial erosion resulting in the development of parallel and subparallel, steep-sided, and narrow ravines in both consolidated and unconsolidated materials.

The assumed process status is active.

Example: gullied lacustrine terrace.

Washed: Modification of a deposit or feature by wave action in a body of standing water resulting in lag deposits, beaches of lag materials, and wave-cut platforms.

It occurs most commonly in areas of former marine inundation or glacial lakes. Active washing occurs along present shorelines. The assumed process status is inactive.

Example: terrace or beach cut or deposited on morainal blanket.

QUALIFYING DESCRIPTORS

A number of descriptors have been introduced to qualify either the genetic materials or the modifying process terms. The descriptors supply additional information about the mode of formation or depositional environment. They also qualify the status of the genetic and modifying processes. Included in the definitions of the categories are statements concerning the commonly assumed status of their processes. Where the process status is contrary to the common assumption, it is indicated.

Clastic: G Glacial, Glaciofluvial, etc.

Process: A Active, I Inactive

Glacial: Used to qualify nonglacial genetic materials or process modifiers where there is direct evidence that glacier ice exerted a strong but secondary or indirect control upon the mode of origin of the materials or mode of operation of the process. The use of this qualifying descriptor implies that glacier ice was close to the site of the deposition of a material or the site of operation of a process.

Glaciofluvial: To be used only where fluvial materials show clear evidence of having been deposited either directly in front of or in contact with glacier ice. At least one of the following characteristics must be present.

1. Kettles, or otherwise irregular (possibly hummocky or ridged) surface that resulted from the melting of buried or partially buried ice, e.g. pitted outwash, knob and kettle topography.
2. Slump structures or their equivalent topographic expression or both indicating partial collapse of a depositional landform due to melting of supporting ice, e.g. kame terrace, delta kame.
3. Ice-contact and molded forms such as gravelly or sandy crevasse fillings and eskers.
4. Nonsorted and nonbedded gravel of an extreme range of particle sizes, such as results from very rapid aggradation at an ice front, e.g. ice-contact gravels.
5. Flowtills.

Glaciolacustrine: To be used where there is evidence that the lacustrine materials were deposited in contact with glacial ice. One of the following characteristics must be present.

1. Kettles or an otherwise irregular surface that is not simply the result of normal settling and compaction in silt nor the result of piping.
2. Slump structures resulting from loss of support due to melting of retaining ice.
3. Presence of numerous ice-rafted stones in the lacustrine silts.

Glaciomarine: To be used only where there is clear evidence that materials of glacial origin were laid down in a marine environment, but settled through the waters from melting, floating ice and ice shelves. Sediments may be poorly sorted and poorly stratified to nonsorted and massive; shells present will generally be whole and in growth positions.

Meltwater channels: To be used to indicate the presence of glacial meltwater channels in a unit where they are too small or too numerous or both to show individually by an on-site symbol.

Active: To be used to indicate any evidence of the recurrent nature of a modifying process or of the contemporary nature of the process forming a genetic material.

Inactive: To be used to indicate no evidence that the modifying process is recurrent and that the processes of formation of the genetic materials have ceased.

MAPPING CONVENTIONS

Map symbols

The following example serves to illustrate a system for ordering symbols in map edits. It assumes that all components of the system (genetic materials and their particle-size or fiber class, surface expression and related slope, modifying processes, and qualifying descriptors) are to be utilized.

$$\frac{t \; G^Q \; e^Q \; / \; t \; G^Q \; e^Q \; 1 - P^Q}{G^Q e}$$

$t \; G^Q \; e^Q$ is the dominant ($>50\%$) surficial material and $t \; G^Q \; e^Q \; 1 - P^Q$ is the subdominant material. Rarely will materials occupying less than 15% of the map area be recognized in the edit. (On-site symbols provide a mechanism for depicting many of these).

- t—genetic material modifier (particle size of clastic materials and fiber content of organic materials).
- G—genetic materials
- e—surface expression
- l—slope qualifiers (numeric)
- P—modifying processes
- Q—qualifying descriptor (superscript)
- $G^Q e$—in the denominator represents an underlying stratigraphic unit.

Composite units

Not all terrain can be presented as simple units because terrain units commonly occur that are of small areal extent and cannot be delimited individually at the scale of mapping. Consequently, a system of composite units is employed whereby up to three types of terrain may be designated within a common unit boundary. The relative amounts of each terrain type are indicated by the use of the symbols =, /, and //. The components are always indicated in decreasing order of abundance.

= components on either side of this symbol are approximately equal; each represents 45–55% of the area.

/ the component in front of this symbol is more abundant than the one that follows; the first represents 55–70% of the area and the second 30–45%.

// the component in front of the symbol is considerably more abundant than the component that follows; the first represents 70–90% and the second 10–30% of the area.

Stratigraphic data

Stratigraphic data may be presented to supplement the surficial data. Stratigraphic information should be given for veneers and blankets. In addition, where the depth of the surface unit is such that the nature of the underlying unit may be important or where it is deemed necessary to show the character of the underlying unit or both, then stratigraphic information should be shown.

For map presentation a horizontal bar is used to separate the components that are arranged in stratigraphic order. Surface expressions may be attached to underlying units if appropriate.

If the type of unconsolidated material underlying a blanket of different genetic material is not known, then only the surface expression of that underlying material is given. For example, Mb/h indicates hummocky unconsolidated material of unknown specific type underlying a blanket of morainal materials.

On-site symbols

On-site symbols or map symbols (Fig. 67) are used to describe features or processes in the terrain that express either a limited (by scale), areal function or are simply point observations. These may be linear features such as eskers or moraine ridges, site specific information such as gravel locations or kettle holes, or to add details of Quaternary history such as striae, glacial meltwater channels, or abandoned shorelines.

The size of the on-site symbols will vary with the type of symbol. For example, the symbols that connote an areal extent such as failing or block fields will vary in size whereas those that are point observations and have no relation to areal extent, such as fossil locality or karst, will be of a standard size. The symbols that have linear connotations, such as eskers, gullying, or end moraines, will vary in length but will be of standard width.

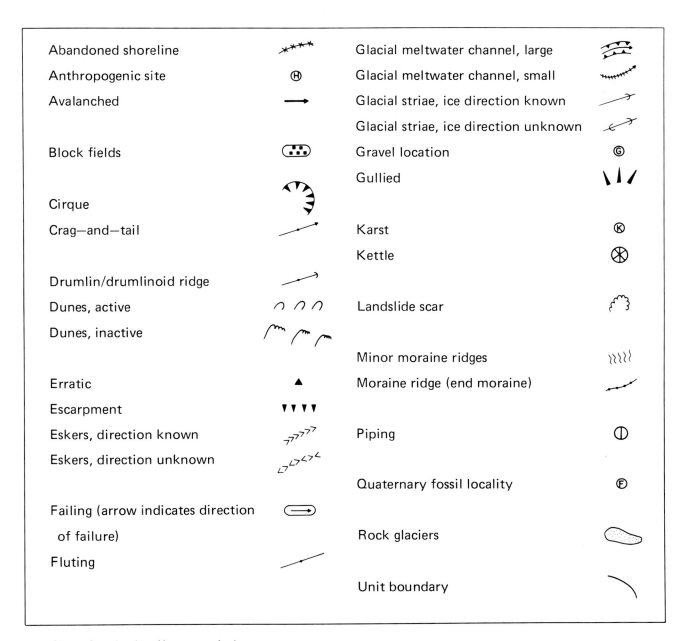

Abandoned shoreline		Glacial meltwater channel, large	
Anthropogenic site		Glacial meltwater channel, small	
Avalanched		Glacial striae, ice direction known	
		Glacial striae, ice direction unknown	
Block fields		Gravel location	
		Gullied	
Cirque			
Crag—and—tail		Karst	
		Kettle	
Drumlin/drumlinoid ridge			
Dunes, active		Landslide scar	
Dunes, inactive			
		Minor moraine ridges	
Erratic		Moraine ridge (end moraine)	
Escarpment			
Eskers, direction known		Piping	
Eskers, direction unknown			
		Quaternary fossil locality	
Failing (arrow indicates direction of failure)		Rock glaciers	
Fluting			
		Unit boundary	

Fig. 67.   On-site landform symbols.

REFERENCES

American Geological Institute. 1960*a*. Glossary of geology and related sciences, 2nd ed. American Geological Institute, Washington, D.C. 397 pp.

American Geological Institute. 1960*b*. Dictionary of geological terms. Doubleday & Company, Inc., Garden City, N.Y. 545 pp.

Baldwin, M., Kellogg, C. E., and Thorp, J. 1938. Soil classification. Pages 979–1001 *in* U.S. Dep. Agric. Soils and men, yearbook of agriculture 1938. U.S. Government Printing Office, Washington, D.C.

Brown, R. J. E., and Kupsch, W. O. 1974. Permafrost terminology, N.R.C., Canada, Tech. Memo. 111. 62 pp.

Canada Department of Agriculture. 1974. A system of soil classification for Canada. Publ. 1455. Revised. Information Canada, Ottawa, Ont. 255 pp.

Canada Department of Agriculture. 1976. Glossary of terms in soil science. Publ. 1459. Revised. 44 pp.

Canada Soil Survey Committee (and National Soil Survey Committee). Proceedings of meetings in 1945, 1955, 1958, 1960, 1963, 1965, 1968, 1970, 1973, and 1976.

Clayton, J. S., Ehrlich, W. A., Cann, D. B., Day, J. H., and Marshall, I. B. 1977. Soils of Canada. Can. Dep. Agric. Publ. 1544. Supply and Services Canada, Ottawa, Ont. 2 vols.

Cline, M. G. 1949. Basic principles of soil classification. Soil Sci. 67: 81–91.

Cline, M. G. 1961. The changing model of soil. Soil Sci. Soc. Am. Proc. 25: 442–446.

Cline, M. G. 1963. Logic of the new system of soil classification. Soil Sci. 96: 17–22.

De Bakker, H. 1970. Purposes of soil classification. Geoderma 4: 195–208.

Ellis, J. H. 1932. A field classification of soils for use in soil survey. Sci. Agric. 12: 338–345.

Ellis, J. H. 1971. The birth of agronomic research at the Manitoba Agricultural College. 181 pp.

E.L.U.C. Secretariat. 1976. Terrain classification system. Government of British Columbia, Victoria, B.C. 54 pp.

Food and Agriculture Organization of the United Nations. 1974. FAO-Unesco Soil map of the world. Vol. 1 Legend. Unesco, Paris, France. 59 pp.

Glinka, K. D. 1927. The great soil groups of the world and their development. (Translated from the German by C. F. Marbut). Edwards Brothers, Ann Arbor, Mich. 235 pp.

Jenny, H. 1961. E. W. Hilgard and the birth of modern soil science. Collana Della Rivista Agrochimica, Pisa, Italy. 144 pp.

Joel, A. H. 1926. Changing viewpoints and methods in soil classification. Sci. Agric. 6: 225–232.

Kellogg, C. E. 1941. The soils that support us. The Macmillan Co., New York, N.Y. 309 pp.

Knox, E. G. 1965. Soil individuals and soil classification. Soil Sci. Soc. Am. Proc. 29: 79–84.

McKeague, J. A., ed. 1976. Manual on soil sampling and methods of analysis. Soil Res. Inst., Can. Dep. Agric., Ottawa, Ont. 212 pp.

Pihlainen, J. A., and Johnston, G. H. 1963. Guide to a field description of permafrost for engineering purposes. N.R.C., Canada, Tech. Memo. 79. 21 pp.

Ruhnke, G. N. 1926. The soil survey of southern Ontario. Sci. Agric. 7: 117–124.

Simonson, R. W. 1968. Concept of a soil. Adv. Agron. 20: 1–47.

Soil Survey Staff. 1951. Soil survey manual. U.S. Dep. Agric. Handbook No. 18. U.S. Government Printing Office, Washington, D.C. 503 pp.

Soil Survey Staff. 1960. Soil classification, a comprehensive system, 7th approximation. U.S. Dep. Agric., U.S. Government Printing Office, Washington, D.C. 265 pp.

Soil Survey Staff. 1975. Soil taxonomy. U.S. Dep. Agric. Handbook No. 436. U.S. Government Printing Office, Washington, D.C. 754 pp.

Working Group on Soil Survey Data. 1975. The Canadian soil information system (CanSIS) manual for describing soils in the field. Soil Res. Inst., Can. Dep. Agric., Ottawa, Ont. 170 pp.

INDEX

Subgroups are listed in alphabetical order under the great group name.